PEARSON CUSTOM
BUSINESS RESOURCES

Compiled by

PEARSON

This special edition published in cooperation with Pearson Learning Solutions.

Printed in the United States of America.

V092

Please visit our website at *www.pearsonlearningsolutions.com*.

Attention bookstores: For permission to return any unsold stock, contact us at *pe-uscustomreturns@pearson.com*.

Pearson Learning Solutions, 501 Boylston Street, Suite 900, Boston, MA 02116
A Pearson Education Company
www.pearsoned.com

ISBN 10: 1-256-59607-8
ISBN 13: 978-1-256-59607-3

Table of Contents

Chapter 1

Ethics: The Foundation for Relationships in Selling

From Chapter 5 of *Selling Today: Partnering to Create Value*, 12/e. Gerald L. Manning. Michael Ahearne.
Barry L. Reece. Copyright © 2012 by Pearson Education. Published by Prentice Hall. All rights reserved.

Ethics: The Foundation for Relationships in Selling

Reality Selling Today Video Series

Edith Botello (pictured above) started her career as a salesperson with Mattress Firm (www.mattressfirm.com), one of the world's largest and most successful retailers in the specialty bedding market. Edith, a recent university graduate, is currently the assistant manager of one of the company's 560 nationwide stores. She is responsible for the sales productivity, maintenance, and merchandising of the store. Within her district, she is also an in-market trainer, recruiter, and intern coordinator.

Edith believes that *qualifying* (the term Mattress Firm uses to describe need identification) and *listening* are the most important skills to be a successful salesperson in her industry. Therefore, she really tries to understand why customers come to visit her and what will make them get a great night's sleep. People come into her store with a wide variety of different needs: Their bed is 20 years old; they are upgrading to a different size; they are buying a college bed; they need a bed for a guest bedroom; their current bed has dips and sags; they are going in for surgery next week and would like to recover on a supportive mattress, and so forth. Accordingly, Edith's goal is to ask the right questions so that she can sell them a solution based on their individual needs. Mattress Firm has taught Edith techniques on how to sell to different types of people. Edith believes that the main reason why many salespeople are successful is that they get their customer to believe in them by educating them and making them feel great about their purchase. Edith feels very fortunate to work for a company that values training and customer service.

Building relationships with customers is very important for Edith because people typically buy from salespeople they like and trust. One way she builds relationships is by getting to know her customers and talking to them about things that interest them. As Edith puts it, you cannot expect your customers to open up to you unless you kick things off by asking questions. Edith also makes use of testimonials to demonstrate how previous customers have resolved their needs with particular sleep products. Customers like to hear that their salesperson has experience dealing with, and finding solutions to, problems they are encountering. ●

Making Ethical Decisions

Business ethics comprise principles and standards that guide behavior in the world of business. They help translate your values into appropriate and effective behaviors in your day-to-day life. Whether a specific behavior is right or wrong, ethical or unethical, is often determined by company leaders, customers, investors, the legal system, and the community.[1] Of course, the views of various stakeholders may be in conflict. Kickbacks and secret payoffs may be acceptable practices to the vice president of sales and marketing, yet may be viewed as unethical by members of the sales force, the board of directors, investors, and the general public.

There is no one uniform code of ethics for all salespeople as societal and relational norms can vary from person to person.[2] However, a large number of business organizations, professional associations, and certification agencies have established written codes. For example, the National Association of Sales Professionals (NASP) states that members must abide by its Standards of Professional Conduct[3] (Figure 1).

Today, we recognize that character and integrity strongly influence relationships in personal selling. Character is composed of your personal standards of behavior, including your honesty and integrity. Your character is based on your internal values and the resulting judgments you make about what is right and what is wrong. The ethical decisions you make reflect your character strength.

We are indebted to Stephen Covey, author of *The Seven Habits of Highly Effective People*, for helping us better understand the relationship between character strength and success in personal selling. In his best-selling book, Covey says that there are basic principles that must be integrated into our character. One example is to always do what you say you are going to do. "As we make and keep commitments, even small commitments, we begin to establish an inner integrity that gives us the awareness of self-control and courage and strength to accept more of the responsibility for our own lives."[4] Fulfilling your commitments builds trust, and trust is the most important precondition of partnering.

Character Development

Colleges and universities are beginning to play a more active role in character development. Courses that focus on ethics are becoming quite common. When a new ethics course was developed at the University of Virginia, the faculty indicated that the purpose of the course is not to point out what is right and what is wrong. The course is designed to help students understand the consequences of their actions when they face an ethical dilemma.[5]

Despite a growing interest in business ethics, unethical behavior has become all too common. A survey conducted by *Newsweek* suggests that the current generation of workers may be more tolerant of deception. Many of those involved in the survey did not view lying and cheating as unacceptable.[6] Employees who are involved in unethical behavior often report that they were under pressure to act unethically or illegally on the job.

The Erosion of Character

As the past decade unfolded, many large, inflexible corporations were transformed into smaller, more nimble competitors. New economy thinking prevailed as business firms, large and small, worked hard to become lean, innovative, and profitable. We witnessed an almost unrelenting emphasis on earnings that was driven, in some cases, by executive greed. It was during this period that some of America's most respected companies began to cross the ethical divide.[7]

A company cannot enjoy long-term success unless its employees are honest, ethical, and uncompromising about values and principles. Yet many employees engage in dishonest practices

PREAMBLE

The American Marketing Association commits itself to promoting the highest standard of professional ethical norms and values for its members (practitioners, academics and students). Norms are established standards of conduct that are expected and maintained by society and/or professional organizations. Values represent the collective conception of what communities find desirable, important and morally proper. Values also serve as the criteria for evaluating our own personal actions and the actions of others. As marketers, we recognize that we not only serve our organizations but also act as stewards of society in creating, facilitating and executing the transactions that are part of the greater economy. In this role, marketers are expected to embrace the highest professional ethical norms and the ethical values implied by our responsibility toward multiple stakeholders (e.g., customers, employees, investors, peers, channel members, regulators and the host community).

ETHICAL NORMS

As Marketers, we must:

1. Do no harm. This means consciously avoiding harmful actions or omissions by embodying high ethical standards and adhering to all applicable laws and regulations in the choices we make.
2. Foster trust in the marketing system. This means striving for good faith and fair dealing so as to contribute toward the efficacy of the exchange process as well as avoiding deception in product design, pricing, communication, and delivery of distribution.
3. Embrace ethical values. This means building relationships and enhancing consumer confidence in the integrity of marketing by affirming these core values: honesty, responsibility, fairness, respect, transparency and citizenship.

ETHICAL VALUES

Honesty – to be forthright in dealings with customers and stakeholders. To this end, we will:
- Strive to be truthful in all situations and at all times.
- Offer products of value that do what we claim in our communications.
- Stand behind our products if they fail to deliver their claimed benefits.
- Honor our explicit and implicit commitments and promises.

Responsibility – to accept the consequences of our marketing decisions and strategies. To this end, we will:
- Strive to serve the needs of customers.
- Avoid using coercion with all stakeholders.
- Acknowledge the social obligations to stakeholders that come with increased marketing and economic power.
- Recognize our special commitments to vulnerable market segments such as children, seniors, the economically impoverished, market illiterates and others who may be substantially disadvantaged.
- Consider environmental stewardship in our decision-making.

Fairness – to balance justly the needs of the buyer with the interests of the seller. To this end, we will:
- Represent products in a clear way in selling, advertising and other forms of communication; this includes the avoidance of false, misleading and deceptive promotion.
- Reject manipulations and sales tactics that harm customer trust. Refuse to engage in price fixing, predatory pricing, price gouging or "bait-and-switch" tactics.
- Avoid knowing participation in conflicts of interest. Seek to protect the private information of customers, employees and partners.

Respect – to acknowledge the basic human dignity of all stakeholders. To this end, we will:
- Value individual differences and avoid stereotyping customers or depicting demographic groups (e.g., gender, race, sexual orientation) in a negative or dehumanizing way.
- Listen to the needs of customers and make all reasonable efforts to monitor and improve their satisfaction on an ongoing basis.
- Make every effort to understand and respectfully treat buyers, suppliers, intermediaries and distributors from all cultures.
- Acknowledge the contributions of others, such as consultants, employees and coworkers, to marketing endeavors.
- Treat everyone, including our competitors, as we would wish to be treated.

Transparency – to create a spirit of openness in marketing operations. To this end, we will:
- Strive to communicate clearly with all constituencies.
- Accept constructive criticism from customers and other stakeholders.
- Explain and take appropriate action regarding significant product or service risks, component substitutions or other foreseeable eventualities that could affect customers or their perception of the purchase decision.
- Disclose list prices and terms of financing as well as available price deals and adjustments.

Citizenship – to fulfill the economic, legal, philanthropic and societal responsibilities that serve stakeholders. To this end, we will:
- Strive to protect the ecological environment in the execution of marketing campaigns.
- Give back to the community through volunteerism and charitable donations. Contribute to the overall betterment of marketing and its reputation.
- Urge supply chain members to ensure that trade is fair for all participants, including producers in developing countries.

IMPLEMENTATION

We expect AMA members to be courageous and proactive in leading and/or aiding their organizations in the fulfillment of the explicit and implicit promises made to those stakeholders. We recognize that every industry sector and marketing sub-discipline (e.g., marketing research, e-commerce, Internet selling, direct marketing, and advertising) has its own specific ethical issues that require policies and commentary. An array of such codes can be accessed through links on the AMA Web site. Consistent with the principle of subsidiarity (solving issues at the level where the expertise resides), we encourage all such groups to develop and/or refine their industry and discipline-specific codes of ethics to supplement these guiding ethical norms and values.

FIGURE 1

This code of ethics serves as a foundation for the members of the American Medical Association (AMA).

Source: American Marketing Association Code of Ethics. Used by permission of American Marketing Association.

that erode character. The collapse of Lehman Bros., one of the largest U.S. corporations ever to file for bankruptcy, can be traced to a culture that emphasized risk taking, personal ambition over teamwork, and earnings growth at any cost. The new economy depends on innovation and aggressive development of markets, but actions that weaken the moral contract with employees, customers, and shareholders can bring serious consequences. Let's examine some "half-truths" that have influenced the erosion of character in a business setting.

- *We are only in it for ourselves.* Some critics of today's moral climate feel that the current moral decline began when society's focus shifted from "what is right" to "what is right for me." In personal selling, this point of view can quickly subtract rather than add value to a relationship with the customer. Fortunately, there are many salespeople for whom integrity and self-respect are basic values. Darryl Ashley, a pharmaceutical representative for Eli Lilly Company, suspected that a pharmacist (a customer) was diluting chemotherapy drugs in order to increase profit margins. Ashley shared his suspicions with one of the cancer doctors who were purchasing the drug from the pharmacist. Tests indicated that the drug had been diluted.[8]

- *Corporations exist to maximize shareholder value.* In the past, corporations were more often viewed as *economic* and *social* institutions—organizations that served a balanced group of stakeholders. In recent years, analysts, stock traders, CEOs, and the media have too often focused on a single standard of performance—share price.[9] Marjorie Kelly, former editor of *Business Ethics*, says, "Managing a company solely for maximum share price can destroy both share price and the entire company."[10]

    Pressure to increase "numbers" led to sales abuses at WorldCom Incorporated. Some salespeople double-booked accounts in order to make their quota and collect increased commissions. The false reporting was identified by an internal company probe and the guilty sales representatives were fired.[11]

- *Companies need to be lean and mean.*[12] Downsizing has become a common practice even when the economy is strong. After the layoffs, companies must deal with serious problems of low morale and mistrust of management. Those employees who remain after a company reduces its ranks often feel demoralized, overworked, and fearful. The stress of long hours and a faster pace can result in quality losses and bad service that alienate customers. Richard Sennett, author of *The Corrosion of Character*, says that the decline of character strength can be traced to conditions that have grown out of our fast-paced, high-stress, information-driven economy. He states that character strength builds in a climate that encourages loyalty, mutual commitment, and the pursuit of long-term goals.[13] These are the qualities needed to build strong buyer–seller relationships.

Character strength builds as we display loyalty, mutual commitment, and the pursuit of long-term goals. These are the qualities needed to build strong buyer–seller relationships.

Source: PhotoAlto/Superstock Royalty Free

The Ethical Use of Social Media

When new, the Internet was often looked upon as an unregulated "Wild West," harboring users of unknown identities with questionable motives. As people grew more familiar with the Internet, it became easier to identify *some* of the disreputable sites, yet user skepticism continued. Dishonest personas and practices can frequently be found on the Internet. E-mails from strangers still improperly solicit money, and the true motives of bloggers may not be known. Originators of Twitter messages (tweets) are often not who they appear to be.

This means that users of social media should be skeptical. Their biases must be managed by salespeople using social media for promotion. The burden is on the salesperson to establish and maintain high ethical standards in all presentations and messages. It is not difficult for a user to discover discrepancies among the Web sites, Facebook pages, e-mails, and tweets generated by a salesperson and his or her sales organization. Just like a reputation, one's social media credibility is difficult to repair once damaged.

Social media is a two-edged sword regarding one's business reputation and credibility. Postings and messages can reach hundreds of people within a very short period of time. This can be advantageous for a sales organization when the communication is positive. It can also be extremely damaging if the information is negative.

Today, many business firms are struggling to align their values, ethics, and principles with the expectations of their salespeople and their customers. The process of negotiating ethical standards and practices must be ongoing. Citigroup Incorporated, the world's largest financial services firm, is working hard to move beyond regulatory scandals. Charles Prince, Citigroup CEO, wants the company to better balance its "delivering-the-numbers" culture with a long-term attention to reputation. He readily admits that " . . . at times, our actions have put at risk our most precious commodity—the trust of our clients, the patience of our employees, and the faith of our shareholders."[14]

Can moral behavior be taught? The National Business Ethics Survey, conducted annually by the Ethics Resource Center (www.ethics.org), found that 90 percent of employees said that ethics training is useful or somewhat useful to them. A growing number of students are completing business ethics courses as part of their undergraduate or graduate programs.[15]

Factors Influencing the Ethics of Salespeople

In the field of personal selling, the temptation to maximize short-term gains by some type of unethical conduct is always present. Salespeople are especially vulnerable to moral corruption because they are subject to many temptations. A few examples follow:

> The competition is using exaggerated claims to increase the sale of its product. Should you counteract this action by using exaggerated claims of your own to build a stronger case for your product?

> You have visited the buyer twice, and each time the person displayed a great deal of interest in your product. During the last visit the buyer hinted that the order might be signed if you could provide a small gift. Your company has a long-standing policy that gifts are not to be given under any circumstances. What do you do?

> Your sales manager is under great pressure to increase sales. At a recent meeting of the entire sales staff, this person said, "We have to hit our numbers no matter what it takes!" Does this emotional appeal change your way of dealing with customers?

> During a recent business trip you met an old friend and decided to have dinner together. At the end of the meal, you paid for the entire bill and left a generous tip. Do you now put these non–business-related expenses on your expense account?

These ethical dilemmas arise frequently in the field of selling. How do salespeople respond? Some ignore company policy, cast aside personal standards of conduct, and yield to the pressure. However, a surprising number of salespeople are able to resist. They are aided by a series of factors that help them distinguish right from wrong. Figure 2 outlines the forces that can help them deal honestly and openly with prospects at all times. Next, we discuss each of these factors.

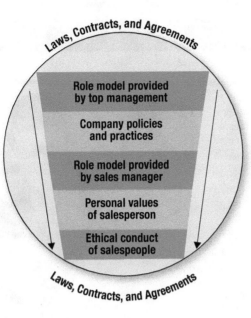

FIGURE 2

Factors Influencing the Ethical Behavior of Salespeople

In personal selling the temptation to maximize short-term gains by some type of unethical conduct is always present. The forces in this figure can help salespeople deal honestly and openly with prospects at all times.

Top Management as Role Model

Ethical standards tend to filter down from the top of an organization. Employees look to company leaders for guidance. The organization's moral tone, as established by management personnel, is the most important single determinant of employee ethics. At Best Buy, Richard Schulze, founder and chairman, is the person who must put ethics concerns on the front burner and make sure that employees stay focused on that priority. The most influential ethics spokesman at Timberland is CEO Jeffrey Swartz, a third-generation CEO whose grandfather founded the company. With pride, he points out Timberland's slogan: "Boots, Brand, Belief."[16]

In recent years, top management has often been guided by advice from professional service firms such as McKinsey & Company, Arthur Andersen, and Merrill Lynch and Company. Too often these firms are recommending strategies that result in quick, short-term gains. Alan M. Webber, who has been studying professional service firms for 20 years, notes, "They want the money right now." He says, " . . . to make the most money, you actually have to believe in the product or service you offer and care for the customers or clients whom you serve."[17]

Minnesota Life Insurance Company has been able to steer clear of scandal for more than 100 years by adopting a values-based management philosophy that rewards integrity and honesty. Success at the management level requires commitment to the company's core values. Managers must demonstrate their ability to infuse ethical values in their subordinates. The Minnesota Life Insurance Company mission and values statement includes the following statement on integrity: "We keep our promises. In all our activities, we adhere to the highest standards of ethical conduct."[18]

Company Policies and Practices

Company policies and practices can have a major impact on the ethical conduct of salespeople. Many employees do not have well-developed moral sensitivity and, therefore, need the guidance of ethics policies. These policies should cover distributor relations, customer service, pricing, product development, and related areas.[19]

Developing policy statements forces a firm to "take a stand" on various business practices. Distinguishing right from wrong can be a healthy activity for any organization. The outcome is a more clear-cut philosophy of how to conduct business transactions. Furthermore, the efforts of salespeople can be compromised by the unethical actions of their companies. Selling products for a company that condones unethical practices is very difficult for the salesperson who maintains high ethical standards.[20]

Doing Business in China

China has entered the World Trade Organization, and its leaders have promised to tear down the barriers that have frustrated foreign business representatives for so long. This country provides a huge market for foreign brands. However, doing business in China begins with a careful study of Chinese business customs.

- Patience is critical when doing business in China. Avoid taking the initiative until you fully understand the rules.
- Business entertaining is frequently done banquet style. If you host a banquet, plan your menu carefully because foods have different meanings. You will be in complete control and no one will eat or drink until you give the signal. Toasting is a ritual in China.
- Chinese businesspeople do not make deals quickly. They prefer to spend time building relationships that will last for years. Harmony is important.
- When making introductions, the oldest and highest-ranking person is introduced first. Chinese bow slightly when greeting another person and the handshake follows.
- Gift giving is a complex process in China. Gifts should be given after all business transactions have been completed.

Source: Eastwest Imaging/Dreamstime

Avoid gifts that suggest death in the Chinese culture: clocks, knife openers, and handkerchiefs, for example.[a]

Mutual of Omaha Executives provides its employees with a carefully worded document titled "Values for Success." Several of these values form the foundation for a corporate culture that encourages ethical behavior:[21]

- **Openness and Trust**   We encourage an open sharing of ideas and information, displaying a fundamental respect for each other as well as our cultural diversity.
- **Honesty and Integrity**   We are honest and ethical with others, maintaining the highest standards of personal and professional conduct.
- **Customer-Focus**   We never lose sight of our customers, and constantly challenge ourselves to meet their requirements even better.

Most marketing companies provide salespeople with guidelines in such areas as sharing confidential information, reciprocity, bribery, gift giving, entertainment, and business defamation.

SHARING CONFIDENTIAL INFORMATION Personal selling, by its very nature, promotes close working relationships. Customers often turn to salespeople for advice. They disclose confidential information freely to someone they trust. It is important that salespeople preserve the confidentiality of the information they receive.

It is not unusual for a customer to disclose information that may be of great value to a competitor. This might include the development of new products, plans to expand into new markets, or anticipated changes in personnel. A salesperson may be tempted to share confidential information with a representative of a competing firm. This breach of confidence might be seen as a means of gaining favor. In most cases this action backfires. The person who receives the confidential information quickly loses respect for the salesperson. A gossipy salesperson seldom develops a trusting relationship with a customer.

RECIPROCITY **Reciprocity** is a mutual exchange of benefits, as when a firm buys products from its own customers. Some business firms actually maintain a policy of reciprocity. For example, the manufacturer of commercial sheets and blankets may purchase hotel services from firms that use its products.

Trust *is not being afraid even if you're vulnerable.*

Is there someone who understands how frightening a situation can be? Someone who believes fear can be dismantled when we are armed with confidence? Is there an insurance company that is consistently rated superior by independent rating services — a company with a 146 year history of providing strength in the face of uncertainty? Without Question.

Without Question. **The St Paul**

Property and Liability Insurance

For more information contact your independent insurance agent or broker or visit www.stpaul.com.

Salespeople representing The St. Paul Property and Liability Insurance Company (www.stpaul.com) can be proud of the firm's record of high ratings.

Source: Courtesy of The St. Paul.

Is there anything wrong with the "you scratch my back and I'll scratch yours" approach to doing business? The answer is sometimes yes. In some cases, the use of reciprocity borders on commercial blackmail. Salespeople have been known to approach firms that supply their company and encourage them to buy out of obligation. Reciprocity agreements are illegal when one company pressures another company to join in the agreement.

A business relationship based on reciprocity has other drawbacks. There is the ever-present temptation to take such customers for granted. A customer who buys out of obligation may take a backseat to customers who were won in the open market.

BRIBERY The book *Arrogance and Accords: The Inside Story of the Honda Scandal* describes one of the largest commercial corruption cases in U.S. history. Over a 15-year period, Honda officials received more than $50 million in cash and gifts from dealers eager to obtain fast-selling Honda cars and profitable franchises. Eighteen former Honda executives were convicted of obtaining kickbacks; most went to prison.[22]

In some cases, a bribe is wrong from a legal standpoint. In almost all cases, the bribe is wrong from an ethical point of view. However, bribery does exist, and a salesperson must be prepared to cope with it. It helps to have a well-established company policy to use as a reference point for what is not acceptable.[23]

Personal selling, by its nature, promotes close working relationships. It is important that salespeople preserve the confidentiality of information they receive. Violation of this ethical responsibility will quickly erode a relationship with the customer.

Source: © Otnaydur

Salespeople who sell products in foreign markets need to know that giving bribes is viewed as an acceptable business practice in some cultures. However, bribes or payoffs may violate the U.S. Foreign Corrupt Practices Act (FCPA). Lucent Technologies Incorporated dismissed two high-ranking executives in China after it found potential violations of the FCPA.[24]

GIFT GIVING Gift giving is a common practice in America. However, some companies do maintain a "no gift" policy. Many companies report that their policy is either no gifts or nothing of real value. Some gifts, such as advertising novelties, planning calendars, or a meal, are of limited value and cannot be construed as a bribe or payoff.

There are some gray areas that separate a gift from a bribe. Most people agree that a token of insignificant price, such as a pen imprinted with a company logo or a desk calendar, is appropriate. These types of gifts are meant to foster goodwill. A bribe, on the other hand, is an attempt to influence the person receiving the gift.

Are there right and wrong ways to handle gift giving? The answer is yes. The following guidelines are helpful to any salesperson who is considering giving gifts to customers:

1. Do not give gifts before doing business with a customer. Do not use the gift as a substitute for effective selling methods.
2. Never convey the impression you are "buying" the customer's business with gifts. When this happens, the gift becomes nothing more than a bribe.
3. When gift giving is done correctly, the customer clearly views it as symbolic of your appreciation—a "no strings attached" goodwill gesture.
4. Be sure the gift is not a violation of the policies of your firm or of your customer's firm. Some firms do not allow employees to accept gifts at all. Other firms place a dollar limit on a gift's value.

In summary, if you have second thoughts about giving a gift, do not do it. When you are sure some token is appropriate, keep it simple and thoughtful.

ENTERTAINMENT Entertainment is a widespread practice in the field of selling and may be viewed as a bribe by some people. The line dividing gifts, bribes, and entertainment is often quite arbitrary.

Salespeople must frequently decide how to handle entertaining. A few industries see entertainment as part of the approach used to obtain new accounts. This is especially true when competing products are nearly identical. A good example is the cardboard box industry. These products vary little in price and quality. Winning an account may involve knowing who to entertain and how to entertain.

Entertainment is a highly individualized process. One prospect might enjoy a professional football game, while another would be impressed most by a quiet meal at a good restaurant. The key is to get to know your prospect's preferences. How does the person spend leisure time? How much time can the person spare for entertainment? You need to answer these and other questions before you invest time and money in entertainment.

BUSINESS DEFAMATION Salespeople frequently compare their product's qualities and characteristics with those of a competitor during the sales presentation. If such comparisons are inaccurate, misleading, or slander a company's business reputation, such conduct is illegal. Competitors have sued hundreds of companies and manufacturers' representatives for making slanderous statements while selling.

What constitutes business defamation? Steven M. Sack, coauthor of *The Salesperson's Legal Guide*, provides the following examples:

1. *Business slander.* This arises when an unfair and untrue oral statement is made about a competitor. The statement becomes actionable when it is communicated to a third party and can be interpreted as damaging the competitor's business reputation or the personal reputation of an individual in that business.
2. *Business libel.* This may be incurred when an unfair and untrue statement is made about a competitor in writing. The statement becomes actionable when it is communicated to a third party and can be interpreted as damaging the company.
3. *Product disparagement.* This occurs when false or deceptive comparisons or distorted claims are made concerning a competitor's product, services, or property.[25]

USE OF THE INTERNET Use of the Internet offers salespeople many advantages, but it can also create a number of ethical dilemmas. For example, e-mail abuse has become a modern-day problem because some employees forget that their employer owns the e-mail system. E-mail messages that contain inflammatory or abusive content, embarrassing gossip, or breaches of confidentiality can lead to legal liabilities. A growing number of companies are developing policies that define permissible uses of their e-mail system.[26]

Some resourceful salespeople have created their own Web sites to alert, attract, or support clients. The rise of these "extranets" has created some problems because they often function outside of the company's jurisdiction. What should top management do if a top salesperson encourages her customers to participate in a special Web auction for a backlogged product? What if the salesperson makes exaggerated claims about a new product? Every marketing firm needs to carefully monitor the development and use of extranets.[27]

The effectiveness of company policies as a deterrent to unethical behavior depends on two factors. The first is the firm's attitude toward employees who violate these policies. If violations are routinely ignored, the policy's effect soon erodes. Second, policies that influence personal selling need the support of the entire sales staff. Salespeople should have some voice in policy decisions; they are more apt to support policies they have helped develop.

Sales Manager as Role Model

The salesperson's actions often mirror the sales manager's behavior and expectations. This is not surprising when you consider the relationship between salespeople and their supervisors. They look to their supervisors for guidance and direction. The sales manager is generally the company's closest point of contact with the sales staff. This person is usually viewed as the chief spokesperson for top management.

SELLING IN ACTION

When the Competition Uses Negative Practices

Negative selling practices create two problems for companies with integrity. First, the salesperson must use valuable time correcting misinformation presented by the competition. Second, a sale may be delayed until the customer rejects the untruth. Jim Galtan, director of sales for Schick Technologies, Inc., the leading manufacturer of digital dental X-ray technology, often learns that the competition has said something negative about his product. When this happens, he looks the customer in the eye and says, "Having the best product often frustrates our competition." He also tells customers that if the competition is honest in their assessment, they should be willing to prepare a letter outlining their concerns. Galtan says documentation is the easiest way to cope with negative selling because no one's going to document untruth.[b]

Sales managers influence the ethical behavior of salespeople by virtue of what they say and what they do.

Source: © Smilla/Dreamstime

Sales managers generally provide new salespeople with their first orientation to company operations. They are responsible for interpreting company policy. On a continuing basis, the sales manager monitors the salesperson's work and provides important feedback concerning conduct. If a salesperson violates company policy, it is usually the sales manager who is responsible for administering reprimands. If the moral fiber of a sales force begins to break down, the sales manager must shoulder a great deal of responsibility, even if it goes against "standard practice."[28]

Sales managers influence the ethical behavior of salespeople by virtue of what they say and what they do. From time to time, managers must review their expectations of ethical behavior. Salespeople are under continuous pressure to abandon their personal ethical standards to achieve sales goals. Values such as integrity and honesty must receive ongoing support from the sales manager.

Salesperson's Personal Values

Ann Kilpatrick, a sales representative in the transportation industry, encountered an unexpected experience when entertaining a potential client. The client said, "Let's go to Johnny's." She was not familiar with Johnny's, but on arrival discovered it was a raunchy bar. Kilpatrick related that she sat there for five minutes and then said, "This is not what I was expecting. This is a sleazy place. Let's go somewhere else where we can talk." She was not willing to compromise her personal values to win a new account.[29]

Values represent the ultimate reasons people have for acting as they do. Values are your deep personal beliefs and preferences that influence your behavior. To discover what really motivates you, carefully examine what you value.[30] Values serve as a foundation for our attitudes, and our attitudes serve as a foundation for our behavior (Figure 3). We do not adopt or discard values quickly. In fact, the development and refinement of values is a lifelong process.

FIGURE 3

Values represent the ultimate reasons salespeople have for acting as they do. Values serve as a foundation for our attitudes, and our attitudes serve as a foundation for our behavior.

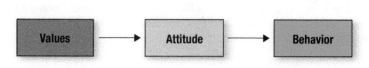

Customers have a very negative view of salespeople who lack integrity. Yet, the temptation to lie about a product's features or benefits grows when you are trying to meet sales quotas. John Craig, a pharmacist at Hancock Drugs in Scottsburg, Indiana, describes a meeting with a pushy sales representative employed by a pharmaceutical company. The salesperson emphasized the wonders of a powerful, expensive painkiller but failed to describe its side effects. Craig said, "He was very pushy at the beginning," and this behavior revealed a character flaw.[31]

VALUES CONFLICT Values help us establish our own personal standards concerning what is right and what is wrong. Ron Willingham, author of *Integrity Selling for the 21st Century*, says, "Selling success is more an issue of who you are than what you know."[32] A salesperson's ethics and values contribute more to sales success than do techniques or strategies. Some salespeople discover a values conflict between themselves and their employer. If you view your employer's instructions or influence as improper, you have three choices:

1. Ignore the influence of your values and engage in the unethical behavior. However, even with success, inattention to values will result in a loss of self-respect and feelings of guilt.[33] When salespeople experience conflicts between their actions and values, they also feel a loss of confidence and energy.[34] Positive energy is the result of creating value for the customer. Negative energy is experienced when salespeople fail to honor and embrace their ethical values.
2. Voice strong opposition to the practice that is in conflict with your values system. Take a stand and state your beliefs. When ethical infractions occur, it's best to bring them up internally and try to influence decisions made by your peers or superiors. In some cases, doing the right thing may not be popular with others. Price Pritchett, the author of *The Ethics of Excellence*, says, "Not everybody will be on your side in your struggle to do the right thing."[35]
3. Refuse to compromise your values and be prepared to deal with the consequences. This may mean leaving the job. It also may mean that you will be fired.

Salespeople face ethical problems and decisions every day. In this respect they are no different from the doctor, the lawyer, the teacher, or any other professional. Ideally, they make decisions on the basis of the values they hold.[36]

Laws, Contracts, and Agreements

Take another look at Figure 2 and you will notice that all of the key elements, personnel, and policies are influenced by laws, contracts, and agreements. Everyone involved in sales and marketing is guided by legal as well as ethical standards. We live in a society in which the legal system plays a key role in preventing people from engaging in unethical behavior.

LAWS The specific obligations imposed by government on the way business operates take the form of *statutes*, laws passed by Congress or state legislatures. Some of the most common laws deal with price competition, credit reporting, debt collection practices, contract enforcement, and land sales disclosure. The Uniform Commercial Code (UCC) is a major law influencing sales throughout the United States (see Table 1). The UCC is a legal guide to a wide range of transactions between the seller and the buyer. This law has been adopted throughout the United States and, therefore, has implications for most salespeople.

A majority of the states have passed legislation that establishes a cooling-off period during which the consumer may void a contract to purchase goods or services. Although the provisions of **cooling-off laws** vary from state to state, their primary purpose is to

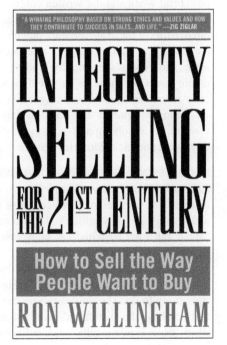

Ron Willingham says a salesperson's ethics and values contribute more to sales success than do techniques and strategies.

Source: Jacket Cover copyright © 2003 by Doubleday, a division of Random House, Inc., from *Integrity Selling for the 21st Century* by Ron Willingham. Used with permission of Doubleday, a division of Random House, Inc.

TABLE 1 Uniform Commercial Code Defines Legal Side of Selling

Any list of the major developments in American law would have near its top the adoption of the Uniform Commercial Code (UCC), a body of statutes that replaces several areas of business law formerly covered individually by each state's common law of contracts.

The Uniform Commercial Code (UCC) is the source of the major laws influencing sales throughout the United States. Several areas featured in the UCC focus directly on the seller–buyer relationship. Some of the primary areas follow:

1. *Definition of a sale.* The code defines the legal dimensions of a sale. It clearly states that salespeople have the authority to legally obligate the company they represent.
2. *Warranties and guarantees.* The code distinguishes between express warranties and implied warranties. Express warranties are those that are described by the express language of the seller. Implied warranties are the obligations imposed by law on the seller that are not assumed in express language.
3. *Salesperson and reseller.* In many cases, the salesperson has resellers as customers or prospects. Salespeople must be aware of their employer's obligations to the reseller.
4. *Financing of sales.* Often salespeople work for firms that are directly involved in financing products or services or in arranging such financing from outside sources. A salesperson needs to be familiar with the legal aspects of these credit arrangements.
5. *Product consignment.* In some cases, goods are delivered to the buyer, but the title remains with the seller. This type of transaction can become complicated if the goods have a limited life span. Depreciation may occur with the passing of time. Salespeople should be familiar with the company's rights in cases in which goods are sold on consignment.

give customers an opportunity to reconsider a buying decision made under a salesperson's persuasive influence. Many laws are designed to deal specifically with sales made in the consumer's home. For example, the Federal Trade Commission (FTC) established the National Do Not Call Registry in an attempt to reduce the number of telemarketing calls.

CONTRACTS AND AGREEMENTS The word *contract* may bring to mind the familiar multipage, single-spaced documents that no ordinary person seems able to understand. In fact, contracts can be oral or written. A **contract** is simply a promise or promises that the courts will enforce. Oral contracts are enforceable, but written contracts are preferable. They reduce the possibility of disagreement and the courts give them great weight in a lawsuit. A written contract can consist of a sales slip, a notation on a check, or any other writing that evidences the promises that the parties made.[37]

Salespeople are sometimes the legal representatives of their company and, therefore, must be careful when signing written contracts. They often oversee contracts with customers, suppliers, and resellers. Salespeople also frequently sign employment contracts at the time they are hired. Most of these agreements include a noncompete clause. One of the most common clauses, a noncompete clause prohibits salespeople from joining a competing firm for a year after they leave. Most clauses are legally binding even when an employee's position is cut. Employers see employment contracts as an effective way to protect intellectual property, customer lists, and other resources an employee might take to a competing firm.[38]

Many companies are learning that resolving legal disputes can be very costly and time-consuming. Resolving a dispute in the courts can sometimes take several years. A serious effort to prevent unethical activities can prevent costly litigation.

ETHICS BEYOND THE LETTER OF THE LAW Too often people confuse ethical standards with legal standards. They believe that if you are not breaking the law, then you are acting in an ethical manner.[39] A salesperson's ethical sense must extend beyond the legal definition of what is right and wrong. To view ethics only in terms of what is legally proper encourages the question, "What can I get by with?" A salesperson must develop a personal code of ethics that extends beyond the letter of the law.

Bruce Weinstein, a professional ethicist who is often introduced as "The Ethics Guy," offers sound advice on living an ethical life. He says we should do the right thing simply because it's the right thing to do. The only way you can build a loyal and growing client base is to demonstrate that you have the customers' own best interests at heart. You are trying to make things better for them. "Here is where ethics differs from the law. It demands more of us," says Weinstein.[40]

A Personal Code of Ethics That Adds Value

Many people considering a career in selling are troubled by the thought that they may be pressured into compromising their personal standards of right and wrong. These fears may be justified. The authors of *The Ethical Edge*, a book that examines organizations that have faced moral crises, contend that business firms have given too little thought to the issue of helping employees to function ethically within organizations.[41] Many salespeople wonder whether their own ethical philosophy can survive in the business world. These are some of their questions:

"Can a profitable business and good ethics coexist?"

"Are there still business firms that value adherence to high ethical standards?"

"Is honesty still a valued personal trait in the business community?"

In the field of athletic competition, the participants rely heavily on a written set of rules. The referee or umpire is ever present to detect rule violations and assess a penalty. In the field of personal selling, there is no universal code of ethics. However, some general guidelines can serve as a foundation for a personal code of business ethics.

1. *Personal selling must be viewed as an exchange of value.* Salespeople who maintain a value focus are searching for ways to create value for their prospects or customers. This value may take the form of increased productivity, greater profit, enjoyment, or security. The value focus motivates the salesperson to carefully identify the prospects' wants and needs.[42] Salespeople who accept this ethical guideline view personal selling as something you do *for* customers, not something you do *to* customers. The role of the salesperson is to diagnose buyer needs and determine whether value can be created. Always be prepared to add value.

2. *Relationship comes first, task second.* Sharon Drew Morgan, author of *Selling with Integrity*, says that you can't sell a product unless there is a level of comfort between you and the prospect. She encourages salespeople to take the time to create a level of comfort, rapport, and collaboration that encourages open communication.[43] Placing task before relationship is based on the belief that the salesperson knows more than the customer. Morgan reminds us, "The buyer has the answers, and the seller has the questions."[44] These answers surface only when the buyer–seller relationship is characterized by rapport and trust.

3. *Be honest with yourself and with others.* To achieve excellence in terms of ethical practices, you have to believe that everything you do counts. Tom Peters in *Thriving on Chaos* said,

---

CUSTOMER RELATIONSHIP MANAGEMENT WITH TECHNOLOGY

Ethical and Legal Issues with Recording CRM Data

Customer relationship management systems enable you to collect information about people with whom you maintain relationships, including the taking of notes. It is a good practice to record more than basic transaction information, such as personal details about your customers. Reviewing your observations about the customers' behavior and your recording of their statements can help you understand them and their needs. Rereading their comments about ethical issues can assist you in assessing the value of maintaining a business relationship with them.

To be fair, it is important to record only the facts concerning your observations, not necessarily your conclusions, especially if negative. Information in an electronic database can last a long time and, for reasons such as litigation or company acquisitions, can be "mobile." This means that others may form an opinion about your customer based on your recorded conclusions, with potential detrimental consequences for your customer. Because the customer may not be aware of the existence of the information in your database,

that person does not have a fair opportunity to correct any erroneous conclusions. Another reason to carefully record only the facts is the possibility that any inappropriate information may come to the attention of the customer. For example, there are reported instances in which a customer later joined the sales organization and gained access to the customer relationship management (CRM) system.

Most CRM systems contain scheduling functions, which means that you can set aside time on your calendar to attend meetings, make phone calls, and perform tasks. The scheduling tools usually include alarms, which remind you that a deadline is approaching. The disciplined use of these features can help you get your work accomplished on time. Taking advantage of the system's reminder tools can be especially important when it involves fulfilling your commitments. The system can help you build trust by reminding you to always do what you said you would do. Application Exercise "Using CRM Data to Prepare Mailing Lists" shows how to generate a list of contacts.

Personal selling must be viewed as an exchange of value. Salespeople who accept this ethical guideline view personal selling as something you do for customers, not something you do to customers.

Source: Kablonk/SuperStock, Inc.

"Integrity may be about little things as much as or more than big ones."[45] Integrity is about accuracy in completing your expense account. There is always the temptation to inflate the expense report for personal gain. Integrity is also about avoiding the temptation to stretch the truth, to exaggerate, or to withhold information. Paul Ekman, author of *Telling Lies*, says that withholding important information is one of the primary ways of lying.[46] A complete and informative sales presentation may include information concerning the product's limitations. If you let your character and integrity be revealed in the little things, others can see you as one who acts ethically in all things. Any violation of honesty, however small, dilutes your ethical strength, leaving you weaker for the big challenges you will face sooner or later.[47]

The Trust Factor

Everyone involved in personal selling must work hard to build relationships based on trust. Customers are more apt to trust salespeople they believe to be ethical, leading to a much more productive partnership.[48] Although trust is an essential element of every sale, the meaning of trust changes with the type of sale.[49]

- *Trust in transactional sales.* The primary customer focus in this type of sale is trust in the product. Is the product reliable? Is the product priced as low as possible? Can the product be delivered in a timely fashion? The transactional buyer may purchase a product from a salesperson they do not feel totally comfortable with if it meets their purchase criteria.
- *Trust in consultative sales.* In a consultative sale, the customer focus shifts from the product to the person who sells the product. The consultative buyer is thinking, "Can I trust this salesperson to identify my problem and offer me one or more solutions?" Customers involved in a consultative sale usually do not separate the product from the person selling it. They want to do business with a salesperson who displays such positive qualities as warmth, empathy, genuineness, competence, and integrity.
- *Trust in strategic alliance sales.* The strategic alliance buyer wants to do business with an institution that can be trusted. This buyer looks beyond the well-qualified salesperson and assesses the entire organization. A strategic alliance customer will not feel comfortable partnering with a company whose values differ greatly from their own. Ethical accountability will greatly influence the way an alliance partner is judged and valued.

Trust exists when we strongly believe in the integrity, ability, and character of a person or an organization. Although trust is an intangible, it is at the very core of all meaningful relationships. Trust is quickly lost and slowly won.[50]

Ethical and Legal Issues in International Business

Ethical and legal issues that are quite complex on the domestic scene become even more complicated at the international level. International business is growing, and the United States is deeply involved in the global marketplace. Thomas Friedman, author of the best-selling book *The World Is Flat: A Brief History of the Twenty-First Century*, says today's highly competitive and global marketplace is flattening the world of international business. In order to compete with China, India, and other dynamic economics, U.S.-based companies must adopt a more aggressive global focus.[51]

Culture Issues

Today's global marketplace reflects a kaleidoscope of cultures, each with its own unique qualities. **Culture** is the sum total of beliefs, values, knowledge, ethnic customs, and objects that people use to adapt to their environment. Cultural barriers can impede acceptance of products in foreign countries and weaken interpersonal relationships. When the salesperson understands the cultural background of the foreign customer, communication problems are less likely. Many people from Asia, Arab countries, and much of Africa prefer a more indirect style of communication and therefore value harmony, subtlety, sensitivity, and tact more than brevity.[52] The customer who seems to be agreeing with everything you say may have no intention of buying your product. This person may simply be displaying polite and tactful behaviors.

Perceptions of time differ from country to country. Americans value promptness, but businesspeople from other countries often approach meetings in a more relaxed manner. Arriving late for a meeting may not be viewed as a problem. Many companies are spending thousands of dollars to make sure that employees sent abroad are culturally prepared. Eastman Chemical Company, for example, has developed a highly successful orientation program for employees who have accepted overseas assignments.[53]

Legal Issues

Doing business in the global marketplace continues to be an ethical minefield. Illegal demands for bribes, kickbacks, or special fees may stand in the way of successful transactions. The Foreign Corrupt Practices Act prohibits U.S. companies from using bribes or kickbacks to influence foreign officials. But monitoring illegal activities throughout the world is a very difficult task.[54] Motorola and some other U.S. businesses are using software to analyze invoices and payments in order to uncover possible payoffs. Gifts from suppliers to U.S. companies can also be a problem. Each year United Technologies sends a letter to foreign suppliers saying "we don't want gifts."[55]

American businesses acknowledge that it is difficult to compete with organizations from other countries that are not bound by U.S. laws. However, the International Business Ethics Institute (www.business-ethics.org) believes that U.S. companies have been a very positive role model for rest of the business world. As noted previously in this chapter, high ethical standards depend on strong leadership provided by management personnel at all levels of the organization. Integrity starts at the top.

CHAPTER LEARNING ACTIVITIES

Reviewing Key Concepts

Describe how ethical decisions influence relationships in selling

Character and integrity strongly influence relationships in personal selling. Unethical sales practices will ultimately destroy relationships with customers. These practices undermine trust, which is at the very core of all meaningful relationships.

Discuss factors that influence character development

Many colleges and universities are playing a more active role in character development. Character education is often integrated into courses that focus on ethics. Character is composed of personal standards of behavior, so all of us can do things that build character. Keeping our commitments to others provides just one example of how character is built.

Describe the factors that influence the ethical conduct of sales personnel

Salespeople can benefit from the stabilizing influence of good role models. Although top management personnel are usually far removed from day-to-day selling activities, they can have a major impact on salespeople's conduct. Dishonesty at the top of an organization can cause an erosion of ethical standards at the lower echelons. Sales managers provide another important role model. They interpret company policies and help establish guidelines for acceptable and unacceptable selling practices.

Discuss guidelines for developing a personal code of ethics

Salespeople must establish their own standards of personal conduct. They must decide how best to serve their company and build strong partnerships with their customers. The pressure to compromise one's ethical standards surfaces almost daily. The primary deterrent is a strong sense of right and wrong. Three general guidelines can serve as a foundation for a personal code of ethics:

a. Personal selling must be viewed as an exchange of value.

b. Relationship comes first; task, second.

c. Be honest with yourself and with others.

Describe ethical and legal issues in international business

At the international level, ethical and legal issues can be very complex. The global marketplace reflects a great number of cultures, each with its unique qualities. Coping with illegal activities throughout the world is also very challenging. Illegal demands for bribes, kickbacks, or special fees can serve as a barrier to business transactions.

Key Terms

Business ethics	Values	Contract
Reciprocity	Cooling-off laws	Culture

Review Questions

1. What is the definition of *business ethics*? Why is this topic receiving so much attention today?
2. Carefully review the Standards of Professional Conduct developed by the National Association of Sales Professionals (NASP). Select the three standards you feel would present the greatest challenge to salespeople. Explain your answer.
3. How does business slander differ from business libel?
4. What major factors help influence salespeople's ethical conduct?
5. What is the Uniform Commercial Code? Why is it needed?
6. Why must a salesperson's ethical sense extend beyond the legal definition of what is right and wrong?
7. Explain why the sales manager plays such an important role in influencing the ethical behavior of salespeople.
8. A company policy on ethics should cover several major areas. What are they?
9. Is it ever appropriate to give gifts to customers? Explain.
10. List and describe three guidelines used as a foundation of a self-imposed code of business ethics.

Application Exercises

1. You find that you have significantly overcharged one of your clients. The error was discovered when you received payment. It is unlikely that the customer or your company will become aware of the overcharge. Because of this error, the company realized a higher net profit on the sale. Your commissions are based on this profit. What, if anything, will you do about the overcharge?
2. Access the National Association of Sales Professionals Web site at www.nasp.com. Click on the sales certification link and examine the steps to becoming a certified sales professional. Also click "Registry of Accredited Salespeople" and "Directory of Members." Examine the backgrounds of several members of the NASP. After reviewing the Standards of Professional Conduct printed in this chapter, discuss your views on the impact professional certification has on the ethical behavior of salespeople. Do you think the designation CPSP would affect the impression a customer might have of a salesperson?

3. You work for a supplier of medical equipment. Your sales manager informs you that he wants you to capture a certain hospital account. He also tells you to put on your expense account anything it costs to secure the firm as a client. When you ask him to be more specific, he tells you to use your own judgment. Up to this time you have never questioned your sales manager's personal code of ethics. Make a list of the items you believe can be legitimately charged to the company on your expense account.

4. For some time your strongest competitor has been making untrue derogatory statements about your product and about your company. You know for a fact that her product is not as good as yours, yet hers has a higher price. Several of your best customers have confronted you with these charges. Describe how you plan to answer them.

5. Sales managers must approve expense reports turned in by members of the sales force. Assume the role of sales manager for a sales force that includes 12 salespeople who travel frequently and average about two overnight trips each week. Recently you noticed that the expense reports turned in by two of your salespeople seem quite high. You suspect that these salespeople are padding their expense reports. What steps should you take to determine whether cheating is occurring? How can a sales manager prevent the padding of expense reports?

Role-Play Exercise

This morning you met with a customer who has purchased office supplies from you for almost three years. You are quite surprised when she says, "I am prepared to place a $10,500 order, but you must match an offer I received from a competitor." She then explains that the competitor is offering *new* customers a seven-day trip to Disney World in Orlando if they place an order of more than $10,000. All expenses will be paid. What would you do?

Prepare to role-play your response with another student. Review the material in this chapter, paying special attention to ways you can add value and build long-term relationships with ethical decision making.

CRM Application Exercise

Using CRM Data to Prepare Mailing Lists

Log onto Salesforce.com, and click on the Reports tab. Choose "SimNet Reports" from the Report Folder drop-down menu and click on the "SimNet Mailing Lists" report.

✓ SimNet Reports	
Edit | Del | Export	Contacts by Communication Style
Edit | Del | Export	Contacts by Location
Edit | Del | Export	Sales Pipeline
Edit | Del | Export	Sales Stage Pipeline
Edit | Del | Export	SimNet Mailing Lists

On the following screen, select the button labeled "Printable View."

| Run Report ▼ | Hide Details | Customize | Save | Save As | Delete | Printable View | Export Details |

Printable View will download to your computer a mailing list of all contacts in Microsoft Excel format.

Save As

File name: report1281831804786.xls

Save as type: Microsoft Office Excel 97-2003 Worksheet

If prompted to save the file, do so and remember where it is stored on your computer. You may open and print the file or, if your instructor requests, you may attach it to an e-mail to your instructor.

Reality Selling Today Video Case Problem: Mattress Firm

Mattress Firm (www.mattressfirm.com) is one of the largest and most successful specialty bedding companies in the world. It offers sleep solutions, including conventional and specialty mattresses, as well as bedding-related products. The company has grown to become one of the largest and fastest growing retailers in the nation. The company operates more than 560 stores in 38 markets nationwide and carries the top mattress brands. From the very beginning, the company, which only hires college graduates, set out to be a different kind of mattress retailer, focused on creating a unique shopping experience.

According to Edith Botello, featured at the beginning of this chapter, the biggest differentiator between Mattress Firm and its competitors is the sales process. As Edith puts it, buying a mattress can be overwhelming: How do you know which one is the best if all you see when you walk into a store are dozens of white rectangles? At Mattress Firm, sales reps make it simple for their customers to pick out their mattress without trying out every single bed. The process invites customers to get fitted for a mattress, just as with suits, shoes, and gowns. This is done through the company's Sleep Diagnostic System, which asks the customer a series of questions about their sleep quality and then measures their weight distribution and postural alignment. The system then recommends a type of support and eliminates 80 percent of the beds in the showroom. Taking the risk out of buying a mattress by letting the customer know what mattresses are best for them is something that only Mattress Firm offers.

How can ethical aspects of selling come into play in Edith's job as a retail salesperson? One example would be that sometimes salespeople have the opportunity to write up a sale where they would get credit but have not earned the right to do so. At times, customers shop around and end up at the same store and want the same product that was offered to them previously. In such a case, the customer may request the particular salesperson who helped him or her previously. If that salesperson is not there, the new salesperson could choose to not give her/him credit. Another example might be a customer who tries to get greater price discounts by making untrue statements about a competitor's price offering or shopping around at different Mattress Firm locations in order to get the lowest possible price. In many cases, however, the salesperson will recognize this behavior and act accordingly.

Being ethical is a core value at Mattress Firm. New hires are made aware of Mattress Firm's expectations from the beginning of their employment to ensure that they are ethical with their customers and other salespeople. Mattress Firm's Code of Conduct is a guide to the general principles that permeate the employees' relationships with customers, business partners, and, last but not least, each other. The Code goes far beyond compliance with laws and regulations. It is also a set of practical instructions to help employees in their day-to-day work. It explains, for example, how to manage potential conflicts of interest and how to report suspected violations of the rules.

At Mattress Firm, several policies and elements in the incentive compensation system exist that also help to safeguard ethical behavior. The Standard Operating Procedure (SOP) dedicates an entire section to commission sales and how to handle different situations such as team selling, ticket trading, SPIFFS, bonuses, etc. For example, the commission system encourages sales reps to hold the line on price concessions. National sales contests are also audited to ensure ethical behavior. The SOP and Employee Code of Conduct are housed on the company's intranet and are available to view at any time. (See the chapter opener and Reality *Selling Today* Role-Play 4 in the appendix at the end of this chapter for more information.)

Questions

1. Put yourself in Edith Botello's place as a sales rep selling mattresses. Can you imagine situations in your job that might challenge your ethical conduct?
2. For retailers such as Mattress Firm, what are the major areas that should be covered in a company policy on ethics?

3. Revenue-based incentive compensation plans, by their very nature, pressure sales reps to generate high sales, which might cause unethical sales practices. How could an incentive compensation system be designed that stimulates sales generation, but safeguards ethical sales behavior at the same time?

4. Imagine you were a salesperson for Mattress Firm, just like Edith Botello. A customer walks into your store and, after awhile, shows great interest in a specific Tempur-Pedic. When it comes to the price, the customer mentions that your competitor across the street offered him exactly that mattress at a 10 percent lower price than Mattress Firm. You have some doubts that this statement is actually true, but you do not want to disgruntle and compromise the customer. How would you react?

ROLE-PLAY EXERCISE

Developing a Relationship Strategy

Scenario

You are an experienced sales representative employed by American Steel Processing, a company that has been in business for more than 25 years. American is an ISO 9002–certified manufacturing company that has earned many accolades, including three consecutive J.D. Power and Associates awards for customer satisfaction. Over the years the company has invested heavily in automation technology as a means of ensuring consistent manufacturing quality. The American Steel processing sales force understands that the company will not be the lowest bidder in most sales situations because the highest quality can never be obtained at the lowest price.

Customer Profile

Tyler Hensman has held the position of senior purchasing agent at Regina Steel Fabricators for several years. Throughout this period of time, Tyler has negotiated more than a dozen purchase agreements with Dana Davis, senior account representative with American Steel Processing. Tyler takes pride in purchasing quality steel products at the best price.

Salesperson Profile

Dana Davis began working for American Steel Processing Company about four years ago. After completion of an extensive sales training program, Dana was assigned to a territory in central Ohio. After three successful years, Dana Davis was promoted to senior account representative.

Product

American Steel Processing sells a wide range of steel products. Many of the orders filled are for high-stress steel beams, stainless steel bolts and nuts, and structural tubing used in commercial building construction. Most orders specify a certain quality of steel.

Instructions

For this role-play you will assume the role of Dana Davis, senior account representative employed by American Steel Processing. To prepare for the role-play, you should carefully read the case problem at the end of this chapter. This information will help you understand the issues that need to be addressed during the role-play. During the early stages of the role-play, you will want to obtain more information from the customer and resolve any misunderstandings. You want to obtain the order for type 316 stainless steel bolts and nuts, and maintain a good relationship with this important customer. Keep in mind that ethical decisions can greatly influence the relationship between a salesperson and the customer. Reflect on the important information covered in this chapter prior to meeting with Tyler Hensman.

Appendix: Reality Selling Today Role-Play Scenario
Reality Selling Today Role-Play 4, Mattress Firm

Edith Botello
Mattress Firm

(This mock sales call role-play scenario is created exclusively for use with this chapter.)

Your Role at Mattress Firm

You will be a sales representative for Mattress Firm (see Web site at www.mattressfirm.com), working in the same store as Edith Botello, featured in the chapter opener and Reality *Selling Today* Video. Your company offers sleep solutions, including conventional and specialty mattresses, as well as bedding-related products. Mattress Firm carries the top mattress brands like Sealy, Stearns & Foster, Tempur-Pedic, Simmons, Serta, Sleep to Live, and more. From the very beginning, the company set out to be a different kind of mattress retailer, focused on creating a unique shopping experience.

One aspect that sets Mattress Firm apart from competition is the buying process. Customers are invited to get fitted for a mattress, just like you do with suits, shoes, and gowns. This is accomplished through the company's so-called Sleep Diagnostic System, which asks the customer a series of questions about their sleep quality and then measures their weight distribution and postural alignment. After this is done, it recommends a type of support and eliminates 80 percent of the beds in the showroom, thus making it simpler for customers to find the right mattress without trying out every single bed. Taking the risk out of buying a mattress by letting the customer know what mattresses are best for them is something that only the Mattress Firm offers. (Refer to the chapter opening vignette, and review the end-of-chapter Reality *Selling Today* Video Case for more information.)

Your Customer: Mark Boomershine

Mark and Kelly Boomershine have been married for eight years. They have two kids, Lisa and Marcus, ages 3 and 5. The Boomershines are a typical mid-class family, living in a residential area on the outskirts of Nashville, Tennessee. They have an Airedale Terrier that Kelly loves and that occupies their bed quite frequently. Mark works as a motor mechanic, and Kelly is a nurse at the Nashville General Hospital, where she is primarily on night duty. Mark is into sports, but he has had some severe problems with his back recently due to a slipped disk. He went into the hospital just a week ago and is now recovering from the surgery at home. For the last couple of days, he has been waking up stiff and hurting. Mark and Kelly have had a relatively inexpensive queen-size mattress for the last six years. They were not planning to replace that mattress, but Mark's back problems have forced them to find a supportive mattress for his recovery as soon as possible. Kelly dislikes sleeping on firm mattresses. That is why their current mattress is fairly soft. However, the couple has doubts that a soft mattress would be the ideal solution for Mark, as friends have been telling them that Mark would need a very firm mattress to support his recovery. Today, Mark enters your store to try out some mattresses that would fit his needs. He needs a supportive mattress quite urgently, but wonders whether Kelly and he would actually need two separate mattresses to fit both of their needs.

Your Call Objectives

In your sales call with Mark Boomershine, you hope to build rapport with him, identify his sleeping needs, and sell him a sleeping solution based on these needs. You have to overcome two major objections raised by Mark: (1) What if his back pain persists over a longer time—even on the new mattress that you recommend? Can he simply exchange the mattress at your store for a new one? (2) Since the mattresses that you offer him as possible solutions would mean a fairly high expenditure for the couple, he asks you for a substantial rebate of around 20 percent in case of a purchase. However, the particular mattresses that come into consideration are price-regulated (i.e., the contract with the manufacturer dictates that price negotiation is not allowed). If you manage to overcome these objections and present a good solution, Mark would be ready to buy. Since he needs a supportive mattress urgently, Mark would bring Kelly into your store tomorrow to get her blessings and just make the final choice among the options under consideration.

Endnotes

1. O. C. Ferrell, John Fraedrich, and Linda Ferrell, *Business Ethics*, 5th ed. (Boston: Houghton Mifflin Company, 2002), p. 6. The importance of character at the leadership level is described in Noel M. Tichy and Warren G. Bennis, "Making the Tough Call," *Inc.*, November 2007, pp. 36–38.

2. Shankar Ganesan, Steven P. Brown, Babu John Mariadoss, and Hillbun (Dixon) Ho (2010), "Buffering and Amplifying Effects of Relationship Commitment in Business-to-Business Relationships," *Journal of Marketing Research*, 47(2), pp. 361–373.

3. NASP Membership Information, www.nasp.com (accessed July 6, 2010).

4. Stephen R. Covey, *The Seven Habits of Highly Effective People* (New York: Simon & Schuster, 1989), pp. 18, 92. See Adam Hanft, "The New Lust for Integrity," *Inc.*, February 2004, p. 104.

5. Jan Yager, *Business Protocol* (Stamford, CT: Hannacroix Creek Books, 2001), pp. 199–200.

6. Sharon Begley, "A World of Their Own," *Newsweek*, May 8, 2000, pp. 53–56; Jaren Sandberg, "Office Sticky Fingers Can Turn the Rest of Us into Joe Fridays," *Wall Street Journal*, November 19, 2005, p. Bl.

7. John A. Byrne, "How to Fix Corporate Governance," *BusinessWeek*, May 6, 2002, pp. 69–78.

8. Josh Freed, "Investigators: Drug Salesman Foiled Pharmacist," *The News & Observer*, August 26, 2001, p. 12A.

9. Robert Simons, Henry Mintzburg, and Kunal Basu, "Memo to: CEOs," *Fast Company*, June 2002, pp. 117–121.

10. Marjorie Kelly, "Waving Goodbye to the Invisible Hand," *Business Ethics*, March/April 2002, p. 4. For a somewhat different point of view, see George Stalk, "Warm and Fuzzy Doesn't Cut It," *Wall Street Journal*, February 15, 2005, p. B2.

11. Yochi J. Dreazen, "Pressure for Sales Fostered Abuses at WorldCom," *Wall Street Journal*, May 16, 2002, p. B1. See Norm Kamikow, "Ethics & Performance," *Workforce Performance Solutions*, March 2006, p. 4.

12. Robert Simons, Henry Mintzburg, and Kunal Basu, "Memo to: CEOs," *Fast Company*, June 2002 pp. 120–121.

13. Patrick Smith, "You Have a Job, But How About a Life?" *BusinessWeek*, November 16, 1998, p. 30.

14. Mitchell Pacelle, "Citigroup Works on Reputation," *Wall Street Journal*, February 17, 2005, p. C3.

15. Patricia B. Gray, "Business Class," *Fortune*, April 17, 2006, p. 336; Margery Weinstein, "Survey Says: Ethics Training Works," *Training*, November 2005, p. 15; "ERC Survey & Benchmarking," www.ethics.org (accessed July 6, 2010).

16. Patricia Gray, "Business Class," *Fortune*, April 17, 2006, p. 336; Philip Kotler and Gary Armstrong, *Principles of Marketing*, 12th ed. (Upper Saddle River, NJ: Prentice Hall, 2008), p. 568.

17. Alan M. Webber, "Are All Consultants Corrupt?" *Fast Company*, May 2002, pp. 130–134.

18. Mary Ellen Egan, "Old Enough to Know Better," *Business Ethics*, January–February 1995, p. 19; "Our Mission and Values," www.minnesotamutual.com (accessed July 6, 2010).

19. Gary Armstrong and Philip Kotler, *Marketing*, 6th ed. (Upper Saddle River, NJ: Prentice Hall, 2003), p. 619.

20. Betsy Cummings, "Ethical Breach," *Sales & Marketing Management*, July 2004, p. 10.

21. O. C. Ferrell, John Fraedrich, and Linda Ferrell, *Business Ethics*, 5th ed. (Boston: Houghton Mifflin Company, 2002), p. 128.

22. Michele Krebs, "All the Marketing Men," *Autoweek*, February 16, 1998, p. 11.

23. Joseph A. McKinney and Carlos W. Moore (2008), "International Bribery: Does a Written Code of Ethics Make a Difference in Perceptions of Business," *Journal of Business Ethics*, 79(1–2), pp. 103–111.

24. Ken Brown and Gee L. Lee, "Lucent Fires Top China Executives," *Wall Street Journal*, April 7, 2004, p. A8; Carl F. Fey, "How to Do Business in Russia," *Wall Street Journal*, October 27, 2007, p. R4.

25. Steve Sack, "Watch the Words," *Sales & Marketing Management*, July 1, 1985, p. 56.

26. Patricia S. Eyres, "Steps for Staying Out of Court and Trouble," *Selling*, April 2002, p. 10.

27. Michael Schrage, "Internet: Internal Threat?" *Fortune*, July 9, 2001, p. 184.

28. Mary C. Gentile, "Managing Yourself: Keeping Your Colleagues Honest," *Harvard Business Review*, March 2010, http://hbr.org/2010/03/managing-yourself-keeping-your-colleagues-honest/ar/1 (accessed July 7, 2010).

29. Rob Zeiger, "Sex, Sales & Stereotypes," *Sales & Marketing Management*, July 1995, pp. 52–53.

30. Barry L. Reece and Rhonda Brandt, *Effective Human Relations—Personal and Organizational Applications*, 10th ed. (Boston: Houghton Mifflin Company, 2008), p. 110.

31. Betsy Cummings, "Do Customers Hate Salespeople?" *Sales & Marketing Management*, June 2001, pp. 50–51.

32. Ron Willingham, *Integrity Selling for the 21st Century* (New York: Currency Doubleday, 2003), p. 1.

33. Nina Mazar, On Amir, and Dan Ariely (2008), "The Dishonesty of Honest People: A Theory of Self-Concept Maintenance," *Journal of Marketing Research*, 45(4), pp. 633–644.

34. Ron Willingham, "Four Traits All Highly Successful Salespeople Have in Common" (audiotape presentation), Phoenix, AZ, 1998.

35. Price Pritchett, *The Ethics of Excellence* (Dallas, TX: Pritchett & Associates, Inc., n.d.), p. 14.

36. Research on how cheaters justify their actions is cited in Romy Drucker, "The Devil Made Me Do It," *BusinessWeek,* July 24, 2006, p. 10.

37. Robert Kreitner, Barry Reece, and James P. O'Grady, *Business*, 2nd ed. (Boston: Houghton Mifflin Company, 1990), pp. 647–648.

38. Karin Schill Rives, "Workers Find Clause Has Teeth," *News & Observer*, July 29, 2001, p. E-1.

39. Dawn Marie Driscoll, "Don't Confuse Legal and Ethical Standards," *BusinessWeek*, July–August 1996, p. 44.

40. Nancy Henderson Wurst, "Who's Afraid of Ethics?" *Hemisphere Magazine,* November 2006, pp. 120–123.

41. Carol Wheeler, "Getting the Edge on Ethics," *Executive Female*, May–June 1996, p. 47.

42. Ron Willingham, *Integrity Selling for the 21st Century* (New York: Currency Doubleday, 2003), p. 11.

43. Sharon Drew Morgan, *Selling with Integrity* (San Francisco: Berrett-Koehler, 1997), pp. 25–27.

44. Ibid., pp. 27–28.

45. Tom Peters, *Thriving on Chaos* (New York: Alfred A. Knopf, 1988), p. 521.

46. Gerhard Gschwandtner, "Lies and Deception in Selling," *Personal Selling Power*, 15th Anniversary Issue, 1995, p. 62.

47. Price Pritchett, *The Ethics of Excellence* (Dallas, TX: Pritchett & Associates, Inc., n.d.), p. 18.

48. John D. Hansen and Robert J. Riggle (2009), "Ethical Salesperson Behavior in Sales Relationships," *Journal of Personal Selling and Sales Management*, 29(2), pp. 151–166.

49. Neil Rackham and John R. DeVincentis, *Rethinking the Sales Force* (New York: McGraw-Hill, 1999), pp. 83–84. A discussion of the trust factor is included in Jacqueline Durett, "A Matter of Trust," *Sales & Marketing Management*, January/February 2007, pp. 36–37.

50. Geoffrey Colvin, "The Verdict on Business: Presumed Guilty," *Fortune*, November 15, 2004, p. 78.

51. "The World Is Flat: A Brief History of the Twenty-First Century," www.thomaslfriedman.com (accessed July 10, 2010).

52. Matthew McKay, Martha Davis, and Patrick Fanning, *Messages: The Communication Skills Book* (Oakland, CA: New Harbinger, 1995), p. 108.

53. O. C. Ferrell, John Fraedrich, and Linda Ferrell, *Business Ethics: Ethical Decision Making and Cases*, 5th ed. (Boston: Houghton Mifflin Company, 2002), p. 208.

54. Barry L. Reece and Rhonda Brandt, *Effective Human Relations: Personal and Organizational Applications* (Boston: Houghton Mifflin Company, 2008), pp. 125–126.

55. William M. Pride, Robert J. Hughes, and Jack R. Kapoor, *Business*, 7th ed. (Boston: Houghton Mifflin Company, 2002), p. 40.

Endnotes for Boxed Features

a. Michael T. Kenny, "Research, Observe Chinese Protocol to Land Sale," *Selling*, May 2001, p. 10; Jan Yager, *Business Protocol*, 2nd ed. (Stamford, CT: Hannacroix Creek Books, 2001), p. 113.

b. Based on Renee Houston Zemanski, "When the Competition Gets Tough," *Selling Power*, April 2006, pp. 17–19.

Chapter 2

Product-Selling Strategies That Add Value

Chapter Preview

When you finish reading this chapter, you should be able to

1 Describe positioning as a product-selling strategy

2 Explain the cluster of satisfactions concept

3 Discuss product-positioning options

4 Explain how to sell your product with a price strategy

5 Explain how to sell your product with a value-added strategy

Introduction

You have just finished paying off your college loans and it's time to replace that old rust bucket with a new car. You have looked at the sport-compact cars available, but they all seem so small. Now you are eagerly looking at cars in the sports-sedan category. The cars in this niche offer a good blend of comfort, design, and performance. However, there are almost too many choices. *Road & Track* says there are 11 different automobiles in this group. The list price for these cars ranges from $29,000 to $40,000. The Audi A4 and Saab 9-3 offer all-wheel drive; all the rest offer front- or rear-wheel drive. As you learn more about the choices available, it becomes clear that each manufacturer has taken steps to differentiate its product.[1]

Several years ago, automobile manufacturers from around the world began to develop and position cars for the sports-sedan segment. Research indicated that demand for these cars would increase. The result was the introduction of 11 different marques, each with its own unique characteristics. At the dealer level, the process of product differentiation continues. If you want something more than standard equipment, the salesperson can describe a variety of options that can add $7,000 to $10,000 to the price. Each car can be accessorized to meet your personal needs. The dealer can also help position this product with modern facilities, customer-friendly service policies, and a reputation for honesty and integrity.

Some automobile manufacturers see the sports-sedan category as critical to their success. At BMW, the 3 Series sports sedan accounts for nearly half of the company's sales worldwide. Sports sedans can be very profitable because many buyers purchase expensive options such as special wheel and tire packages, anti-skid electronics, ground-effects trim, and top-of-the line audio systems.

Salespeople at the dealer level in the crowded sports-sedan market play an important role in positioning their brand for competitive advantage. Adding value depends on the salesperson's ability to provide a competitive analysis using knowledge of the manufacturer, the automobile, and the dealership.

Source: Transtock/SuperStock, Inc.

Design can play a major role in the sports-sedan market segment. BMW and Audi recently unveiled completely redesigned cars. These new cars will face off against the Infiniti G37 and the Cadillac CTS, two cars noted for advanced design.[2]

Salespeople at the dealer level can play an important role in positioning the automobile for competitive advantage. They can describe the quality control process that ensures the build quality of the BMW 330i or demonstrate the sports car driving characteristics of the Lexus IS 350. Adding value depends on the salesperson's ability to provide a competitive analysis using knowledge of the manufacturer, the automobile, and the dealership. ●

Product Positioning—A Product-Selling Strategy

Long-term success in today's dynamic global economy requires the continuous positioning and repositioning of products.[3] **Positioning** involves those decisions and activities intended to create and maintain a certain concept of the firm's product in the customer's mind. It requires developing a marketing strategy aimed at influencing how a particular market segment perceives a product in comparison to the competition.[4] In a market that has been flooded with various types of sport-utility vehicles (SUVs), Land Rover has been positioned as a dependable vehicle that can climb a steep, rock-covered hillside with ease. Every effort has been made to create the perception of safety, durability, and security. To give sales representatives increased confidence in the Land Rover, the company has arranged plant tours and the opportunity to observe actual testing of the Land Rover vehicles under extremely demanding conditions.

Good positioning means that the product's name, reputation, and niche are well recognized. However, a good positioning strategy does not last forever. The positioning process must be continually modified to match the customer's changing wants and needs.[5]

Essentials of Product Positioning

Most companies use a combination of marketing and sales strategies to give their products a unique position in the marketplace. Every salesperson needs a good understanding of the fundamental practices that contribute to product positioning. The chapter begins with a brief introduction to the concept of product differentiation. This is followed by an explanation of how products have been redefined in the age of information. The remainder of the chapter is devoted to three product-selling strategies that can be used to position a product. Emphasis is placed on positioning your product with a value-added strategy. In the age of information, salespeople who cannot add value to the products they sell will diminish in number and influence.

Michael Dell's Early Years

At the age of 12, Michael Dell, CEO of Dell Computer Corporation, was displaying the characteristics of an opportunistic entrepreneur. He turned his stamp-collecting hobby into a mail-order business that netted $2,000. This money was used to purchase his first computer. He also developed his personal selling skills at an early age. At age 16, he was selling subscriptions to his hometown paper, the *Houston Post*. Later he enrolled in college but had difficulty focusing on his coursework. He often cut classes in order to spend more time assembling and selling computers. When Dell's parents discovered his newest enterprise, they pressured him to stay focused on completing his degree. Dell completed the spring semester and then spent the summer expanding his business. In the month prior to the fall semester, he sold $180,000 worth of computers. He did not return to college.[a]

Source: Dell/Getty Images/Getty Images, Inc. - Getty News

Achieving Product Differentiation in Personal Selling

One of the basic tenets of sales and marketing is the principle of product differentiation. **Differentiation** refers to your ability to separate yourself and your product from that of your competitors. It is the key to building and maintaining a competitive advantage.[6] The competitors in virtually all industries are moving toward differentiating themselves on the basis of quality, price, convenience, economy, or some other factor. Salespeople, who are on the front line of many marketing efforts, assume an important role in the product differentiation process.

Differentiating your product helps you stand out from the crowd. It often allows you to distance yourself from the competition. In many cases, the process of differentiation creates barriers that make it difficult for the buyer to choose a competing product simply on the basis of price.[7]

Creating a Value Proposition

A well-informed customer will usually choose the product that offers the most value. Therefore, salespeople need to position their product with a value proposition. A **value proposition** is the set of benefits and values the company promises to deliver to customers to satisfy their needs. The value proposition presented by Porsche promises driving performance and excitement.[8] Kinko's, which is now part of FedEx, is attempting to differentiate itself from Sir Speedy, AlphaGraphics, and print shops found at Office Depot, OfficeMax, and Staples. The new value proposition promises that 1,200 FedEx Kinko's locations offer a breadth of services unparalleled in the industry. These new centers leverage the traditional strengths and brand awareness of FedEx and Kinko's.[9]

In many situations salespeople must quantify the value proposition. This is especially true when the customer is a business buyer. The value quantification process raises customers' comprehension levels as they discover the merits of buying your product or service.[10] Let's assume you are selling Kenworth trucks and one of your customers is Contract Freighters, Inc., based in Joplin, Missouri. This large company is planning to purchase 700 new trucks. Your Kenworth diesel trucks cost 10 percent more than rivals' trucks. Within your proposal you should try to quantify the benefits of buying Kenworth trucks, which may include greater reliability, higher trade-in value, and the plush interiors that will help the buyer attract better drivers.[11]

The Cluster of Satisfactions Concept

Ted Levitt, former editor of the *Harvard Business Review*, says that products are problem-solving tools. People buy products if they fulfill a problem-solving need. Today's better-educated and more demanding customers are seeking a *cluster of satisfactions*. **Satisfactions** arise from the product itself, from the company that makes or distributes the product, and from the salesperson who sells and services the product.[12] Figure 1 provides a description of a three-dimensional Product-Selling Model. Many companies are attempting to transform themselves from *product selling* to *solution selling*. To develop and sell solutions, salespeople must be familiar with the satisfactions that meet the needs of each customer.

To illustrate how the cluster of satisfactions concept works in a business setting, let us examine a complex buying decision. Elaine Parker, a sales representative for Elmore Industries Incorporated, sells metals for manufacturing operations. Over a period of six months, she frequently called on a prospect that had the potential to become a valued customer. During every call, the buyer's receptionist told her they were happy with their current supplier. She refused to give up and finally the buyer agreed to see her. At first she was greeted with cool silence, so she decided to ask him some questions about his business: "How's the slow economy affecting your sales?" The buyer's answers focused on materials costs. He said his company could not raise prices or cut quality. He wanted to lower costs, but was unsure how it could be done. Parker suggested he consider trying some new alloys that were less expensive than the standard metals he had been purchasing. As she described the new alloys, the buyer's interest began to build. She offered to make a full presentation to the buyer and his engineers at a follow-up meeting. The second meeting was a success. Soon after that meeting, Parker received her first order from the customer. Within a year, she had become the customer's most trusted advisor on technological developments in the industry and his exclusive supplier.[13]

Elaine Parker used questions to engage the customer and identify his problem. She also provided satisfactory answers to questions raised by the customers:

Questions Related to the Product

What product is best for our type of operation?

Does the product meet our quality standards?

Given the cost of this product, will we maintain our competitive position in the marketplace?

FIGURE 1

Product-Selling Model

The product strategy should include a cluster of satisfactions that meets the needs of today's better-educated and more demanding customers. Drawing from this cluster, the salesperson can configure value-added solutions that meet individual customer's needs.

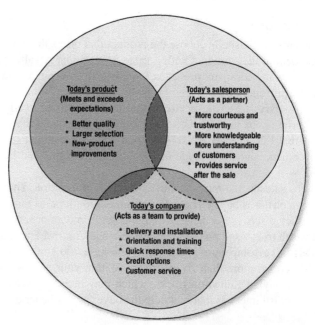

Questions Related to the Company

Does this company provide the most advanced technology?

What is the company's reputation for quality products?

What is the company's reputation for standing behind the products it sells?

Questions Related to the Salesperson

Does this salesperson possess the knowledge and experience needed to recommend the right product?

Can the salesperson clearly communicate specific buyer benefits?

Can this salesperson serve as a trusted advisor?

Will this salesperson provide support services after the sale?

Salespeople who are knowledgeable in all areas of the Product-Selling Model are better able to position a product. Knowledge helps you achieve product differentiation, understand the competition, and prepare an effective value proposition. The competitive analysis worksheet (Table 1) can help you discover ways to position your product as the superior choice over your competition.

A WORD OF CAUTION Because many of today's information age products are very complex, product differentiation must be handled with care. Salespeople are sometimes tempted to use technical lingo, real and invented, to impress the buyer. This problem often surfaces in a situation in which

TABLE 1 Competitive Analysis Worksheet

A value-added product-selling strategy is enhanced when salespeople analyze product, company, and salesperson attributes of the competition in relation to the benefits they offer. This information helps the salesperson create value within the sales process.

	MY COMPANY	COMPETITOR A	COMPETITOR B
Product Attributes			
Quality			
Durability			
Reliability			
Performance			
Packaging flexibility			
Warranty			
Brand			
Company Attributes			
Reputation			
Industry leadership			
Facilities			
Ease of doing business			
Distribution channels			
Ordering convenience			
Returns, credits, etc.			
Salesperson Attributes			
Knowledge/expertise			
Responsiveness			
Pricing authority			
Customer orientation			
Honesty/integrity			
Follow-through			
Presentation skills			

the salesperson is not sure how to describe the value-added features of the product. Robert Notte, technology chief for travel outfitter Backroads, says that during the telecom boom salespeople representing WorldCom (now MCI) and other firms babbled endlessly, using industry jargon that was often unintelligible. "They wanted you to be impressed," Mr. Notte says. Some customers were so intimidated they were afraid to ask questions . . . or make a buying decision.[14]

Product-Positioning Options

Product positioning is a concept that applies to both new and existing products. Given the dynamics of most markets, it may be necessary to reposition products several times in their lives because even solid, popular products can lose market position quickly. Salespeople have assumed an important and expanding role in differentiating products. To succeed in our overcommunicated society, marketers must use a direct and personalized form of communication with customers. Advertising directed toward a mass market often fails to position a complex product.

Throughout the remainder of this chapter, we discuss specific ways to use various product-positioning strategies. We explain how salespeople can (1) position new and emerging products versus well-established products, (2) position products with price strategies, and (3) position products with value-added strategies.

Selling New and Emerging Products Versus Mature and Well-Established Products

In many ways, products are like human beings. They are born, grow up, mature, and grow old. In marketing, this process is known as the **product life cycle**. The product life cycle includes the stages a product goes through from the time it is first introduced to the market until it is discontinued. As the product moves through its cycle, the strategies relating to competition, promotion, pricing, and other factors must be evaluated and possibly changed. The nature and extent of each stage in the product life cycle are determined by several factors, including:

1. The product's perceived advantage over available substitutes
2. The product's benefits and the importance of the needs it fulfills
3. Competitive activity, including pricing, substitute product development and improvement, and effectiveness of competing advertising and promotion
4. Changes in technology, fashion, or demographics[15]

As we attempt to develop a product-selling strategy, we must consider where the product is positioned in terms of the life cycle. The sales strategy used to sell a new and emerging product is much different from the strategy used to sell a mature, well-established product (Figure 2).

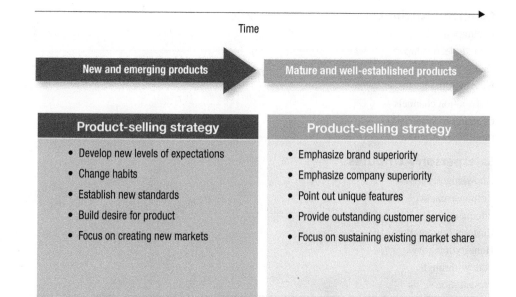

FIGURE 2

Product-Selling Strategies for Positioning New and Emerging Products Versus Mature and Well-Established Products

Distributing Product Information with CRM

Today salespeople are challenged to manage a steady stream of information about customers (needs) and products (solutions). From this stream of information, the salesperson must select product information that is relevant to a specific customer and deliver the information in a manner that can be understood by the customer. Customer relationship management (CRM) assists the busy salesperson by providing tools that can collect information and rapidly link it to those who need it. Most CRM systems can receive and organize information from many sources, within and outside the organization. For example, Salesforce.com is linked to Google AdWords, an online advertising service. Advertisements placed on search engines, including Google, direct users to pages with forms to complete for more information. The data entered on these forms are downloaded directly into Salesforce.com. The statistics generated by the service permits a quick analysis of online advertising. Once information is received from the various sources, sales professionals can add value to this information by summarizing, combining, and tailoring the information to meet a customer's needs.

When new information about a product is received, the customer database can be quickly searched to find those customers who might have an interest. The new product data can be merged into an e-mail, fax, or letter to those customers, along with other information (benefits) that can help the recipients assess its value. Later, the CRM system can display an alert, reminding the sales professional to follow up on the information that was shared with the customer. CRM Application Exercise "Distributing Product Information with CRM" describes how product information can be shared between customers.

SELLING NEW AND EMERGING PRODUCTS Selling strategies used during the new and emerging stage (see Figure 2) are designed to develop a new level of expectation, change habits, and in some cases establish a new standard of quality.[16] The goal is to build desire for the product. Highly talented and resourceful salespeople are needed during the product initiation phase.[17] Salespeople must be resourceful, possess information regarding every aspect of the product, and be able to present a convincing value proposition.[18]

When Brother International Corporation introduced its line of Multi-Function Center (MFC) machines, the goal was to convince buyers that one machine could replace five separate machines. However, before buyers would give up their copy machine, fax machine, laser printer, and other machines, they asked some hard questions. Is a multifunction machine reliable? Does the quality match that of the current machines? Finding the best machine for each customer is challenging because Brother offers more than 10 different MFC models to choose from.

In some cases the new product is not a tangible item. Several years ago IntraLinks closed its first big sale, a $50,000 contract, with J.P. Morgan. The company got its start providing the financial services industry with the secure transmission of highly confidential information across the Internet. Patrick Wack and his business partners convinced J.P. Morgan and other financial firms that they did not need to rely on an army of foot messengers and FedEx trucks to deliver sensitive documents. They were not only selling a new product; they were selling a vision that included new levels of expectations. The value proposition focused on faster, more secure document transfer, which, in the customer's mind, translated into improved customer service and cost savings. Today Patrick Wack is selling this document transfer concept to customers in a variety of business communities.[19]

SELLING MATURE AND WELL-ESTABLISHED PRODUCTS Mature and well-established products are usually characterized by intense competition as new brands enter the market. Customers who currently buy your product will become aware of competing products. With new and emerging products, salespeople may initially have little or no competition and may dominate the market; however, this condition may not last long.

New York Life Insurance Company provides its sales agents with new products almost every year. The product portfolio was recently expanded to include the Asset Preserver, which allows the policy death benefit to be accelerated, on an income tax–free basis, to pay for long-term care services. The company also developed the Universal Life Protector, which offers long-term protection at lower prices. New products offered by a market leader are quickly copied by competing insurance companies. When competing products enter the market, New York Life agents must adopt new strategies. One positioning strategy is to emphasize the company's 150 years of outstanding service to policyholders. They can also note that New York Life is a "mutual" company; it is owned by policyholders, not corporate shareholders. The objective is to create in the customer's mind the perception that New York Life is a solid company that will be strong and solvent when it's time to pay premiums.[20]

The relationship strategy is often critical in selling mature and well-established products. To maintain market share and ward off competitors, many salespeople work hard to maintain a strong relationship with the customer. At New York Life, salespeople have found that good service after the sale is one of the best selling strategies because it builds customer loyalty.

Selling Products with a Price Strategy

Price, promotion, product, and place are the four elements that make up the marketing mix. Pricing decisions must be made at each stage of the product life cycle. Therefore, setting the price can be a complex process. The first step in establishing price is to determine the firm's pricing objectives. Some firms set their prices to maximize their profits. They aim for a price as high as possible without causing a disproportionate reduction in unit sales. Other firms set a market share objective. Management may decide that the strategic advantage of an increased market share outweighs a temporary reduction in profits. Many of the new companies doing business on the Internet adopt this approach.

Pricing strategies often reflect the product's position in the product life cycle. When large, high-definition flat-screen TVs were in the new and emerging stage, customers who wanted this innovative product were willing to pay $5,000 or more for a unit.

TRANSACTIONAL SELLING TACTICS THAT EMPHASIZE LOW PRICE Some marketers have established a positioning plan that emphasizes low price and the use of transactional selling tactics. These companies maintain a basic strategy that focuses on meeting competition. If the firm has meeting competition as its pricing goal, it makes every effort to charge prices that are identical or close to those of the competition. Once this positioning strategy has been adopted, the sales force is given several price tactics to use. Salespeople can alter (lower) the base price through the use of discounts and allowances. Discounts and allowances can take a variety of forms. A few of the more common ones follow:

Quantity discount. The quantity discount allows the buyer a lower price for purchasing in multiple units or above a specified dollar amount.

Seasonal discount. With seasonal pricing, the salesperson adjusts the price up or down during specific times to spur or acknowledge changes in demand. Off-season travel and lodging prices provide examples.

Promotional allowance. A promotional allowance is a price reduction given to a customer who participates in an advertising or a sales support program. Many salespeople give supermarkets promotional allowances for advertising or displaying a manufacturer's products.

Trade or functional discounts. Channel intermediaries, such as wholesalers, often perform credit, storage, or transportation services. Trade or functional discounts cover the cost of these services.[21]

Another option available to salespeople facing a buyer with a low-price buying strategy is to "unbundle" product features. Let's assume that a price-conscious customer wants to schedule a conference that will be accompanied by a banquet-style meal. To achieve a lower price, the salesperson might suggest a cafeteria-style meal, thereby eliminating the need for servers. This product configuration involves less cost to the seller, and cost savings can be passed on to the buyer. Timken Company, a century-old bearing maker, has adopted bundling as a way to compete with other manufacturers around the world. The company now surrounds its basic products with additional components in order to provide customers with exactly what they need. These components can take the form of electronic sensors, lubrication systems, castings, or installation and maintenance. Giving customers bundling options has given Timken a big advantage over foreign competitors who often focus on the basic product. Salespeople who represent Timken have flexible pricing options.[22]

These examples represent only a small sample of the many discounts and allowances salespeople use to compete on the basis of price. Price discounting is a competitive tool available to large numbers of salespeople. Excessive focus on low prices and generous discounts, however, can have a negative impact on profits and sales commissions.

SELLING IN ACTION

How Do Customers Judge Service Quality?

In the growing service industry, there is intense price competition. From a distance, one gets the impression that every buyer decision hinges on price alone. However, a closer examination of service purchases indicates that service quality is an important factor when it comes to developing a long-term relationship with customers.

How do customers judge service quality? Researchers at Texas A&M University have discovered valuable insights about customer perceptions of service quality. They surveyed hundreds of customers in a variety of service industries and discovered that five service-quality dimensions emerged:

1. *Tangibles:* Details the customers can see, such as the appearance of personnel and equipment.
2. *Reliability:* The ability to perform the desired service dependably, accurately, and consistently.

3. *Responsiveness:* The willingness of sales and customer service personnel to provide prompt service and help customers.
4. *Assurance:* The employees' knowledge, courtesy, and ability to convey trust and confidence.
5. *Empathy:* The provision of caring, individualized attention to customers.

Customers apparently judge the quality of each service transaction in terms of these five quality dimensions. Companies need to review these service-quality dimensions and make sure that each area measures up to customers' expectations. Salespeople should recognize that these dimensions have the potential to add value to the services they sell.[b]

CONSEQUENCES OF USING LOW-PRICE TACTICS Pricing is a critical factor in the sale of many products and services. In markets where competition is extremely strong, setting a product's price may be a firm's most complicated and important decision.

The authors of *The Discipline of Market Leaders* encourage business firms to pick one of three disciplines—best price, best product, or best service—and then do whatever is necessary to outdistance the competition. However, the authors warn us not to ignore the other two disciplines: "You design your business to excel in one direction, but you also have to strive to hit the minimum in the others."[23] Prior to using low-price tactics, everyone involved in sales and marketing should answer these questions:

- *Are you selling to high- or low-involvement buyers?* Some people are emotionally involved with respected brands such as BMW, Sony, and Macintosh computers. A part of their identity depends on buying the product they consider the best. Low-involvement buyers care mostly about price.[24]

" WE HAVE QUALITY AND WE HAVE LOW PRICES...
WHICH DO YOU WANT ? "

Source: Agency Sales Magazine from the Manufacturing Agent National Association (MANA). Used with permission.

- *How important is quality in the minds of buyers?* If buyers do not fully understand the price–quality relationship, they may judge the product by its price. For a growing number of customers, long-term value is more important than short-term savings that result from low prices.
- *How important is service?* For many buyers, service is a critical factor. Even online customers, thought to be very interested in price, rate quality of service very highly. This is especially true in business-to-business sales. A survey conducted by Accenture reports that 80 percent of nearly 1,000 corporate buyers rate a strong brand and reliable customer service ahead of low prices when deciding which companies to do business with online.[25]

INFLUENCE OF ELECTRONIC COMMERCE ON PRICING Companies large and small are racing to discover new sales and marketing opportunities on the Internet. Products ranging from personal computers to term insurance can be purchased from various Web sites. Salespeople who are involved primarily in transactional selling and add little or no value to the sales transaction often are not able to compete with online vendors. To illustrate, consider the purchase of insurance. At the present time it is possible to purchase basic term insurance online from InsureMarket.com, AccuQuote.com, and other Web sites. A well-informed buyer, willing to visit several Web sites, can select a policy with a minimum amount of risk. In the case of long-term care insurance, which can pay for health care at home or in a nursing home, the buyer needs the help of a well-trained agent. These policies are complex and the premiums are high.

Investors now have more choices than they have had in the past. Persons who need little or no assistance buying stocks can visit the E*Trade Web site or a similar online discount vendor. The person who wants help selecting a stock can turn to a broker, such as Merrill Lynch or UBS PaineWebber, that offers both full-service and online options. Full-service brokers can survive and may prosper as long as they can add value to the sales transaction. The new economy is reshaping the world of commerce and every buyer has more choices.

Selling Your Product with a Value-Added Strategy

Many progressive marketers have adopted a market plan that emphasizes *value-added strategies*. Companies can add value to their product with one or more intangibles such as better-trained salespeople, increased levels of courtesy, more dependable product deliveries, better service after the sale, and innovations that truly improve the product's value in the eyes of the customer. In today's highly competitive marketplace, these value-added benefits give the company a unique niche and a competitive edge. Companies that don't make selling and delivering high-value solutions a high priority will consistently lose sales to competitors.[26]

To understand fully the importance of the value-added concept in selling, and how to apply it in a variety of selling situations, it helps to visualize every product as being four dimensional. The *total product* is made up of four "possible" products: the generic product, the expected product, the value-added product, and the potential product (Figure 3).[27]

GENERIC PRODUCT The **generic product** is the basic, substantive product you are selling. Generic product describes only the product category, for example, life insurance, rental cars, or personal computers. Every Ritz-Carlton hotel offers guest rooms, one or more full-service restaurants, meeting rooms, guest parking, and other basic services. For Yellow Freight System, a company that provides shipping services, the generic product is the truck and trailer that moves the customer's freight. At the generic level, Nordstrom provides categories of goods traditional to an upscale specialty-clothing retailer. The generic products at a bank are money that can be loaned to customers and basic checking account services.

The capability of delivering a generic product simply gives the marketer the right to play in the game, to compete in the marketplace.[28] Generic products, even the lowest-priced ones, often cannot compete with products that are "expected" by the customer.

EXPECTED PRODUCT Every customer has minimal purchase expectations that exceed the generic product itself.[29] Ritz-Carlton must offer not only a comfortable guest room but also a clean one. Some customers expect a "super" clean room. Yellow Freight System must provide clean, well-maintained trucks *and* well-trained drivers. The **expected product** is everything that represents the customer's minimal expectations. The customer at a Nordstrom store *expects* current fashions and well-informed salespeople.

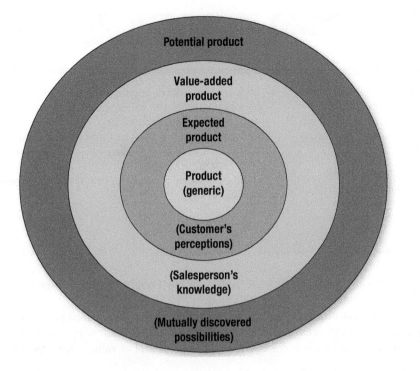

FIGURE 3

The Total Product Concept

An understanding of the four "possible" products is helpful when the salesperson develops a presentation for specific types of customers.

The minimal purchase conditions vary among customers, so the salesperson must acquire information concerning the expected product that exists in the customer's mind. When the customer expects more than the generic product, the product can be sold *only* if those expectations are met. Every customer perceives the product in individualized terms, which a salesperson cannot anticipate.

Determining each customer's expectations requires the salesperson to make observations, conduct background checks, ask questions, and listen to what the customer is saying. You are attempting to discover both feelings and facts. Top salespeople encourage customers to think more deeply about the problems they face and discover for themselves the value of a solution. They *avoid* offering solutions until the needs are clearly spelled out. If the buyer says, "The average gas mileage for our fleet of delivery trucks is only 17 miles per gallon," the salesperson might respond with this question: "How does this low mileage rate affect your profitability?" To move the customer's attention from the expected product to a value-added product, you need to keep the customer focused on solutions.[30]

Research reported in the *Harvard Business Review* indicates that it is very difficult to build customer loyalty if you are selling only the expected product. Customer satisfaction and loyalty do not always move in tandem.[31] The customer who purchases the services of Ernst & Young Consulting may feel satisfied after the project is completed but never do business with the company again. Customer loyalty is more likely to increase when the purchase involves a value-added product.[32]

VALUE-ADDED PRODUCT The **value-added product** exists when salespeople offer customers more than they expect. Coupling CRM with a differentiation strategy provides one way for a salesperson to add value.[33] When you make a reservation at one of the Ritz-Carlton hotels and request a special amenity such as a tennis lesson, a record of this request is maintained in the computer system. If you make a reservation at another Ritz-Carlton at some future date, the agent informs you of the availability of a tennis court. The guest who buys chocolate chip cookies in the lobby gift shop in New Orleans may find a basket of them waiting in his room in Boston two weeks later. The hotel company uses modern technology to surprise and delight guests.[34]

In the mid-1990s, Yellow Freight System was a troubled long-haul carrier offering customers a generic product. Bill Zollars was hired to transform the company by adding a variety of services built around unprecedented customer service. The new services positioned the company to satisfy a broader range of transportation needs. For example, the company launched Yellow's Exact Express, its first time-definite, guaranteed service. Exact Express is now Yellow's most

GLOBAL BUSINESS INSIGHT

Doing Business in India

India is a very large country that is growing in importance in terms of international trade. Indians' customs are often dictated by their religious beliefs. In addition to Hindus and Muslims, there are dozens of other religious groups. Study the Indian culture carefully before your first business trip to this country.

- Customs of food and drink are an important consideration when you do business in India. Avoid eating meat in the presence of Hindus because they are vegetarians and consider the cow a sacred animal. Muslims will not eat pork or drink alcoholic beverages.

- There is a very strict caste system in India so be aware of the caste of the clients with whom you are dealing and any restrictions that may apply to that caste.
- Most members of the Indian business community speak English.
- Indians tend to be careful buyers who seek quality and durability. They respect a salesperson who is caring and well informed. Personal relationships in business transactions are very important.

expensive and most profitable service. Today, Yellow Freight System salespeople are able to offer its 300,000 customers a value-added product.[35]

Among the most important factors that contribute to the value-added product is the overall quality of employees the customer has contact with. Sales and sales support staff who display enthusiasm and commitment to the customer add a great deal of value to the product.[36]

POTENTIAL PRODUCT After the value-added product has been developed, the salesperson should begin to conceptualize the **potential product**. The potential product refers to what may remain to be done, that is, what is possible.[37] As the level of competition increases, especially in the case of mature products, salespeople must look to the future and explore new possibilities.

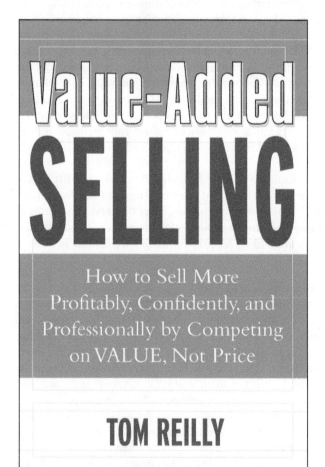

In his book *Value-Added Selling*, Tom Reilly states that "Value-added selling is a business philosophy. It's proactively looking for ways to enhance, augment, or enlarge your bundled package for the customer. Value-added salespeople sell a three-dimensional bundle of values: the product, the company, and themselves."

Source: Book cover of *Value-Added Selling* by Tom Reilly. Copyright © 2003. Reprinted by permission of The McGraw-Hill Companies, Inc.

In the highly competitive food services industry, restaurant owners like to do business with a distribution sales representative (DSR) who wants to help make the business profitable. The DSR who assumes this role becomes a true partner and looks beyond the customer's immediate and basic needs. The potential product might be identified after a careful study of the restaurant's current menu and customer base. To deliver the potential product, a salesperson must discover and satisfy new customer needs, which requires imagination and creativity.

Steelcase Incorporated, a leading manufacturer of office furniture, has developed the "Think" chair, which is 99 percent recyclable and can be disassembled with basic hand tools in about five minutes. This $900 chair meets a growing demand for products made of parts that can be recycled several times and manufactured in ways least harmful to the environment. Steelcase developed this "potential product" after learning that customers are increasingly seeking environmentally safe products and are sometimes willing to pay a premium for them.[38]

The potential product is more likely to be developed by salespeople who are close to their customers. Many high-performing salespeople explore product possibilities with their customers on a regular basis. Potential products are often mutually discovered during these exchanges.

Every indication points toward product-selling strategies that add value becoming more important in the future. New product life cycles are shrinking, so more companies are searching for ways to add value during the new and emerging stage. Some companies that have experienced low profits selling low-priced products are reinventing those products. They search for product features that provide benefits customers think are worth paying for. Maytag Corporation developed the expensive environment-friendly Neptune washing machine for customers who will pay more for a washer that uses less water. Yellow Freight System created value for customers with the addition of Yellow's Exact Express and other service options.

Herman Miller salespeople can assure customers of a custom solution with their CEO's commitment.

Source: Courtesy of Parametric Technology Corporation.

37

Pricing Your Professional Fees

The age of information has created many career opportunities for people who want to sell professional services. Strong demand for professional services has surfaced in such diverse fields as telecommunications, banking, computer technology, training, and health care. Dana Martin spent 18 years working in the human resources division of Allstate Insurance Company. His specialty was the design and delivery of training programs. He decided to leave the corporate environment and start his own training firm. Martin, like thousands of other professional service providers, had to decide how much to charge for his service. Before he could sell the first training program, he had to decide how much to charge. Should he price his service on an hourly basis or on a project basis? Here are some points to consider when determining fees:

- *Experience:* In the case of Dana Martin, new clients benefit from what he has learned during many years at Allstate.

- *Exclusivity:* If you are one of only a small number of people with a particular capability, you may be able to charge more. Specialists often charge higher fees than generalists.
- *Target market:* Some markets are very price sensitive. If you are selling your services to large corporations that are used to paying high fees, you may be able to set your fees higher. If you are providing your services to small business clients, expect resistance to high fees.
- *Value:* How important is your service to the client? In the late 1990s, many companies needed help preparing their computers for transition to the year 2000. This was known as the "Y2K" problem. These firms were willing to pay high fees for this assistance. Some service providers charge higher fees because they add value in one form or another.[c]

Value Creation Investments for Transactional, Consultative, and Strategic Alliance Buyers

In most cases, value creation investments during the transactional sale are minimal. Emphasis is usually placed on finding ways to eliminate any unnecessary costs associated with the sale and avoiding delays in processing the order. Technology investments can sometimes play a big role in improving efficiencies.[39] For example, customers may be encouraged to order products online.

A considerable amount of value creation takes place in consultative sales. Higher investments in value creation are permitted because companies need to invest in developing a good understanding of the customer's needs and problems. This is especially true in large, complex sales. The opportunity to create custom-tailored solutions and deliver more real benefits to the customer provides the opportunity for high margins. If your company is selling mobile autonomous robots, for example, the sales cycle will be quite long and investments will be quite high. It may take several weeks to study the applications of this product in a hospital, a manufacturing plant, or a large warehouse facility. The use of these robots may ultimately result in significant cost savings for the customer.[40]

Value creation investments in strategic alliance sales are the highest. Strategic alliances represent the highest form of partnering. Building an alliance is always preceded by a careful study of the proposed partner. Creating value often requires leveraging the full assets of the company, so investments go well beyond the sales force. Alliances are often developed by a team of specialists from such areas as finance, engineering, and marketing. A proposed alliance may require investments in new technology, manufacturing facilities, and warehouses.[41]

WHAT IS LEXUS?

Lexus is... Engineering sophistication and manufacturing quality.

Lexus is... Luxury and performance.

Lexus is... An image and an expectation of excellence.

Lexus is... Valuing the customer as an important individual.

Lexus is... Treating customers the way THEY want to be treated.

Lexus is... A total experience that reflects professionalism and a sincere commitment to satisfaction.

Lexus is... "Doing it right the first time".

Lexus is... Caring on a personal level.

Lexus is... Exceeding customer expectations.

And... In the eyes of the customer I AM LEXUS !!!

LEXUS

00-LTT-034

Lexus, a major success story in the automobile industry, offers the customer a value-added strategy that encompasses the product, the company, and the salesperson.

Source: Courtesy of Lexus.

CHAPTER LEARNING ACTIVITIES

Reviewing Key Concepts

Describe positioning as a product-selling strategy
Success in today's dynamic global economy requires the continuous positioning and repositioning of products. Product positioning involves those decisions and activities intended to create and maintain a certain concept of the firm's product in the customer's mind. Salespeople can make an important contribution to the process of product positioning.

Explain the cluster of satisfactions concept
Today's better-educated customers are often seeking a cluster of satisfactions. They seek satisfactions that arise from the product itself, from the company that makes or distributes the product, and from the salesperson who sells and services the product.

Discuss product-positioning options
We described the major product-positioning strategies available to salespeople: positioning new and emerging products versus mature and well-established products; positioning with a price strategy; and positioning with a value-added strategy.

Explain how to sell your product with a price strategy
Pricing decisions must be made at each stage of the product life cycle. Some companies use transactional selling tactics that emphasize low price. Salespeople are often given permission to alter (lower) the base price through the use of discounts and allowances. Consequences of using low-price tactics are discussed in this chapter.

Explain how to sell your product with a value-added strategy
To understand fully the importance of the value-added concept in selling, it helps to visualize every product as being four dimensional. This range of possibilities includes the generic product, the expected product, the value-added product, and the potential product.

Key Terms

Positioning	Quantity discount	Generic product
Differentiation	Seasonal discount	Expected product
Value proposition	Promotional allowance	Value-added product
Satisfactions	Trade or functional discount	Potential product
Product life cycle		

Review Questions

1. Why has product differentiation become so important in sales and marketing?
2. According to Ted Levitt, what is the definition of a product? What satisfactions do customers want?
3. Explain what is meant by *positioning* as a product-selling strategy. What is a value proposition?
4. Why have salespeople assumed an important role in positioning products?
5. Briefly describe the influence of electronic commerce on pricing. What types of products are likely to be sold on the Internet?
6. What are the possible consequences a salesperson might experience when using low-price tactics?
7. Read the Selling in Action feature titled "How Do Customers Judge Service Quality?". How might this information help a salesperson who wants to adopt the value-added selling strategy?

8. What are some of the common ways salespeople add value to the products they sell?
9. What are the four possible products that make up the *total product* concept?
10. Describe the difference between a generic product and a value-added product.
11. What is the relationship between value-added selling strategies and the cluster of satisfactions?
12. Is it true that selling products with a price strategy largely ignores customer satisfaction? Discuss.

Application Exercises

1. Study catalogs from two competing industrial supply firms or two competing direct-mail catalog companies. Assume one of the represented businesses is your employer. After studying the catalogs, make a comparative analysis of your company's competitive advantages.
2. Several weeks ago Erin Neff fell in love with the Scion tC coupe. After reading about the car in a magazine, she decided to visit a local Scion dealer. A test drive convinced her to place an order. What happened next was very frustrating. The salesperson, Tim Downey, immediately started recommending options she should add to the basic car: sporting wheel and tire package ($1,565), ground-effects trim ($995), performance exhaust system ($525), and a satellite radio tuner and antenna ($449). Suddenly the price of $15,950 jumped to nearly $19,000, way more than she had planned to spend. Erin returned home without placing an order. Assume the role of sales trainer and suggest ways that Tim can improve his ability to position this product so it meets the customer's needs.
3. The Ritz-Carlton hotel chain illustrates the total product concept discussed in this chapter. Research value-added information on the Ritz-Carlton chain by accessing www.ritzcarlton.com. Choose a location and click "Meetings." Click "Quick Facts" and print the information presented. Circle at least five features you consider to be value-added features. Examine the room rates by clicking "Accommodations." On the fact sheet you printed, record the room rate for single- and double-occupancy rooms.
4. Call a local financial services representative specializing in stock, bond, or equity fund transactions. Ask what percentage of clients rely on the information given to make complex decisions on their investments. Also ask this person if customers believe that advice on custom-fitting investment programs adds value to their decision making. Find out whether financial products are getting more or less complex and what effect this will have on providing value-added service in the future.

Role-Play Exercise

Study the Convention Center information in Part 1 of Appendix: Partnership Selling. Analyze this information and determine the value-added product that would appeal to a meeting planner (customer). Prepare a value proposition that summarizes the mix of key benefits on which your product is positioned. The proposition might include, for example, the free limousine service to and from the airport. Present your value proposition to another class member who will assume the role of the customer. Consider using information sheets, pictures, and other materials that will enhance your presentation.

CRM Application Exercise

Distributing Product Information with CRM

Testimonials and demonstrations have a strong influence on a buyer's decisions. Owners of a product often appear to be more objective and credible than those selling it. Demos allow prospective customers to see for themselves how a product performs. Your chance of selling a specific product is increased if you arrange for the prospective customer to visit the site where the product is in use. In this exercise you will connect a satisfied customer of a SimNet product with someone considering its purchase.

Timothy Ellis of Ellis Enterprises just called you to talk about Extranets. He read in one of his trade publications that companies like his improve their competitive position through an Extranet connection with their clients. You tried to explain that SimNet could help confirm his potential benefits with a needs analysis. However, Mr. Ellis insisted the article convinced him and he wants to see an operating Extranet right away. You told him you would arrange it and notify him by e-mail.

Click on the Documents tab and select "Pat Silva Notes." On the following Document Detail record, choosing "View file" will open a PDF file of the notes taken during sales calls by the previous salesperson. Use PDF search to review the references to Extranet until you find a customer who said she would "be happy to show their Extranet to others." Make a note of this customer's name, return to the Salesforce.com database, and search for the contact record of Timothy Ellis. When it is displayed, click on "Send An Email."

On the e-mail form choose the Select Template button and click on the "Product Inquiry" link. You will note the Subject field and e-mail body will be completed.

Click on the body of the e-mail template, remove the blank line, and replace it with "Extranet." Highlight and delete the following paragraphs:

You and your people are invited to visit our demonstration center at any time to observe this powerful system and ask our experts all of the questions you wish. Others who have implemented this product are very satisfied with their results of improved communications and increased production.

Should you decide to enhance your operation by adding this system, your people will receive training designed to best meet their needs and to assure you obtain optimal value from your investment.

Please let me know how I can assist you in evaluating this product. I look forward to serving you.

Replace these paragraphs with the following:

Kerri Mathers, the MIS Coordinator at Mercy Hospital, is the satisfied owner of an Extranet system and said she would be happy to let you and your people observe it in operation. Please provide a few dates in the future that would be convenient for you, and I will coordinate arrangements with Ms. Mathers.

When finished, type in the e-mail address for Kerri Mathers: kmathers@pearson-sellingtoday. com, in the "CC:" field so she will be aware of your plan.

Click on the Attach File button and select the Extranets link.

Name	Author	Size
Extranets	PSilv	64KB
Pat Silva Notes	PSilv	224KB
SimNet Systems Networks	PSilva	76KB

Once you have made your changes, you may send the e-mail. First find out whether a copy is to be sent to your instructor. You should send a copy to your own e-mail address to confirm the message was sent. When ready, click on the Send button at the top of the screen.

Case Problem

Many of the most profitable companies have discovered that there are "riches in market niches." They have developed products and services that meet the needs of a well-defined or newly created market. Steelcase Incorporated, a leading source of information and expertise on work effectiveness, has been working hard to develop products that meet the needs of people who do most of their work in an office environment. The company's motto is "the office environment company." One of its newest products is the "Think" chair. Steelcase also developed the Personal Harbor Workspaces, a self-contained, fully equipped, and totally private podlike workstation. Steelcase sales literature describes the product as ideal for companies that are tired of waiting for the future:

> They were developed to support the individual within a highly collaborative team environment, and they work best when clustered around common work areas equipped with mobile tables, carts, benches, screens, and other Steelcase Activity Products. These "commons" are meant to be flexible spaces that enhance communication and facilitate interaction.

Steelcase realized that selling this advanced product would not be easy, so a decision was made to develop an advanced sales team to presell the Personal Harbor before its major introduction. Once the team started making sales calls, it became evident that a traditional product-oriented sales presentation would not work. The Personal Harbor was a departure from conventional office design, so many customers were perplexed. Sue Sacks, a team member, said, "People acted like we had fallen from Mars." Team members soon realized that to explain the features and benefits of the product they had to begin studying new organizational developments such as team-oriented workforces and corporate reengineering. The advanced sales team was renamed the "advanced solutions team." Sales calls put more emphasis on learning about the customers' problems and identification of possible solutions. Members of the team viewed themselves as consultants who were in a position to discuss solutions to complex business problems.

The consultative approach soon began to pay off in sales. One customer, a hospital, was preparing to build a new office building and needed workstations for 400 employees. The hospital had formed a committee to make decisions concerning the purchase of office equipment. After an initial meeting between the Steelcase sales team and the hospital committee, a visit to Steelcase headquarters in Grand Rapids, Michigan, was arranged. The hospital committee members were able to tour the plant and meet with selected Steelcase experts. With knowledge of the hospital's goals and directions, Sue Sacks was able to arrange meetings with Steelcase technical personnel who could answer specific questions. The hospital ultimately placed an order worth more than a million dollars.

Questions

1. To fulfill a problem-solving need, salespeople must often be prepared to communicate effectively with customers who are seeking a cluster of satisfactions (see Figure 1). Is it likely that a customer who is considering the Personal Harbor Workspaces will seek information concerning all three dimensions of the Product-Selling Model? Explain your answer.

2. What product-selling strategies are most effective when selling a new and emerging product such as the Personal Harbor Workspaces?

3. Sue Sacks and other members of her sales team discovered that a traditional product-oriented presentation would not work when selling the Personal Harbor Workspaces. Success came only after the team adopted the consultative style of selling. Why was the product-oriented presentation ineffective?

4. Sue Sacks and other members of the advanced solutions team found that the consultative approach resulted in meetings with people higher in the customer's organization. "We get to call on a higher level of buyer," she said. Also, the team was more likely to position the product with a value-added strategy instead of a price strategy. In what ways did the advanced solutions team members add value to their product? Why was less emphasis placed on price during meetings with the customer?

ROLE-PLAY EXERCISE

Developing a Product Strategy

Scenario

First National Bank is a full-service bank with a reputation for excellent customer service. Personal selling efforts by tellers, loan officers, and financial consultants are considered an integral part of the bank's customer service program.

Customer Profile

At age 45, Gianni Diaz is looking forward to early retirement. To supplement a company-sponsored retirement program, a certificate of deposit (CD) in the amount of $4,000 is purchased each year. The annual percentage yield earned on CDs is currently in the range of 3.75 to 4.00 percent. Diaz is not interested in stocks and bonds because these products represent high-risk investments.

Salesperson Profile

Deaven Ray is a senior investment officer with First National Bank. Ray represents a wide range of financial products such as stock and bond mutual funds, blue chip stocks, diversified mutual funds, fixed annuities, money market funds, and certificates of deposit. Ray feels that Gianni Diaz may be a good candidate for an investment in fixed annuities. Diaz has agreed to meet and discuss investment options.

Product

Electric Capital Assurance Company offers a guaranteed-growth annuity at an annual percentage yield of 5.0 percent for a term of five years. This product gives the customer a guaranteed principal and a fixed rate of return. At the contract maturity date, the customer can select several payout options. This is a tax-deferred annuity, which means you won't pay income taxes on earnings until you choose to withdraw the funds. You can add funds to your account throughout the contract period. You need not close the account at the end of the contract period. You can allow your money to continue to grow at the same interest rate. If funds are withdrawn prior to the end of the contract, a withdrawal charge will be assessed. The minimum single premium purchase is $5,000.

Instructions

For this role-play activity, you will meet with Gianni Diaz and discuss current and future financial plans. You will determine whether Diaz might benefit by investing in a guaranteed-growth annuity. Prior to meeting with the customer, review the following material:

- Adding value with a feature–benefit strategy
- Use of bridge statements
- General versus specific benefits

Also, think about the implications of the Product-Selling Model (Figure 1). At the beginning of the role-play, use appropriate questions to acquire information regarding the customer's needs. Be prepared to recommend this product and close the sale if you feel the customer will benefit from this purchase.

Endnotes

1. Peter Egan, "The Best of All Worlds Bunch," *Road & Track,* July 2002, pp. 52–78; "2005 Geneva: Lexus Finesses Next IS Sport Sedan," www.autoweek.com (accessed July 6, 2010); Greg Kable, "Audi A4 Debuts at Frankfurt," *Autoweek,* September 3, 2007, p. 10; Joe Rusz, "Saab 9–3 & XWD," *Road & Track,* October 2007, p. 60.

2. Neal E. Boudette, "The Luxury-Car Market Gets More Crowded," *Wall Street Journal,* March 3, 2005, p. Dl; J. P. Vettraino, "2006 BMW 3 Series: Technology Update," www.autoweek.com (accessed July 6, 2010).

3. Wayne S. Desarbo, Rajdeep Grewal, and Crystal J. Scott (2008), "A Clusterwise Bilinear Multidimensional Scaling Methodology for Simultaneous Segmentation and Positioning Analyses," *Journal of Marketing Research,* 45(2), pp. 280–292.

4. Michael R. Solomon, Grey W. Marshall, and Elnora W. Stuart, *Marketing: Real People, Real Choices,* 5th ed. (Upper Saddle River, NJ: Pearson Education, 2008), p. 220.

5. D. Lee Carpenter, "Return on Innovation—The Power of Being Different," *Retailing Issues Letter,* May 1998, p. 3.

6. Brian Tracy, "Keeping the Customers You Make," *Selling,* November 2003, pp. 1, 4.

7. Tom Reilly, "You Must Differentiate to Win," *Selling,* April 2001, pp. 1, 10.

8. Gary Armstrong and Philip Kotler, *Marketing: An Introduction,* 7th ed. (Upper Saddle River, NJ: Prentice Hall, 2005), p. 12.

9. Tom Leverton, "Five Questions," *Sales & Marketing Management,* July 2004, p. 13.

10. Theodore Kinni, "The Value Proposition," *Selling Power,* July/August 2005, p. 75.

11. Michael Arndt, "Built for the Long Haul," *BusinessWeek,* January 30, 2006, p. 66.

12. Carl K. Clayton, "Sell Quality, Service, Your Company, Yourself," *Personal Selling Power,* January–February 1990, p. 47.

13. Elaine Parker, "How I Made the Sale," *Value-Added Selling* 21, June 17, 2003, pp. 1–2.

14. Suein L. Hwang, "It Was a WOMBAT for the Meatware, But It Was a Good Sell," *Wall Street Journal,* May 15, 2002, p. B1.

15. J. Thomas Russell and W. Ronald Lane, *Kleppner's Advertising Procedure* (Upper Saddle River, NJ: Prentice Hall, 1996), pp. 46–47.

16. Kevin Zheng Zhou and Kent Nakamoto (2007), "How Do Enhanced and Unique Features Affect New Product Preference? The Moderating Role of Product Familiarity," *Journal of the Academy of Marketing Science* 35, pp. 53–62.

17. Lawrence B. Chonko and Eli Jones (2005), "The Need for Speed: Agility Selling," *Journal of Personal Selling and Sales Management,* 25(4), pp. 371–382.

18. Mark Leslie and Charles A. Holloway, "The Sales Learning Curve," *Harvard Business Review,* July/August 2006, p. 121.

19. Jess McCuan, "Reeling In the Big One" *Inc.*, August 2004, pp. 43–44; "What Is IntraLinks?" www.Intralinks.com (accessed March 2, 2005).

20. Information was taken from *Report to Policyholders 2004*. This 24-page report was published by New York Life in 2005.

21. Michael R. Solomon and Elnora W. Stuart, *Marketing: Real People, Real Choices,* 4th ed. (Upper Saddle River, NJ: Prentice Hall, 2006), pp. 347–348.

22. Carlos Tejada, "The Allure of Bundling," *Wall Street Journal,* October 7, 2003, p. B1.

23. Michael Treacy, "You Need a Value Discipline—But Which One?" *Fortune,* April 17, 1995, p. 195.

24. Robert Shulman and Richard Miniter, "Discounting Is No Bargain," *Wall Street Journal,* December 7, 1998, p. A30.

25. Andy Cohen, "Survey Says: Service Beats Price Online," *Sales & Marketing Management,* July 2002, p. 18.

26. Geoffrey James, "Solution Selling," *Selling Power,* May 2006, p. 46.

27. Adopted from a model described in "Marketing Success Through Differentiation—of Anything," *Harvard Business Review,* January–February 1980.

28. Joanna Johnson, "A New Perspective on Marketing," *Construction Dimensions,* April 1990, p. 14.

29. Ted Levitt, *Marketing Imagination* (New York: The Free Press, 1983), p. 80.

30. Neil Rackham, "Boost Your Sales 20 Percent by Improving This Skill," *Value-Added Selling* 21, June 17, 2003, pp. 1–2.

31. Beth Davis-Sramek, Cornelia Droge, John T. Mentzer, and Matthew B. Myers (2009), "Creating Commitment and Loyalty Behavior Among Retailers: What Are the Roles of Service Quality and Satisfaction?" *Journal of the Academy of Marketing Science* 37, pp. 440–454.

32. Thomas A. Stewart, "A Satisfied Customer Isn't Enough," *Fortune,* July 21, 1997, pp. 112–113.

33. Martin Reimann, Oliver Schilke, and Jacquelyn S. Thomas (2010), "Customer Relationship Management and Firm Performance: The Mediating Role of Business Strategy," *Journal of the Academy of Marketing Science* 38, pp. 326–346.

34. "Business Bulletin," *Wall Street Journal,* September 24, 1998, p. A1.

35. Chuck Salter, "On the Road Again," *Fast Company,* January 2002, pp. 50–58.

36. "Study: What Really Matters to Your Customers," *Value-Added Selling* 21, February 14, 2005, p. 4.

37. Ted Levitt, *Marketing Imagination* (New York: The Free Press, 1983), p. 84.

38. Rebecca Smith, "Beyond Recycling: Manufacturers Embrace 'C2C' Design," *Wall Street Journal,* March 3, 2005, p. B1.

39. Neil Rackham and John R. DeVincentis, *Rethinking the Sales Force* (New York: McGraw-Hill, 1999), p. 89.

40. Ibid., pp. 89–90.

41. Ibid., p. 90.

Endnotes for Boxed Features

a. Based on Malcolm Fleschner, "Chief Sales Executives," *Selling Power,* April 2002, pp. 58–59.

b. Adapted from discussion in Leonard L. Berry, A. Parasuraman, and Valerie A. Zeithaml, "The Service-Quality Puzzle," *Business Horizons,* September–October 1988, pp. 35–43; Robert Kreitner, *Management,* 5th ed. (Boston: Houghton Mifflin Company, 1992), pp. 613–614.

c. Based on Rhonda M. Abrams, "Problem for Pros: Knowing How Much to Charge," *The Des Moines Register,* January 16, 1998, p.2-B.

Chapter 3

The Buying Process and Buyer Behavior

From Chapter 8 of *Selling Today: Partnering to Create Value*, 12/e. Gerald L. Manning. Michael Ahearne. Barry L. Reece. Copyright © 2012 by Pearson Education. Published by Prentice Hall. All rights reserved.

The Buying Process and Buyer Behavior

Chapter Preview

When you finish reading this chapter, you should be able to

1 Discuss the meaning of a customer strategy

2 Explain the difference between consumer and business buyers

3 Understand the importance of alignment between the selling process and the customer's buying process

4 Understand the buying process of the transactional, consultative, and strategic alliance buyer

5 Discuss the various influences that shape customer buying decisions

Reality Selling Today Video Series

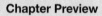

Ashley Pineda is a new home sales representative for the PulteGroup (www.pultegroupinc.com). The company offers different product lines: homes for first-time home buyers, move-up homes, and active adult communities. With three different customer groups, Ashley must have a general understanding of the buying motives of each group. In her work with individual customers in each of these groups she must develop an in-depth understanding of that customer's buying interests.

Most of Ashley's customers are in the first-time home-buyers group who have lived in an apartment but have developed an interest in purchasing a home. Because she has developed an in-depth understanding of this buying group a central purpose of Ashley's sales presentations is to educate her prospects on renting versus owning and the benefits of owning a home. She also understands this customer group often knows little about the logistics of owning a home, therefore she provides her prospects with information and on-site impressions about the neighborhood, the area, the amenities of the community, as well as shopping areas and schools around the neighborhood. All these details help Ashley's customers envision raising their children in one of Pulte's neighborhoods.

Another very important thing Ashley understands about the buying needs of this first-time buying group is the question of the financing of their new home. Ashley typically needs to address the following questions from her customers: What about our credit scores? What qualifies us to buy a new home? Do we need a down payment? What will our monthly payment be? Will it be comfortable with our budget? PulteGroup supplies Ashley with the knowledge to be able to professionally provide and implement that knowledge and make customers feel comfortable with the financial scenario involved in owning their first home.

As is commonly known, buyers tend to buy from people they like and trust. Considering that many customers buy the largest asset they may ever own from sales professionals like Ashley, trust in the seller becomes especially critical. Therefore building rapport and trust throughout the whole buying process is essential for Ashley to be successful. Furthermore, Ashley describes having a positive mindset, good time management, and multi-tasking abilities as the most important skills to be a successful salesperson in her particular business. In essence, sales reps like Ashley have to be able to run their own business in the communities for which they are responsible. ●

Developing a Customer Strategy

The greatest challenge to salespeople in the age of information is to improve responsiveness to customers. In fact, a growing number of sales professionals believe the customer has supplanted the product as the driving force in sales today. This is especially true in those situations in which the products of one company in an industry are becoming more and more similar to those of the competition. Jerry Acuff, author of *Stop Acting Like a Seller and Start Thinking Like a Buyer*, encourages salespeople to think like buyers. In order to think like a buyer, salespeople must understand the buying process and focus on what the customer is looking for.[1]

Adding Value with a Customer Strategy

A **customer strategy** is a carefully conceived plan that results in maximum customer responsiveness. One major dimension of this strategy is to achieve a better understanding of the customer's buying needs and motives. Information has become a strategic resource. When salespeople take time to discover needs and motives, they are in a much better position to offer customers a value-added solution to their buying problem.

Every salesperson who wants to develop repeat business should figure out a way to collect and systematize customer information. The authors of *Reengineering the Corporation* discuss the importance of collecting information about the unique and particular needs of each customer:

> Customers—consumers and corporations alike—demand products and services designed for their unique and particular needs. There is no longer any such notion as the *customer;* there is only this *customer,* the one with whom a seller is dealing at the moment and who now has the capacity to indulge his or her own personal tastes.[2]

The first prescription for developing a customer strategy focuses on the customer's buying process (see Figure 1). Buying procedures and policies can vary greatly from one buyer to another. This is especially true in business-to-business selling. If a salesperson fails to learn how the buyer plans to make the purchase, then there is the danger that the selling process will be out of alignment with the customer's buying process. Keith Eades, author of *The New Solution Selling*, says:

> If we haven't defined how our buyers buy, then we make assumptions that throw us out of alignment with our buyers. Misalignment with buyers is one of selling's most critical mistakes.[3]

The second prescription focuses on why customers buy. This topic will be discussed in detail later in this chapter. The third prescription for developing a customer strategy emphasizes building a strong prospect base.

Complex Nature of Customer Behavior

The forces that motivate customers can be complex. Arch McGill, former vice president of IBM, reminds us that individual customers perceive the product in their own terms and that these terms may be "unique, idiosyncratic, human, emotional, end-of-the-day, irrational, erratic terms."[4] Different people doing the same thing, for example, purchasing a personal computer (PC), may

Strategic/Consultative Selling Model

Strategic Step	Prescription
Develop a Personal Selling Philosophy	☑ Adopt Marketing Concept ☑ Value Personal Selling ☑ Become a Problem Solver/Partner
Develop a Relationship Strategy	☑ Adopt Win-Win Philosophy ☑ Project Professional Image ☑ Maintain High Ethical Standards
Develop a Product Strategy	☑ Become a Product Expert ☑ Sell Benefits ☑ Configure Value-Added Solutions
Develop a Customer Strategy	☐ Understand the Buying Process ☐ Understand Buyer Behavior ☐ Develop Prospect Base

FIGURE 1

Today, one of the greatest challenges to salespeople is improving responsiveness to customers. A well-developed customer strategy is designed to meet this challenge.

have different needs that motivate them, and each person may have several motives for a single action.

The proliferation of market research studies, public opinion polls, surveys, and reports of "averages" makes it easy to fall into the trap of thinking of the customer as a number. The customer is a person, not a statistic. Companies that fully accept this basic truth are likely to adopt a one-to-one marketing strategy. The one-to-one strategy is based on a bedrock concept: Treat different customers differently.[5]

Consumer Versus Business Buyers

Consumer buyer behavior refers to the buying behavior of individuals and households who buy goods and services for personal consumption. Each year, consumers purchase many trillion dollars' worth of goods and services. **Business buyer behavior** refers to the organizations that buy goods and services for use in the production of other products and services that are sold, rented, or supplied to others.[6] In many business buying situations, several people work together to reach a decision. The **buying center** is a cross-functional team of decision makers who often represent several departments. Each team member is likely to have some expertise needed in a particular purchase decision. Salespeople must continually identify which individuals within a firm will be members of the buying center team.[7]

It is not uncommon for salespeople to sell products and services to both consumer and business buyers. A well-established interior decorating firm will likely work with homeowners as well as commercial clients who own hotels, restaurants, or art galleries. A salesperson employed by an automobile dealership will often sell to corporate customers who maintain a fleet of cars or trucks as well as consumers who buy vehicles for personal use.

There are some similarities between consumer markets and business markets. Both involve people who assume the role of buyer and make purchase decisions to satisfy needs. These two markets differ, however, in some important areas. Figure 2 provides a brief review of some of these differences. A business purchase is likely to involve more decision participants and these participants may be well-trained. Most purchasing agents spend time learning how to buy better.[8]

Types of Business Buying Situations

There are three major types of business-to-business buying situations. The amount of time and effort organizational buyers spend on a purchase usually depends on the complexity of the product and how often the decision must be made.[9] At one extreme is the *straight rebuy,* which is a

Consumer Buyers	Organizational Buyers
• Purchases for individual or household consumption	• Purchases made for some purpose other than personal consumption
• Decisions usually made by individuals	• Decisions frequently made by several people
• Purchases often made based on brand reputation or personal recommendations with little or no product expertise	• Purchases made according to precise technical specification based on product expertise
• Purchases based primarily on emotional responses to product or promotions	• Purchases based on primarily rational criteria
• Individual purchasers may make quick decisions	• Purchasers may engage in lengthy decision process
• Products: consumer goods and services for individual use	• Products: often complex; classified based on how organizational customers use them

FIGURE 2

Differences Between Consumer and Organizational Buyers

Adapted from Michael R. Solomon and Elnora W. Stuart, *Marketing: Real People, Real Choices*, 3rd ed. (Upper Saddle River, NJ: Prentice Hall, 2003), p. 193. Reprinted and electronically reproduced by permission of Pearson Education, Inc. Upper Saddle River, New Jersey.

fairly routine decision. At the other extreme is the *new-task buy,* which may require extensive research. In the middle is the *modified rebuy,* which will require some research.[10]

NEW-TASK BUY A first-time purchase of a product or service is a **new-task buy**. Depending on the cost and complexity of this purchase, the buying decision may require several weeks of information gathering and the involvement of numerous decision participants. In some cases, a buying committee is formed to consider the new product's quality, price, and service provided by suppliers. Salespeople who are involved in new-task buying situations must rely heavily on consultative selling skills.

STRAIGHT REBUY A **straight rebuy** is a routine purchase of items needed by a business-to-business customer. Let's assume you have decided to open a new restaurant and need a steady supply of high-quality cooking oil. After talking to several restaurant suppliers, and testing several oils, you select one that meets your needs. Your goal now is to simplify the buying process with the use of a straight rebuy plan. As long as the supplier meets your criteria for price, quality, service, and delivery, future purchases will be very routine. Organizations often use the straight rebuy approach for such items as cleaning supplies, copy paper, and cartridges for computer printers. Salespeople must constantly monitor every straight rebuy situation to be sure the customer is completely satisfied. A competing supplier will be quick to exploit any sign of dissatisfaction by the customer.

MODIFIED REBUY The tide of change is a powerful force in the world of business. From time to time, your customers may wish to modify product specifications, change delivery schedules, or renegotiate prices. Several years ago, American automobile manufacturers, faced with greater competitive pressures from China, Korea, Japan, Germany, and other nations, turned to their suppliers and demanded price reductions. Suppliers were required to become involved in a **modified rebuy** situation or risk loss of the account. A modified rebuy often requires the involvement of several participants.

Well-trained professional salespeople work hard to provide outstanding service after the sale and anticipate changes in customer needs. Some salespeople regularly ask their customers what they value most about the existing buying situation and how improvements can be made in this area.

BUILDING STRATEGIC ALLIANCES Strategic alliances are the highest form of partnering. Alliances are often formed by companies that have similar business interests and believe the partnership will help them gain a mutual competitive advantage. Large companies often form several alliances. Some strategic alliances take the form of systems selling. **Systems selling** appeals to buyers who prefer to purchase a packaged solution to a problem from a single seller, thus avoiding all the separate decisions involved in a complex buying situation.[11]

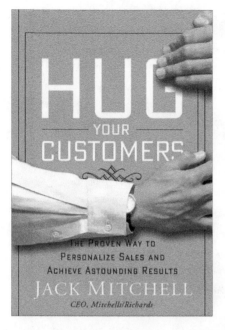

The sales personnel at Mitchells/Richards sells high quality apparel to discriminating customers. Many of these customers are business executives who invest heavily in their business wardrobes. Salespeople at Mitchells/Richards work hard to discover the customer's needs and provide outstanding service after the sale.

Source: Reprinted by permission of Christina B. Bliss.

Several years ago, Kinko's reinvented itself as a document solutions provider for business firms of all sizes. Full-service Kinko's stores began offering the buyer networks of computers equipped with popular software, ultrafast color printers, high-speed Internet connections and, of course, a variety of document preparation services. After Kinko's was purchased by FedEx, a network of 1,200 digitally connected FedEx Kinko's locations began offering a wider selection of customized, needs-based document solutions. One large financial institution consolidated the services of 13 vendors by forming an alliance with FedEx Kinko's.[12] Systems selling efforts at FedEx Kinko's has become an important strategy for winning and holding accounts.

Types of Consumer Buying Situations

As noted previously, consumer buying behavior refers to purchases of products for personal or household use. The amount of time consumers devote to a purchase decision can vary greatly depending on the cost of the product, familiarity with the product, and the importance of the item to the consumer. Few buyers invest much effort in selecting a tube of toothpaste, but the purchase of a new automobile or a home will involve extensive decision making. Consumer buying situations can fall into one of three categories depending on the degree of buyer involvement.

HABITUAL BUYING DECISIONS **Habitual buying decisions** usually require very little consumer involvement and brand differences are usually insignificant.[13] For frequently purchased, low-cost items such as shampoo, copy paper, or laundry detergent, consumer involvement in the decision-making process is very low. Supermarket shoppers often display habitual buying behavior as they select items.

VARIETY-SEEKING BUYING DECISIONS **Variety-seeking buying decisions** are characterized by low customer involvement, but important perceived brand differences.[14] Brand switching is not uncommon among these buyers because they can be influenced by advertising appeals, coupons, or lower prices to try a new brand. Brand switching is usually motivated by the desire for variety rather than dissatisfaction.[15]

COMPLEX BUYING DECISIONS **Complex buying decisions** are characterized by a high degree of involvement by the consumer. Consumers are likely to be highly involved when the product is expensive, purchased infrequently, and highly self-expressive.[16] The purchase of a vacation home, a long-term care insurance policy, an expensive boat, or a costly piece of art would require a complex buying decision. The learning process for some purchases can be very lengthy.

Achieving Alignment with the Customer's Buying Process

The foundation of a successful sales effort comes from knowing how buyers buy. If you don't know what the customer's decision-making process is and you proceed according to your own agenda, you risk losing the sale. If we have not defined how buyers buy, then we make assumptions that throw our sales process out of alignment with the buyer's buying process.[17] Too often salespeople rely on generalizations about the buyer's decision-making process rather than acquiring specific information.

The **buying process** is a systematic series of actions, or a series of defined, repeatable steps intended to achieve a result.[18] Organizational purchasing structures and buying procedures can vary greatly from company to company, so we need to be clear on how decisions are being made within each account. In some cases, the steps in the buying process have been clearly defined by the organization and this information is available to any potential supplier. However, this information may not tell us the whole story. Salespeople need to obtain answers to these types of questions:

- How urgent is my proposal to the buyer? When will a buying decision be made?
- Will any "political" factors within the organization influence how decisions are made?
- Has the money needed to purchase my product been allocated?
- Which person or persons in the buying organization will actually use or supervise the use of the product I am selling?[19]

Customers make buying decisions in many ways, so understanding each individual buyer's decision-making process is central to success in personal selling. Some buyers will have multiple buying processes. Buying decisions involving a straight rebuy, for example, will likely differ from buying decisions involving a new-task buy.[20]

Steps in the Typical Buying Process

The term "process" brings to mind a set formula that applies to every situation. But buying decisions are made in different ways, so it would be inappropriate to view the buying process as a uniform pattern of decision making. However, there is a model—a form of decision making that buyers usually apply to their unique circumstances. Figure 3 shows the typical stages in the buying decision process: needs awareness, evaluation of solutions, resolution of problems, purchase, and implementation. This model is especially helpful in understanding organizational buying decisions and large consumer acquisitions. Consumers who make habitual buying decisions often skip or reverse some of these stages.[21]

NEEDS AWARENESS Needs awareness is the first stage in the buying process. The buyer recognizes that something is imperfect or incomplete. The need for energy conservation technology may surface when oil prices rise to higher levels. The need for a customer service training program may become evident when customer satisfaction survey scores decline. Salespeople can create value at this stage of the buying process if they can help determine the magnitude of the customer's problem and identify a solution. For example, a sales representative may be able to help the buyer estimate the cost of poor customer service and recommend a way to improve

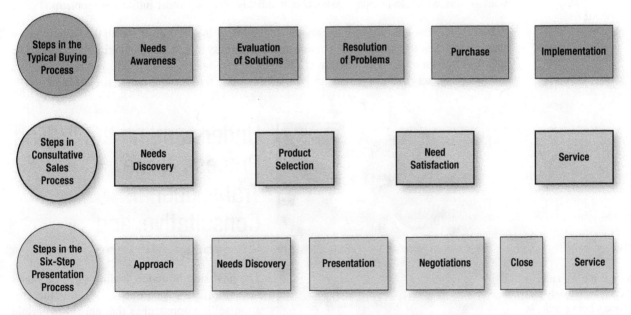

FIGURE 3

Typical Buying Process Model

In this figure, for purposes of illustration, the Typical Buying Process Model is aligned with the two most popular Selling Process Models. It is important salespeople understand the customer's unique buying process, and where the customer is in that buying process, and then align the sales process to satisfy their customer's needs.

service. Customers often need help in determining whether they have a problem large enough to justify the cost of a solution.[22]

EVALUATION OF SOLUTIONS Buyers who experience need awareness usually begin searching for information that will help them evaluate possible problem solutions. They realize, at this point, that the problem they face is amenable to some type of solution. In some cases, there are several solutions that the customer needs to study. Salespeople can add value at this stage by providing useful information that helps the customer make an informed choice. In some cases, the value justification can be presented in terms of cost reduction or increased revenues. In other cases, the value justification may be an intangible such as customer satisfaction, improved security, or reduced stress. In business-to-business selling situations, value justification that can be measured is usually the most powerful.

To establish a true partnership with the customer, you need to be sure that you are offering them information that will help them achieve their objectives. If you possess a good understanding of the customer's buying process, you will know what they are trying to accomplish.[23]

RESOLUTION OF PROBLEMS At this stage of the buying process, the customer is aware of a need and has evaluated one or more solutions. The customer has resolved to do something. However, the customer is likely to have issues and concerns that must be resolved before moving ahead. This is especially true in the case of complex sales.[24]

Some customers will want the proposed solution put in writing. Competitors may be invited to submit written proposals. A well-written proposal is one way to add value. The customer may request specific information that can only be provided by the supplier's engineers or accountants. The customer many insist on visiting the supplier's manufacturing plant so they can see the production process firsthand. Buyers often need help overcoming obstacles that prevent them from moving to the purchase stage of the buying process.[25]

PURCHASE After all the customer's obstacles and concerns have been overcome, the purchase decision is made. Professional salespeople create value in many ways at this stage of the buying process.[26] First, they do whatever is necessary to make sure the purchase is "hassle free." This may mean working with the customer to arrange the best financing or supervising the delivery and installation of the product. Salespeople add value by becoming a "customer advocate" within their own organizations. This may mean negotiating with various departments to expedite the order. Buyers want to work with salespeople who are able to quickly solve any order fulfillment problems.[27]

IMPLEMENTATION The first sale is only the beginning of the relationship with the buyer. Repeat sales occur when the supplier has demonstrated the ability to add value in various ways after the sale. Value creation can take the form of timely delivery, superior installation, accurate invoicing, follow-up contacts by the salesperson, or something else that is important to the customer.

There is no longer any such notion as the customer—there is only this customer, the one whom a seller is dealing with at the moment. Discovering the individual needs of this customer can be challenging.

Source: Yuri Arcurs/Dreamstime

Understanding the Buying Process of the Transactional, Consultative, and Strategic Alliance Buyer

The next step in understanding the customer's buying process is to discuss three value creation selling approaches that appeal to certain types of customers: transactional selling, consultative selling, and strategic alliance selling. We will now discuss how to work effectively with each type of buyer.[28]

Transactional Process Buyer

Transactional buyers are well aware of their needs and usually know a great deal about the products or services they intend to purchase. In a true transactional sale, buyers will become frustrated if the salesperson attempts to use needs assessment, problem solving, or relationship building. They are not looking for new information or advice from the salesperson. Most transactional buyers have conducted their own research and, in most cases, have decided which product best meets their needs. They don't want hand-holding and they don't want the salesperson to waste their time.[29]

How can a salesperson add value to a transactional sale? If the buyer is already aware of his needs, has evaluated solutions, and has no issues or concerns that need to be resolved, then the salesperson needs to focus on the purchase stage of the five-part buying process model (see Figure 3). Do whatever is necessary to facilitate a convenient and hassle-free purchase. Eliminate any unnecessary costs or delays in processing the order. The transactional buyer may quickly turn to a competitor if they experience unnecessary costs or delays.

Consultative Process Buyer

Consultative selling appeals to buyers who lack needs awareness or need help evaluating possible solutions. Some buying decisions require assistance from a consultative salesperson because the product is very complex and/or the cost of the product is very high. The purchase of a new home provides a good example in the consumer arena. Home buyers usually seek the assistance of an experienced realtor. The purchase of Internet phone-calling equipment provides a good example in the business-to-business arena. Organizations that are considering the purchase of complex Internet telephone equipment seek answers to several questions: Can we keep a portion of our traditional phone network or must we adopt an all–Internet phone system? Will the new system provide the same voice quality as our traditional system? Internet phone-calling equipment is available from several suppliers, including Avaya Incorporated and Cisco Systems Incorporated. Some customers will need help comparing the technology available from these and other suppliers.[30]

Successful consultative salespeople focus a great deal of attention on needs awareness, which is step one in the buying process model (see Figure 3). This is where salespeople can create the most value by helping customers gain an understanding of their problems and create solutions that correct these problems.[31] Many customers seek help defining needs and solutions, but avoid dealing with a sales representative who simply wants to sell a product.

Consultative selling encompasses the concept that salespeople should conduct a systematic assessment of the prospect's situation. This usually involves collecting as much information as possible prior to the sales call and using a series of carefully worded questions to obtain the customer's point of view during the sales call. Two-way communication will provide for a mutual exchange of ideas, feelings, and perceptions.

The consultative salesperson will help the customer evaluate solutions and help resolve any problems that surface prior to the purchase stage. Consultative salespeople also work hard to add value at the implementation stage of the sales process. This may involve supervising product delivery and installation, servicing warranties, and providing other services after the sale.

Strategic Alliance Process Buyer

As noted previously, the goal of strategic alliances is to achieve a marketplace advantage by teaming up with another company. Alliances are often formed by companies that have similar business interests and seek to gain a mutual competitive advantage. Dell Computer, for example, formed a partnership with Microsoft and Intel to provide customized e-business solutions. In the highly competitive global market, going it alone is sometimes more difficult.[32]

Step one in building an alliance is a careful study of the proposed partner. This research is often coordinated by senior management and may involve persons working in the areas of sales, marketing, finance, and distribution. At some point, representatives from both companies will meet and explore the mutual benefits of the alliance. Both parties must be prepared to explain how they will add value once the alliance is formed.

Buyer Resolution Theory

This view of the buying process recognizes that a purchase is made only after the prospect has made five buying decisions involving specific affirmative responses to the following questions:

Why Should I Buy?
Realistically, it is sometimes difficult to provide prospects with an answer to this question. In many cases, salespeople fail in their attempt to help customers become aware of a need. Thus, large numbers of potential customers are not sufficiently persuaded to purchase products that provide them with genuine buyer benefits.

What Should I Buy?
If a prospect agrees that a need does exist, then you are ready to address the second buying decision. You must convince the prospect that the product being offered can satisfy the need. In most cases, the buyer can choose from several competing products.

Where Should I Buy?
As products become more complex, consumers are giving more attention to "source" decisions. In a major metropolitan area the person who wants to buy a Laserjet 3160 or a competing product can choose from several sources.

What Is a Fair Price?
Today's better educated and better informed consumers are searching for the right balance between price and value (benefits). They are better able to detect prices that are not competitive or do not correspond in their minds with the product's value.

When Should I Buy?
A sale cannot be closed until a customer has decided when to buy. In some selling situations, the customer may want to postpone the purchase because of reluctance to part with the money.

FIGURE 4

The buyer resolution theory, sometimes referred to as "The 5 W's Theory," focuses attention on questions the customer may need answers to before making a purchase. An absence of an answer to any of these will likely result in a customer objection.

The Buyer Resolution Theory

Several theories explain how customers arrive at a buying decision. One traditional point of view is based on the assumption that a final buying decision is possible only after the prospect has answered five logical questions (see Figure 4). This is called the **buyer resolution theory**. One strength of this buying theory is that it focuses the salesperson's attention on five important factors that the customer is likely to consider before making a purchase. Answers to these five questions provide valuable insights about the customer's buying strategy. One important limitation of this theory is that it is often not possible to anticipate which of the five buying decisions might be most difficult for the prospect to make. If the selling process does not mesh with the buying process, a sale is less likely. There is no established sequence in which prospects make these five decisions, so a highly inflexible sales presentation would not be effective.

Understanding Buyer Behavior

Although every customer is unique, salespeople need an understanding of the important social and psychological influences that tend to shape customer buying decisions. We will review concepts that come from the fields of psychology, sociology, and anthropology. Figure 5 illustrates the many forces that influence buying decisions.

Basic Needs That Influence Buyer Behavior

Basic human needs have changed little throughout our economic history. However, the ways in which needs are fulfilled have changed greatly during the age of information.[33] The starting point for developing an understanding of the forces influencing buying decisions is a review of the individual needs that shape the customer's behavior. To gain insights into customer behavior motivated by both physiological and psychological needs, it is helpful to study the popular hierarchy of needs developed by Abraham Maslow.

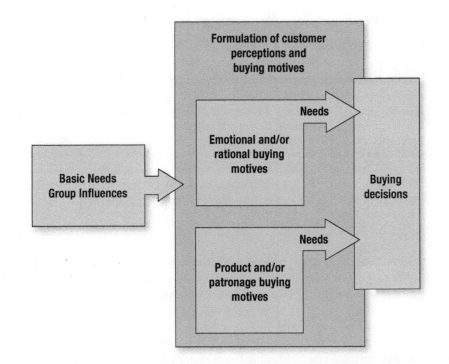

FIGURE 5

The Buyer Behavior Model

This model illustrates the many complex psychological and sociological forces that influence buyer behavior.

MASLOW'S HIERARCHY OF NEEDS According to Abraham Maslow, basic human needs are arranged in a hierarchy according to their strength (Figure 6). His theory rests on the assumption that as each lower-level need is satisfied, the need at the next level demands attention.

Physiological Needs Sometimes called primary needs, **physiological needs** include the needs of food, water, sleep, and shelter. Maslow placed our physiological needs at the bottom of the pyramid because he believed that these basic needs tend to be strong in the minds of most people.

Security Needs After physiological needs have been satisfied, the next need level that tends to dominate is safety and security. **Security needs** represent our desire to be free from danger and uncertainty. The desire to satisfy the need for safety and security often motivates people to purchase such items as medical and life insurance or a security alarm for the home or business.

Social Needs The need to belong, or **social needs**, reflects our desire for identification with a group and approval from others. These needs help explain our continuing search for friendship, social acceptance among one's peers, and long-term business relationships.

Esteem Needs At the fourth level of Maslow's need priority model appear **esteem needs**. Esteem needs reflect our desire to feel worthy in the eyes of others. We seek a sense of personal worth and adequacy, a feeling of competence.[34]

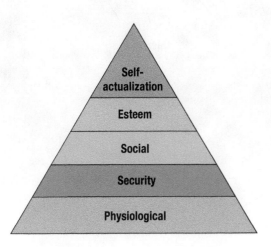

FIGURE 6

Maslow's Hierarchy of Needs Model

The forces that motivate customers to make specific buying decisions are complex. This model illustrates Maslow's hierarchy of needs.

Source: Abraham H. Maslow, Robert D. Frager (editor), and James Fadiman (editor), *Motivation and Personality*, 3rd ed. (Upper Saddle River, NJ: Pearson Education, 1987), p. 193. Printed and electronically reproduced by permission of Pearson Education, Inc. Upper Saddle River, New Jersey.

Selling Across Generation Gaps

It is important to understand the context in which people from different generational groups live and work. After all, success in personal selling requires the ability to create rapport and develop trust with buyers who may differ from us. Picture yourself as a Millennial (Generation Y), who was born between 1977 and 1994. Chances are you welcome the latest high-tech communications technology and do not resent the never-ending sea of information that demands your immediate attention and response. Some of the customers you call on are members of the Baby Boom generation, who were born between 1946 and 1964. These individuals may welcome traditional memos, letters, phone calls, and face-to-face communications and feel uncomfortable working in today's wireless world. Generational differences shaped by sociological, political, and economic conditions can influences our values. Dave Stein, author of *How Winners Sell,* says, "Before you ever meet that prospect, understand that 'different' in terms of cross-generational selling is neither right nor wrong; it's just different."[a]

Self-Actualization Needs   Maslow defined the term **self-actualization** as a need for self-fulfillment, a full tapping of one's potential. It is the need to "be all that you can be," to have mastery over what you are doing. One goal of consultative selling is to help the customer experience self-actualization in terms of the relationship with the salesperson.

The five-level need priority model developed by Maslow is somewhat artificial in certain instances. At times several of our needs are interacting together within us. One example is the business lunch. Not only are you conducting business with a client but you are also satisfying your needs for food and beverages, for engaging in social activities, and perhaps for feeling important in your own eyes and—you hope—in the eyes of your customer. However, the model can provide salespeople with a practical way of understanding which need is most likely to dominate customer behavior in certain situations.

Group Influences That Influence Buying Decisions

As noted earlier, the people around us also influence our buying decisions. These **group influences** can be grouped into four major areas: (1) role influences, (2) reference groups, (3) social class, and (4) culture and subculture.[35] (See Figure 7.) Salespeople who understand these roles and influences can develop the type of insight customers view as being valuable.

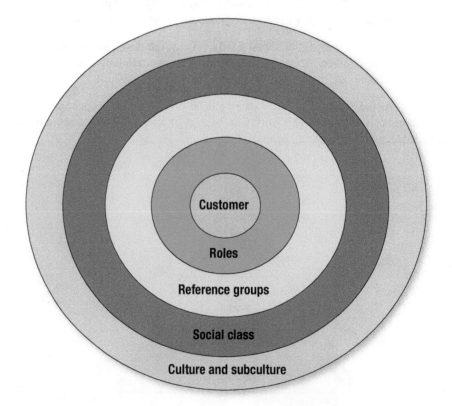

FIGURE 7

Group Influences That Influence Buying Decisions Model

To gain additional insights into customers' motivations, it is helpful to study the group influences that affect buying decisions.

ROLE INFLUENCE Throughout our lives we occupy positions within groups, organizations, and institutions. Closely associated with each position is a **role**: a set of characteristics and expected social behaviors based on the expectations of others. All the roles we assume (student, member of the school board, or position held at work) influence not only our general behavior but also our buying behavior. In today's society, for example, a woman may assume the role of mother at home and purchasing manager at work. In the manager's role, she may feel the need to develop a conservative wardrobe, enroll in a leadership training course, or join a professional association.

REFERENCE GROUP INFLUENCE A **reference group** consists of the categories of people that you see yourself belonging to, and with which you habitually compare yourself. Members of a reference group tend to influence the values, attitudes, and behaviors of one another.[36] The reference group may act as a point of comparison and a source of information for the individual member.[37] For example, Pi Sigma Epsilon, the national fraternity in marketing, sales management, and selling, may serve as a reference group for a college business major. In the business community, a chapter of the American Society for Training and Development, or Sales & Marketing Executives International, may provide a reference group for its members. As members of a reference group, we often observe other people in the group to establish our own norms, and these norms become a guide for our purchasing activity.

SOCIAL CLASS INFLUENCE **Social classes** are society's relatively permanent and ordered divisions whose members share similar values, interests, and behavior.[38] The criteria used to rank people according to social class vary from one society to another. In some societies, land ownership allows entry into a higher social class. In other societies, education is a major key to achieving upper-class status. Social class, in most cases, is not determined by a single factor. It is determined by a combination of factors such as income, education, occupation, and accumulated wealth.

CULTURAL INFLUENCE **Culture** can be defined as the accumulation of values, rules of behavior, forms of expression, religious beliefs, transmitted behavior patterns, and the like for a group of people who share a common language and environment. Culture tends to encourage or discourage particular behaviors and mental processes.[39] We maintain and transmit our culture chiefly through language. Culture has considerable influence on buying behavior. Today, culture is getting more attention because of the rapid increases in immigrant groups. As cultural diversity increases, companies must reexamine their sales and marketing strategies.

Within most cultures are groups whose members share value systems based on common life experiences and situations. We call such a group a **subculture**. Some subcultures, such as mature consumers, Hispanic, African-American, and Generation Y (16- to 24-year-olds), make up important market segments.[40]

Perception—How Customer Needs Are Formed

Perception is the process through which sensations are interpreted, using our knowledge and experience. These sensations are received through sight, hearing, touch, taste, and smell. Buyer behavior is often influenced by perception.[41] When Volkswagen announced that it would build an ultra-luxury car selling for $70,000, many people questioned the merits of this decision.

CUSTOMER RELATIONSHIP MANAGEMENT WITH TECHNOLOGY

Managing Multiple Contacts with CRM

Salespeople often find that groups of their contacts have common interests and buying motives. Customers and prospects may be segmented into groups by buying influences, by the products they purchase, by the industries they are involved in, or by their size. Customer relationship management (CRM) software can enable the salesperson to easily link contacts together as groups and "mass-produce" information that appears custom-fitted to the need of each person in a specific group. For example, each owner of a specific product may receive a telephone call, personalized letter, or report that describes the benefits of a new accessory available from the salesperson. CRM Application Exercise "Managing Multiple Contacts with CRM" describes how common interest groups can be found.

Could the maker of the Beetle and Thing compete in the market segment dominated by Lexus, Mercedes-Benz, Jaguar, and BMW? Thus far, sales of the Volkswagen Phaeton have been slow even though most automobile journalists view it as a true luxury car.[42] Is perception the barrier to sales growth?

We tend to screen out or modify stimuli, a process known as *selective attention*, for two reasons. First, we cannot possibly be conscious of all inputs at one time. Just the commercial messages we see and hear each day are enough to cause sensory overload. Second, we are conditioned by our social and cultural background, and our physical and psychological needs, to use selectivity.

Buyers may screen out or modify information presented by a salesperson if it conflicts with their previously learned attitudes or beliefs. The business buyer who feels the new office furniture designs that combine individual work space will only encourage impromptu employee chitchat is apt to use selective attention when the salesperson begins discussing product features. Salespeople who can anticipate this problem of selective attention should acquire as much background information as possible before meeting with the prospect. During the first meeting with the customer, the salesperson should make every effort to build a strong relationship so that the person opens up and freely discusses personal perceptions. Salespeople who do this have accepted one of the great truisms in sales and marketing: "Facts are negotiable. Perception is rock solid."

Buying Motives

Every buying decision has a motive behind it. A **buying motive** can be thought of as an aroused need, drive, or desire. This motive acts as a force that stimulates behavior intended to satisfy the aroused need. Our perceptions influence or shape this behavior. An understanding of buying motives provides the salesperson with the reasons why customers buy. Unfortunately, some buyers will not or cannot tell you their buying motives. A company may be planning a new product launch and wants to keep this initiative a secret. In some cases revealing important information may make the customer feel vulnerable. And, some customers may not be aware of one or more buying motives that will influence the purchase decision.[43]

As you might expect, some buying decisions are influenced by more than one buying motive. The buyer of catering services may want food of exceptional quality served quickly so all her guests can eat together. This customer also may be quite price conscious. In this situation, the caterer should attempt to discover the *dominant buying motive* (DBM). The DBM may have the greatest influence on the buying decision.[44] If the customer is eager to make a good impression on guests who have discriminating food tastes, then food quality may be the dominant buying motive.

Successful salespeople have adopted a product strategy that involves discovery of the buying motives that influence the purchase decision.

EMOTIONAL VERSUS RATIONAL BUYING MOTIVES A careful study of buyer behavior reveals that people make buying decisions based on both emotional and rational buying motives. An **emotional buying motive** is one that prompts the prospect to act because of an appeal to some sentiment or passion. When customers buy expensive Harley-Davidson motorcycles, they are paying for much more than a high-flying hog. They are purchasing entry into a community of like-minded enthusiasts who share a passion for all things Harley.[45] Emotions can be powerful and often serve as the foundation of the dominant buying motive.[46] A **rational buying motive** usually appeals to the prospect's reason or judgment based on objective thought processes. Some common rational buying motives include profit potential, quality of service, and availability of technical assistance.

Emotional Buying Motives A surprising number of purchases are guided by emotional buying motives. Recent research indicates that buying is a lot more emotional than most marketers thought. Many buyers are guided more by feelings than by logic.[47] Even technology firms sometimes rely on emotional appeals as part of their marketing strategy. Doing business in America, or anyplace else in the world, is never purely a rational or logical process. Recognize that there is an emotional component to every sale and tune in to the emotional cues such as body language,

CEO Glenn Sandberg understands that in the business-to-business market, exact specifications and 24-hour support appeal to those customers who are motivated by rational buying motives.

Source: Courtesy of Formax, Inc.

tone of voice, and emotive words. With the power of empathy you can get on the same page, emotionally, as your customer.[48]

Rational Buying Motives   A purchase based on rational buying motives is generally the result of an objective review of available information. The buyer closely examines product or service information with an attitude that is relatively free of emotion. Business buyers are most likely to be motivated by rational buying motives such as on-time delivery, financial gain, competent installation, saving of time, increased profits, or durability.

Business buyers representing large firms such as Ford Motor Company, IBM, and General Electric rely on a buying process that is more formalized than the consumer buying process. Purchases made by these companies usually call for detailed product specifications, written purchase orders, and formal approval. The business buyer and the salesperson work closely during all stages of the buying process that begins with a precise definition of the customer's problem. Salespeople who sell to business buyers spend a great deal of time gathering, interpreting, and disseminating customer-specific information.[49]

PATRONAGE VERSUS PRODUCT BUYING MOTIVES Another way to help explain buyer behavior is to distinguish between patronage and product buying motives. Patronage buying motives and product buying motives are learned reasons for buying. These buying motives are important because they can stimulate repeat business and referrals.

Selling NASCAR in Manhattan

NASCAR is growing in popularity each year. This form of auto racing, with deep roots in the South, is attracting fans throughout the nation. About 40 million people consider themselves avid fans. Although NASCAR TV ratings are rising and most races are sold out, someone still needs to sell this product to team sponsors. Brett Yormark is a corporate sales representative representing NASCAR in New York City. It now costs from $10 million to $14 million to sponsor a top team, so he is a key member of the NASCAR sales and marketing team. Yormark faces major challenges because he is selling stock car racing to an upscale, urban crowd. Many of his prospects are corporate executives who have never seen a NASCAR race.[b]

Source: CORBIS-NY

Patronage Buying Motives A **patronage buying motive** is one that causes the prospect to buy products from one particular business. The prospect has had prior direct or indirect contact with the business and has judged this contact to be beneficial. In those situations where there is little or no appreciable difference between two products, patronage motives can be highly important. At a time when look-alike products are very common, these motives take on a new degree of importance. Some typical patronage buying motives are superior service, complete selection of products, competence of sales representatives, and ability to buy online.

Product Buying Motives A **product buying motive** is one that leads a prospect to purchase one product in preference to another. Interestingly enough, this decision is sometimes made without direct comparison between competing products. The buyer simply believes that one product is superior to another. There are numerous buying motives that trigger prospects to select one product over another. These include brand preference, quality preference, price preference, and design or engineering preference.

It is hard to imagine how salespeople can create values for customers without first understanding the latter's buying motives. Figure 8 provides various examples of how salespeople can put this understanding into creating values at different stages of the buying process.

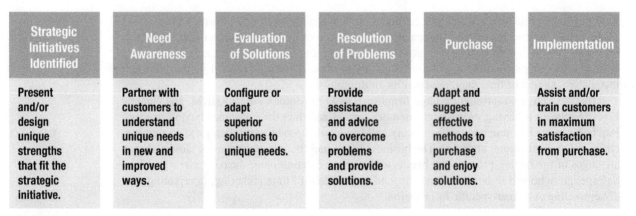

Strategic Initiatives Identified	Need Awareness	Evaluation of Solutions	Resolution of Problems	Purchase	Implementation
Present and/or design unique strengths that fit the strategic initiative.	Partner with customers to understand unique needs in new and improved ways.	Configure or adapt superior solutions to unique needs.	Provide assistance and advice to overcome problems and provide solutions.	Adapt and suggest effective methods to purchase and enjoy solutions.	Assist and/or train customers in maximum satisfaction from purchase.

FIGURE 8

Creating Value Throughout the Buying Process Model

A sample list of methods for creating value throughout each of the steps in the buying process. Specific methods should be created after arriving at a careful understanding of the unique needs of the individual customer.

GLOBAL BUSINESS INSIGHT

Doing Business in France

The French people are very proud of their history, language, social systems, and customs. They expect visitors to respect the many things that make their country unique. Preparation for a business trip to France may take a little extra time.

- Learn basic French and use it often. Although most French businesspeople speak English, some will not admit it.
- Introductions should be made by someone (attorney, banker, or a friend) known to the person with whom you want to do

business. French people tend to be cautious when meeting someone new.

- Be prepared to conduct business over meals at nice restaurants. A business lunch might last for two hours. The French rarely invite business guests to their homes.
- French businesspeople are reluctant to take risks, so negotiations may take a long time. Be well prepared to discuss the merits of your product but avoid the hard sell.[c]

To fully understand the customer's buying strategy the salesperson must conduct a careful needs discovery or assessment. This is done by asking appropriate questions, listening to the customer's responses, and making careful observations.

Source: Deanm1974/Dreamstime LLC-Royalty Free

CHAPTER LEARNING ACTIVITIES

Reviewing Key Concepts

Discuss the meaning of a customer strategy

The importance of developing a customer strategy was introduced in this chapter. This type of planning is necessary to ensure maximum customer responsiveness. Buying procedures and policies can vary greatly from one buyer to another. If a salesperson does not learn how the buyer plans to make the purchase, then there is the strong possibility that the selling process will be out of alignment with the customer's buying process.

Explain the difference between consumer and business buyers

Business buyer behavior was compared to consumer buyer behavior. Three types of business buying situations were described: straight rebuy, new-task buy, and the modified rebuy. Systems selling, a common business buying strategy, was also described. Three types of consumer buying situations were defined: habitual buying decisions, variety-seeking buying decisions, and complex buying decisions.

Understand the importance of alignment between the selling process and the customer's buying process

Customers make buying decisions in many ways, so it would be inappropriate to view the buying process as a uniform pattern of decision making. However, there is a common decision-making model that most buyers apply to their unique circumstances. The typical stages in the buying decision process are needs awareness, evaluation of solutions, resolution of problems, purchase, and implementation.

Understand the buying process of the transactional, consultative, and strategic alliance buyer

Three value creation selling approaches that appeal to certain types of customers were discussed: the transactional process buyer, the consultative process buyer, and the strategic alliance process buyer. The consultative process buyer offers the greatest challenge to most salespeople.

Discuss the various influences that shape customer buying decisions

We noted that buyer behavior is influenced in part by individual (physical and psychological) needs. Maslow's popular model ranks these needs. There are also a number of group influences that shape our psychological needs to various degrees. Buyer behavior is influenced by the roles we assume, reference groups, social class, and culture. *Perception* was defined as the process of selecting, organizing, and interpreting information inputs to produce meaning. We discussed emotional and rational buying motives and compared patronage and product motives.

Key Terms

Customer strategy	Complex buying decisions	Reference group
Consumer buyer behavior	Buying process	Social classes
Business buyer behavior	Buyer resolution theory	Culture
Buying center	Physiological needs	Subculture
New-task buy	Security needs	Buying motive
Straight rebuy	Social needs	Emotional buying motive
Modified rebuy	Esteem needs	Rational buying motive
Systems selling	Self-actualization	Patronage buying motive
Habitual buying decisions	Group influences	Product buying motive
Variety-seeking buying decisions	Role	

Review Questions

1. According to the Strategic/Consultative Selling Model, what are the three prescriptions for the development of a successful customer strategy?
2. List and describe the three most common types of organizational buying situations.
3. Describe the five major stages in the typical buying process.
4. List and describe three value creation selling approaches that appeal to various types of customers.
5. According to the buyer resolution theory, a purchase is made only after the prospect has made five buying decisions. What are they?
6. Explain how Maslow's hierarchy of needs affects buyer behavior.
7. Describe the four group influences that affect buyer behavior.
8. What is meant by the term *perception*?
9. Distinguish between emotional and rational buying motives.
10. J. D. Power, founder of J.D. Power and Associates, says, "We define quality as what the customer wants." Do you agree or disagree with his observations? Explain your answer.

Application Exercises

1. Select several advertisements from a trade magazine. Analyze each one and determine what rational buying motives the advertiser is appealing to. Do any of these advertisements appeal to emotional buying motives? Then select a magazine that is aimed at a particular consumer group, for example, *Architectural Digest*, *Redbook*, or *Better Homes and Gardens*. Study the advertisements and determine what buying motives they appeal to.

2. The $40,000 Hyundai Genesis V8, which entered the U.S. market as a 2009 model, is a far cry from the popular Elantra. Hyundai's new flagship model was designed to compete with Lexus, Mercedes-Benz, Cadillac, and BMW. The Genesis is positioned as another choice in the luxury-car market. Will potential customers accept the Genesis as a true luxury car? Will customer perceptions play a role in acceptance of this new model?

3. J.D. Power and Associates is a global marketing information services firm that helps businesses and consumers make better decisions through credible customer-based information. The company provides an unbiased source of marketing information based on opinions of consumers. Visit www.jdpower.com and become familiar with the type of information services offered.

Role-Play Exercise

In this role-play, you will assume the role of a salesperson working at a Brook's Brothers clothing store. The inventory includes a wide range of business professional clothing such as suits, sport coats, dress shirts, and accessories; the store also offers a full range of business casual clothing. A member of your class will assume the role of a customer who visits your store for the purpose of buying clothing for work. He recently graduated from college and will start work at a new job in about two weeks. In addition to clothing, your store offers complete alteration services and credit plans. During the role-play, you should develop a relationship with the customer using strategies discussed in previous chapters and determine the customer's needs with questions, attentive listening, and observation.

CRM Application Exercise

Managing Multiple Contacts with CRM

The Salesforce.com database contains four new companies identified as prospects. Little information about them is available, which is common when a list of names has been downloaded from a purchased list or a social media network. The fact that they are all financial services firms may mean that SimNet is expanding into this industry sector. These firms are listed as prospects because no contact has been made with them to determine whether they may qualify for SimNet's products or services.

You are to begin the process of qualifying these leads by looking up the companies to arrange an initial contact with them. To find prospects such as these, select the Reports tab, choose "SimNet Reports" from the Folder drop-down list, and click on "Sales Pipeline."

SimNet Reports	
Edit | Del | Export	Contacts by Communication Style
Edit | Del | Export	Contacts by Location
Edit | Del | Export	Sales Pipeline
Edit | Del | Export	Sales Stage Pipeline
Edit | Del | Export	SimNet Mailing Lists

This report displays a section for each stage in the sales funnel and lists the companies in each section. Click on the top of the column labeled "Sales Process Stage" once or twice so all four Prospects are listed at the top.

Click on the last name of the first prospect, which will display the Contact Detail record. Scroll down to the Activity History section. Select the "Send An Email" button,

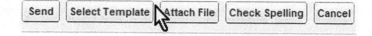

and on the Task screen that is displayed, click on the "Select Template" button.

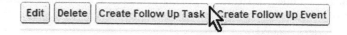

Choosing the Financial Services template will provide the e-mail's subject and body. Clicking the Send button, with a copy to your instructor if directed, will return you to the Contact screen. View the Activity History section and click on the link to the e-mail you just sent. On the Task Detail screen, click "Create Follow Up Task" (not the Create Follow Up *Event*) link.

Choosing the Financial Services template will provide the e-mail's subject and body. Clicking the Send button, with a copy to your instructor if directed, will return you to the Contact screen. View the Activity History section and click on the link to the e-mail you just sent. On the Task Detail screen, click "Create Follow Up Task" (not the Create Follow Up *Event*) link.

On the Task Edit screen, click on the icon to the right of the Subject field.

Selecting "Call" from the pop-up ComboBox list will identify the type of follow-up task you are arranging. When reviewing your future tasks, it might be more helpful to you if the task description is more explicit. In the Subject field, enter "Financial Services Call."

In the Due Date field, enter the date for the Monday following the day you perform this exercise. You will note that the Reminder field below will automatically update to match the date you enter. The Reminder serves as an alarm clock, allowing you to set a date and time to be alerted about the task, which may be days or hours before the scheduled due date. In this case, leave the Reminder at the same date and the hour as 8:00 A.M. When finished, click the Save button on the Task Edit bar.

Repeat this process for all four financial services companies. You may verify these financial services calls have been scheduled for next Monday by clicking on the Home tab. The My Tasks section will display your financial services calls.

Reality Selling Today Video Case Problem

Ashley Pineda, featured at the beginning of this chapter, is a new home sales representative for the PulteGroup (see Web site at www.pultegroupinc.com). The company engages in homebuilding and financial services businesses. Its homebuilding business includes the acquisition and development of land primarily for residential purposes and the construction of housing on such land targeted for first-time, first and second move-up, and active adult home buyers. As of March 31, 2010, its homebuilding operations offered homes for sale in 842 communities. The company's financial services business consists of mortgage banking and title operations. It arranges financing through the origination of mortgage loans for its homebuyers, sells such loans and the related servicing rights, provides title insurance policies as an agent, and provides examination and closing services to its home buyers. PulteGroup offers a one-stop shopping experience for prospective customers. Sales reps help clients to finance their homes (with Pulte Mortgage) and to close their homes with PGP Title. One of PulteGroup's key strengths is the ability to provide customers with an exceptional home-buying experience and, ultimately, satisfaction with their homes. Being able to offer everything under one roof and walk the customers through each step of the entire home-buying process makes their home-buying experience very comfortable.

Ashley Pineda sells the company's Centex product line, which is primarily geared towards first-time home buyers by delivering quality homes at an affordable price. Ashley describes a typical selling process as follows: When a customer walks into the door, she engages with them by welcoming them and building rapport. The company provides its sales reps with a consultative questioning strategy that allows the reps to smoothly walk the customer through the buying process. The questions, for example, may ask the customers about their location preferences or what they consider most important when they buy a home. Ashley asks these types of questions to help her guide first-time home buyers through the variety of different homes available, ranging from one- to two-story homes, from three to five bedrooms, from 1183 to 2600 square feet, and a price range from $95,000 to $150,000. Across various options, the customers are asked how well the different options align with their needs and wants.

The customers are also given the opportunity to touch and feel their future homes. This process typically involves a car tour through the neighborhood, where they are shown the different homes' features and colors, and walk-throughs of both completed homes and homes under construction. The latter type helps to demonstrate the quality of Pulte's workmanship, the insulation, and the energy efficiency of a home. Altogether this allows potential customers to feel comfortable with the construction of the homes and the home-buying process.

In the next step, Ashley typically talks about financing issues with first-time home-buyers such as the amounts of their monthly payments and potential down payments. PulteGroup equips Ashley with the knowledge to be able to professionally provide that information and make customers feel comfortable with the financial scenario involved in owning their first home. Once the customer is comfortable with the financial scenario, Ashley and her customer can move forward toward opening the agreement to buy a home. Generally, when you sign a contract, you are opening the agreement to take the next steps. These steps include financing, completing construction, and ultimately closing on the home and moving in. That entire process typically lasts from 45 days to approximately four months. (See the chapter opener and Reality Selling Today Role-Play 6 in the end-of-chapter appendix for more information).

Questions

1. Which of the prescriptions of the Strategic/Consultative Selling Model (see Figure 1) does Ashley Pineda follow? Please explain.
2. How does Ashley elicit the needs and preferences of the prospective customers? What questions does she ask?
3. Outline a typical buying process that a middle-class couple with two young kids goes through in a first-time home buy. What questions and problems might arise at different stages of the buying process?
4. What might be key influencing factors for the couple's home-buying decisions? To what extent are rational and emotional buying motives important?
5. Put yourself in the position of Ashley Pineda. How can she create value at different stages of the young couple's buying process? Give examples.
6. Ashley sells new homes in the company's Centex product line, which is primarily geared towards first-time home buyers. One of her job responsibilities is to monitor competition. Who might be direct and indirect competitors that Ashley should watch?

Appendix: Reality Selling Today Role-Play Scenario
ScenariosReality Selling Today Role-Play 6, PulteGroup

Ashley Pineda
PulteGroup

(This mock sales call role-play scenario is created exclusively for use with this chapter.)

Your Role at PulteGroup

You will be a sales representative for PulteGroup (www. pultegroupinc.com), working in a similar community as Ashley Pineda, featured in the chapter Reality *Selling Today* Video Case. PulteGroup offers a one-stop shopping experience for prospective customers. Sales reps help clients to finance their homes (with Pulte Mortgage) and to close their homes with PGP Title. Being able to offer everything under one roof and walk the customers through each step of the entire home-buying process makes their home-buying experience very comfortable. PulteGroup offers different product lines: homes for first-time home buyers, move-up homes, and active adult communities. Just like Ashley Pineda, you will sell the company's Centex product line (see www.centex.com), which is primarily geared towards first-time home buyers. One central purpose of your sales presentations is to educate your prospects on renting versus owning and the benefits of owning a home. You also give prospects information about the neighborhood, the area, the schools zoned to the neighborhood, and the amenities of the community, describing the pools and the shopping areas in and around the neighborhood in order to help your customers envision raising their children in one of Pulte's communities. (Refer to the chapter opening vignette and case problem, and review the Reality *Selling Today* Video for more information.)

Your Customer: Mary Bartone

Mary Bartone is 37 years old. She is a single mother and has two little kids, Laura and Fred, ages 4 and 2. Mary had been married to Tom Bartone for almost seven years. The first years of their marriage were happy ones. The Bartones lived in a nice, large apartment in Chicago's Uptown neighborhood. They really enjoyed living in this trendy and vibrant part of the city. Both Mary and Tom liked going out to restaurants, cafes, and bars together with their friends, many of whom also lived in or close to the Uptown area. In their leisure time, Mary and Tom enjoyed horse riding and going to all kinds of cultural events. Money was never a big issue, since Tom made good money as a design engineer for Honeywell Building Solutions, and Mary earned a decent salary as a senior contact representative for the U.S. Social Security Administration. After some years, however, things started to become worse in their relationship, and about one year ago Tom and Mary eventually decided to split up. They went through a painful divorce. After a tedious court battle, custody of the two children was awarded to Mary, with Tom seeing his children every other weekend.

For almost a year now, Mary and her two kids have been living in a 790-square-foot, 2-bedroom apartment close to the Uptown area, just about 3 miles way from their old apartment, where Tom still lives. Mary feels that the apartment is just too small and that the area is not really perfect to raise children. Knowing that the apartment would only be an interim solution, Mary has been dreaming about a new home for quite a while now.

Quick Facts About Mary Bartone's Needs

- Mary is looking for a house with at least 1,200 square feet and 3 bedrooms.
- Like most parents with young children, Mary is very concerned about her children growing up in a safe and sheltered environment with decent daycare facilities and schools in the neighborhood.

- As a single mother who wants to raise her children in the new home, Mary is very much interested in the warranties that PulteGroup can offer as a builder.
- Mary pays great attention to the warmth and feel of a home and having a large backyard for the children to play.
- Mary has bank savings of approximately $60,000. Her annual income (including some alimony) is currently around $55,000. Therefore, a solid financing solution that is comfortable with her budget is needed.
- Mary is a true family person. Her parents and her younger sister Susan, who live in Indianapolis, come to visit her in Chicago quite frequently. Before signing a contract for a new home, she would always make sure to have her father's blessings for that.
- Mary is of two minds concerning the location of the house. On the one hand, she knows that having more square footage, a large backyard, and so forth would require her to move further out of the city. On the other hand, she does not want to move too far away from the Uptown area of Chicago where her office is located, and where Tom and many of her friends still live.

Your Call Objectives

In your meeting with Mary, you hope to build rapport with her and identify her needs and requirements for owning a home. You also hope to convince Mary that you can offer her an excellent home in which to raise her children.

Endnotes

1. "Nighttime Reading for Daytime Success," *Sales & Marketing Management*, May 2007, p. 44.
2. Michael Hammer and James Champy, *Reengineering the Corporation: A Manifest for Business Revolution* (New York: HarperBusiness, 1993), p. 18.
3. Keith M. Eades, *The New Solution Selling* (New York: McGraw-Hill, 2004), pp. 32–33.
4. Tom Peters and Nancy Austin, *A Passion for Excellence* (New York: Random House, 1985), p. 71.
5. "How Well Do You Know Your Customers?" *Sales & Field Force Automation*, January 1999, p. 141.
6. Gary Armstrong and Philip Kotler, *Marketing: An Introduction*, 6th ed. (Upper Saddle River, NJ: Prentice Hall, 2003), pp. 191–192, 215.
7. Michael R. Solomon and Elnora W. Stuart, *Marketing: Real People, Real Choices*, 5th ed. (Upper Saddle River, NJ: Prentice Hall, 2008), p. 184.
8. Gary Armstrong and Philip Kotler, *Marketing: An Introduction*, 6th ed. (Upper Saddle River, NJ: Prentice Hall, 2003), pp. 191–192, 215.
9. Michael R. Solomon and Elnora W. Stuart, *Marketing: Real People, Real Choices*, 5th ed. (Upper Saddle River, NJ: Prentice Hall, 2008), p. 182.
10. Ibid., pp. 182–183.
11. Philip Kotler and Gary Armstrong, *Principles of Marketing*, 12th ed. (Upper Saddle River, NJ: Prentice Hall, 2008), pp. 163–166.
12. FedEx, www.fedex.com (accessed July 6, 2010).
13. Philip Kotler and Gary Armstrong, *Principles of Marketing*, 12th ed. (Upper Saddle River, NJ: Prentice Hall, 2008), pp. 146–147.
14. Ibid., p. 147.
15. S. Sajeesh and Jagmohan S. Raju (2010), "Positioning and Pricing in a Variety Seeking Market," *Management Science*, 56(6), pp. 949–961.
16. Ibid., pp. 145–146.
17. Keith M. Eades, *The New Solution Selling* (New York: McGraw-Hill, 2004), pp. 32–33; Betsy Cummings, "Proving the Sale Process," *Sales & Marketing Management*, June 2006, p. 12.
18. Keith M. Eades, *The New Solution Selling*, p. 31.
19. Stephen E. Heiman and Diane Sanchez, *The New Conceptual Selling* (New York: Warner Books, 1999), pp. 190–191.
20. Research reported in Tom Atkinson and Ron Koprowski, "Sales Reps' Biggest Mistakes," *Harvard Business Review*, July–August 2006, p. 1. This research indicates that 26 percent of the business-to-business buyers say salespeople "don't follow my company's buying process."
21. Gary Armstrong and Philip Kotler, *Marketing: An Introduction*, 7th ed. (Upper Saddle River, NJ: Prentice Hall, 2005), p. 160.
22. Neil Rackham and John R. DeVincentis, *Rethinking the Sales Force* (New York: McGraw-Hill, 1999), p. 66.
23. Bill Stinnett, "Reverse-Engineer the Buying Process," *Selling*, December 2004, p. 16.
24. Neil Rackham and John R. DeVincentis, *Rethinking the Sales Force* (New York: McGraw-Hill, 1999), p. 68.
25. Monika Kukar-Kinney and Angeline G. Close (2010), "The Determinants of Consumers' Online Shopping Cart Abandonment," *Journal of the Academy of Marketing Science* 38, pp. 240–250.
26. Hean Tat Keh and Jun Pang (2010), "Customer Reactions to Service Separation," *Journal of Marketing*, 74(2), pp. 55–70.
27. Ibid., p. 69.

28. Neil Rackham and John DeVincentis provide extensive coverage of these three selling modes in *Rethinking the Sales Force*. Also see "Let the Customer Define Value—and Sales Will Rise," by Neil Rackham and John DeVincentis, *Value-Added Selling* 21, January 13, 2004, pp. 1–2.

29. Neil Rackham and John DeVincentis, *Value-Added Selling* 21, January 13, 2004, pp. 1–2.

30. Ken Brown, "Little-Known Avaya Tackles Cisco in Internet Calling Gear," *Wall Street Journal*, October 26, 2004, p. B1.

31. Neil Rackham and John R. DeVincentis, *Rethinking the Sales Force* (New York: McGraw-Hill, 1999), p. 74.

32. Philip Kotler and Gary Armstrong, *Principles of Marketing*, 10th ed. (Upper Saddle River, NJ: Prentice Hall, 2004), p. 28.

33. Stan Davis and Christopher Meyer, *Blur: The Speed of Change in the Connected Economy* (New York: Addison-Wesley, 1998), p. 16.

34. Leilei Gao, S. Christian Wheeler, and Baba Shiv (2009), "The 'Shaken Self': Product Choices as a Means of Restoring Self-View Confidence," *Journal of Consumer Research*, 36(1), pp. 29–38.

35. William M. Pride and O. C. Ferrell, *Marketing*, 10th ed. (Boston: Houghton Mifflin Company, 1997), pp. 143–148.

36. Douglas A. Bernstein, Alison Clark-Stewart, Louis A. Penner, and Edward J. Roy, *Psychology*, 6th ed. (Boston: Houghton Mifflin Company, 2003), p. 648.

37. C. Page Moreau and Kelly B. Herd (2010), "To Each His Own? How Comparisons with Others Influence Consumers' Evaluations of Their Self-Designed Products," *Journal of Consumer Research*, 36(5), pp. 806–819.

38. Gary Armstrong and Philip Kotler, *Marketing: An Introduction*, 7th ed. (Upper Saddle River, NJ: Prentice Hall, 2005), pp. 147–148.

39. Douglas A. Bernstein, Alison Clark-Stewart, Louis A. Penner, and Edward J. Roy, *Psychology*, 6th ed. (Boston: Houghton Mifflin Company, 2003), p. 21.

40. Gary Armstrong and Philip Kotler, *Marketing: An Introduction*, 7th ed. (Upper Saddle River, NJ: Prentice Hall, 2005), p. 145.

41. Louis E. Boone and David L. Kurtz, *Contemporary Marketing*, 11th ed. (Mason, Ohio: South-Western Publishing, 2004), p. 267.

42. Roger Hart, "Luxury, VW's Way," *Autoweek*, December 27, 2004, pp. 18–19; Tom Reilly, "All Sales Decisions Are Emotional for the Buyer," *Selling*, July 2003, p. 13.

43. Roy Chitwood, "Hidden Buyer Motives: Handle Them with Care," *Value-Added Selling* 21, April 2, 2007, p. 4.

44. Phil Kline, "Dominant Buying Motive Is the Result of Strong Emotions," *Marketing News*, May 24, 1993, p. 4.

45. Stan Davis and Christopher Meyer, *Blur: The Speed of Change in the Connected Economy* (New York: Addison-Wesley, 1998), p. 52.

46. Hakkyun Kim, Kiwan Park, and Norbert Schwarz (2010), "Will This Trip Really Be Exciting? The Role of Incidental Emotions in Product Evaluation," *Journal of Consumer Research*, 36(6), pp. 983–991.

47. Robert McGarvey, "The Buyer's Emotional Side," *Selling Power*, April 2006, p. 35.

48. Ibid., p. 36.

49. Gary Armstrong and Philip Kotler, *Marketing: An Introduction*, 6th ed. (Upper Saddle River, NJ: Prentice Hall, 2003), p. 216; Sid Chadwick, "New Twists in Price vs. Perceived Value," *Sales and Marketing Advisory Magazine*, July/August 2001, p. 6.

Endnotes for Boxed Features

a. Based on Dave Stein, "Selling Across Generation Gaps," *Sales & Marketing Management*, October 2007, p. 9.

b. Based on Sam Walker, "Can Nascar Take Manhattan?" *Wall Street Journal*, March 8, 2002, p. W6.

c. "International Snapshot," *Sales & Marketing Management*, May 2001, p. 74; Jan Yager, *Business Protocol*, 2nd ed. (Stamford, CT: Hannacroix Creek Books, 2001), p. 116.

Chapter 4

Developing and Qualifying a Prospect Base

From Chapter 9 of *Selling Today: Partnering to Create Value*, 12/e. Gerald L. Manning. Michael Ahearne.
Barry L. Reece. Copyright © 2012 by Pearson Education. Published by Prentice Hall. All rights reserved.

Developing and Qualifying a Prospect Base

Chapter Preview

When you finish reading this chapter, you should be able to

1 Discuss the importance of developing a prospect base

2 Identify and assess important sources of prospects

3 Describe criteria for qualifying prospects

4 Explain common methods of collecting and organizing prospect information

5 Describe the steps in managing the prospect base

Reality Selling Today Video Series

Salesforce.com offers hosted applications that manage customer information for sales, marketing, and customer support, providing clients with a rapidly deployable alternative to buying and maintaining enterprise software. The company's applications are used by approximately 80,000 clients for generating sales leads, maintaining customer information, and tracking customer interactions. Dave Levitt (pictured above) joined Salesforce.com as a regional sales manager in 2008, leading a team of six sales representatives.

With prior experience as a direct salesperson in the enterprise software industry, Levitt has profound knowledge about how to approach and qualify prospects in his business. For his sales representatives, there are various ways to get in touch with potential customers: Some prospects will inquire at the company's Web site, and that will be forwarded directly to the sales representative so that he/she can follow up. Direct-response advertising, trade shows, or customer referrals can also be important sources of prospects. Besides having the customers reach out to them, salespeople at Salesforce.com also try to utilize the knowledge on the company's 80,000 customers. For example, if the sales representative has a chemical company as one of his prospects, he/she will take a look at the CRM system and ask: What other chemical companies are current customers, and how did they benefit from using our services? Then the representative could use reference selling and thus demonstrate credibility with the prospect.

According to Dave Levitt, the key to successful selling is empathy, i.e., the ability to understand the customer's business so that the sales representative can identify areas where he can add value. Levitt points out: "We cannot count on the customer to know what we offer, because our services can be applied in many different ways. The burden is on the sales representative to use his industry and product knowledge to probe and uncover opportunities, and then to qualify and pursue them accordingly." Hence, the salesperson has to be able to look at accounts holistically, understand what the real business drivers are at a company, and then apply Salesforce.com's service solutions in different areas. ●

Account-based software vendors such as Salesforce.com, NetSuite, and Oracle Siebel are helping companies develop effective customer relationship management (CRM) systems. These systems are at the heart of every successful one-to-one marketing initiative.

Prospecting—An Introduction

Gerhard Gschwandtner, publisher of *Selling Power*, says, "The main purpose of a salesperson is not to make sales, but to create customers."[1] Identifying potential customers is an important aspect of the customer strategy. In the terminology of personal selling, this process is called **prospecting**. A potential customer, or **prospect**, is someone who meets the qualification criteria established by you or your company.

Finding prospects who can make the purchase is not as easy as it sounds. This is especially true in business-to-business sales. In many situations the salesperson must make the sales presentation to multiple decision makers. One of these decision makers might be the technical expert who wants an answer to the question: "Does the product meet the company's specifications?" Another decision maker may be the person who will actually use the product. The employee who will use the forklift truck you are selling may be involved in the purchase decision. Of course, there is often a "purse-string" decision maker who has the ultimate authority to release funds for the purchase. During periods of economic uncertainty, the decision-making process often moves upward. It is sometimes difficult to make connections with upper-level executives. One solution is to plan a joint sales call involving a higher-level executive from your company.[2]

The goal of prospecting is to build a qualified **prospect base** made up of current customers and potential customers. Building a prospect base involves the use of CRM software to monitor movement of the customer through the sales process. Many successful companies find that current customers account for a large percentage of their sales. Every effort is made to devise and implement a customer strategy that builds, fosters, nurtures, and extends relationships with established customers. CRM software is critical to building this kind of partnership with a large customer base.[3]

Importance of Prospecting

Every salesperson must cope with customer attrition, that is, the inevitable loss of customers over a period of time, which can be attributed to a variety of causes. Unless new prospects are found to replace lost customers, a salesperson eventually faces a reduction in income and possible loss of employment.

To better understand the significance of prospecting, let us examine a few common causes of customer attrition.

The customer may have a one-time need or there is an extended period of time between purchases. Because of this CB Richard Ellis's Susana Rosas realizes new prospects for commercial real estate must be continually added to her prospect base.

The customer may move to a new location outside the salesperson's territory. The American population is very mobile. This cause of attrition is especially common in the retail and service areas and is a major issue experienced by Tom James Company's Alex Homer with many of his successful upwardly mobile clients.

A firm may go out of business or merge with another company. In some areas of business the failure rate is quite high. In recent years, we have witnessed a record number of mergers that have caused massive changes in purchasing plans.

A loyal buyer or purchasing agent may leave the position because of promotion, retirement, resignation, or serious illness. The replacement may prefer to buy from someone else.

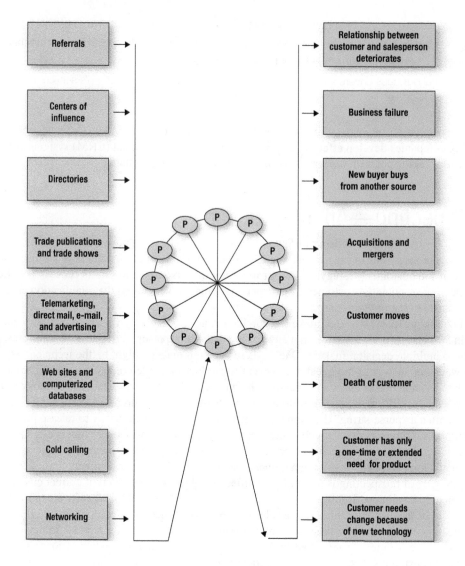

FIGURE 1

The "Ferris wheel" concept, which is aimed at supplying an ongoing list of prospects, is part of world sales record holder Joe Girard's customer strategy.

Sales are lost to the competition. In some cases, the competition offers more value. The added value may take the form of better quality, a better price, a stronger relationship, better service, or some combination of these factors.

Some studies reveal that the average company loses 15 to 20 percent of its customers every year. Depending on the type of selling, this figure might be higher or lower. It becomes clear that many customers are lost for reasons beyond the salesperson's control. If salespeople want to keep their earnings at a stable level, they need to develop new customers.

Joe Girard, once recognized by the *Guinness Book of Records* as the world's greatest salesperson, used the "Ferris wheel" concept to illustrate the relationship between prospecting and loss of customers due to the attrition.[4] As people get off the Ferris wheel, the operator fills their seats one at a time, moves the wheel a little, and continues this process until all the original riders have left the wheel and new ones come aboard (Figure 1). In reality, of course, established customers do not come and go this fast. With the passing of time, however, many customers must be replaced.

Prospecting Requires Planning

Prospecting should be viewed as a systematic process of locating potential customers. Some prospecting efforts can be integrated easily into a regular sales call. Progressive marketers are doing three things to improve the quality of the prospecting effort:

CUSTOMER RELATIONSHIP MANAGEMENT WITH TECHNOLOGY

Using the Same CRM Software as Cisco Systems

Cisco has committed to deploying the Salesforce.com CRM solution to 25,000 global users. Salesforce.com provides Cisco with effective prospect management tools, such as dashboards, account planning tools, and reports regarding partner relationships.

- Dashboards track metrics such as opportunities, lead conversion rates, number of account plans, and top accounts for sales representatives and managers. Salespeople can create their own reports to chart their progress.
- Account planning, which had previously been difficult to manage on a worldwide basis, is increasingly leveraged with Salesforce.com.
- Partners are part of Cisco's customer "eco-system." Overall productivity and effectiveness are improved by extending leads

to partners, such as resellers, and tracking their conversion to opportunities and ultimately to sales.

You have the opportunity to use a demonstration version of the same solution, Salesforce.com, used by Cisco. Just like a Cisco salesperson, you are assigned a number of prospect accounts and given individual and company information about each account's contact person in Salesforce.com. Your participation in the CRM case study and exercises will give you hands-on experience with the use of a customer database, using modern sales technology. You not only will be using the same software being used by thousands of salespeople but also will be working with data derived from authentic selling challenges. (See the CRM Case Study "Reviewing the Prospect Database" for more information).

---

1. *Increase the number of people who board the Ferris wheel.* You want to see a continuous number of potential prospects board the Ferris wheel because they are the source of sales opportunities. If the number of potential prospects declines sharply, the number of sales closed also declines.
2. *Improve the quality of the prospects who board the Ferris wheel.* Companies often establish quality standards that ensure a steady supply of prospects with high profit potential. For example, some companies focus their prospecting efforts on consultative process buyers. These are prospects who often lack need awareness and need help evaluating possible solutions.
3. *Shorten the sales cycle by quickly determining which of the new prospects are qualified prospects—qualified as to need, authority to buy, ability to pay, and authority to purchase the product.* Gerhard Gschwandtner says, "Time is the ultimate scorekeeper in the game of selling." He points out that many salespeople do not meet their sales goals because they do not quickly qualify new prospects.[5] Later in this chapter we examine qualifying practices and discuss how to shorten the sales cycle with sales automation methods.

Prospecting Plans Must Be Assessed Often

In today's dynamic, ever-changing marketplace, prospecting plans must be monitored continuously. Some prospecting techniques that worked well in the past may become ineffective because of changing market conditions. Midwest Training Institute, a firm that helps companies to improve their production and sales efficiency, experienced a dramatic sales decline during the first quarter of the year. This decline came after years of steady sales increases. Joel Pecoraro, president of the company, initiated a thorough investigation and discovered that his sales staff were relying primarily on one prospecting approach that was no longer successful: The salespeople were calling established customers. Pecoraro designed an incentive program that rewarded salespeople who adopted new prospecting techniques such as attending an association meeting where the salesperson could meet potential prospects or speaking at a meeting attended by persons who might need the services offered by Midwest Training Institute.[6]

Sources of Prospects

Every salesperson must develop a prospecting system suited to a particular selling situation. Some of the many sources of prospects follow, and each should be carefully examined:

Referrals

Centers of influence, friends, and family members

Directories

Your request for referrals are more likely to receive a positive response if made after you have built a strong trusting relationship. In most cases referral leads result in higher close rates, larger sales, and shorter sales cycles.

Source: Shutterstock

Trade publications

Trade shows and special events

Telemarketing and e-mail

Direct-response advertising and sales letters

Web site

Computerized database

Cold calling

Networking

Educational seminars

Prospecting by nonsales employees

Referrals

The use of referrals as a prospecting approach has been used successfully in a wide range of selling situations. In most cases, referral leads result in higher close rates, larger sales, and shorter sales cycles. A **referral** is a prospect who has been recommended by a current customer or by someone who is familiar with the product. Satisfied customers, business acquaintances, and even prospects who do not buy often can recommend the names of persons who might benefit from purchasing the product.

Liberty Mutual's Marcus Smith realizes customers are more likely to give a referral if they perceive value in the solution he offers. When you build value into your sales process, you increase the odds that the customer will give you a referral. Steve Lewis, managing partner of New England Financial, says, "Our attitude is that we can't ask for referrals until clients have perceived value in the process."[7]

ENDLESS CHAIN REFERRALS The endless chain approach to obtaining referrals is easy to use because it fits naturally into most sales presentations. A salesperson selling long-term health care insurance might say, "Miss Remano, whom do you know who might be interested in our insurance plan?" This open-ended question gives the person the freedom to recommend several prospects and is less likely to be answered with a no response. Be sure to use your reference's name when you contact the new prospect—"Mary Remano suggested that I call you. . . . "

REFERRAL LETTERS AND CARDS The referral letter method is a variation of the endless chain technique. In addition to requesting the names of prospects, the salesperson asks the customer to prepare a note or letter of introduction that can be delivered to the potential customer. The correspondence is an actual testimonial prepared by a satisfied customer. Some companies use a referral card to introduce the salesperson. The preprinted card features a place for your customer to sign the new prospect's name and his own name, and can be used as part of the sales presentation.

Within the field of personal selling, there is no complete agreement regarding the timing of the referral request. Some sales training programs encourage salespeople to request the referral immediately after closing the sale. Others point out that if you are working with a new customer, it takes time to earn the customer's trust. The customer may feel there is a risk involved in giving you referrals. Once you have built a strong, trusting relationship with the customer, referral requests are more likely to receive a positive response.[8]

REFERRAL ORGANIZATIONS Some salespeople have found that membership in a referral organization is an effective way to obtain good leads. BNI (Business Network International) is one of the largest business networking organizations with more than 3,600 chapters worldwide (www.bni.com). BNI offers members the opportunity to share ideas, contacts, and referrals.[9] In addition, some local organizations such as breakfast clubs offer referrals as a member benefit.

Centers of Influence, Friends, and Family Members

The center-of-influence method involves establishing a relationship with a well-connected, influential person who is willing to provide prospecting information. This person may not make buying decisions but has influence with other people who do. To illustrate, consider the challenge facing Gary Schneider, creator of a powerful software product that would help small farmers optimize their crop selection. After spending several years developing the product, Schneider and his wife began selling the product one copy at a time. During one cold call on a major crop insurer, American Agrisurance, he met a senior researcher who immediately saw the benefits of the software product. This respected researcher is in a position to influence buying decisions at his company and to provide prospect information for other crop insurers.[10]

A person who is new in the field of selling often uses friends and family members as sources of information about potential customers. It is only natural to contact people we know. In many cases these people have contacts with a wide range of potential buyers.

Directories

Directories can help salespeople search out new prospects and determine their buying potential. A list of some of the more popular national directories is provided next:

Middle Market Directory lists 14,000 firms worth between $500,000 and $1 million (available from Dun & Bradstreet, www.dnb.com).

Standard & Poor's Corporation Records Service provides details on more than 11,000 companies (www.spglobal.com).

Thomas Register of American Manufacturers provides a listing of 60,000 manufacturers by product classifications, addresses, and capital ratings (www.thomasregister.com).

Polk City Directory provides detailed information on the citizens of a specific community. Polk, in business for more than 125 years, publishes about 1,100 directories covering 6,500 communities in the United States and Canada (www.citydirectory.com).

The Encyclopedia of Associations lists more than 23,000 U.S. associations and more than 20,000 international organizations with details on membership, publications, and conferences (www.gale.com).

These are just a few of the better-known directories. There are hundreds of additional directories covering business and industrial firms on the regional, state, and local levels. Some directories are free, whereas others must be purchased at a nominal fee. One of the most useful free sources of information is the telephone directory. Most telephone directories have a classified (yellow pages) section that groups businesses and professions by category. Web Yellow Pages (www.bigyellow.com) provides more than 11 million U.S. business listings.

Trade Publications

Trade publications provide a status report on every major industry. If you are a sales representative employed by SuperValu Stores, Fleming Companies Inc., Sysco Corporation, or one of the other huge food wholesaling houses that supplies supermarkets, then you can benefit from a monthly review of *Progressive Grocer* magazine. Each month this trade publication reports on trends in the retail food industry, new products, problems, innovations, and related information. Trade journals such as *Institutional Distribution, Home Furnishings, Hardware Retailer, Modern Tire Dealer,* and *Progressive Architecture* are examples of publications that might help salespeople identify prospects.

SELLING IN ACTION

Prospecting with Your Partners

When Megan Michael sees a new office building going up, she stops her car and makes inquiries about who is to occupy the building. As a sales representative for BKM Total Office, an office furniture supplier in San Diego, she needs to be aware of new office space. However, this approach is not her most important prospecting method. She has found the telephone to be her most effective prospecting tool.

Michael speaks regularly with her customers to find out if they know companies that might need BKM's products. Architects, designers, and builders who have previously worked with Michael have proved to be good sources of referrals. The key to her prospecting success is maintaining a strong relationship with her customers. She realizes that you must be an effective partner before you can ask for help.[a]

Trade Shows and Special Events

A trade show is a large exhibit of products that are, in most cases, common to one industry, such as electronics or office equipment. The prospects walk into the booth or exhibit and talk with those who represent the exhibitor. In some cases, sales personnel invite existing customers and prospects to attend trade shows so they can have an opportunity to demonstrate their newest products.

Research studies indicate that it is much easier to identify good prospects and actually close sales at a trade show. In most cases, fewer sales calls are needed to close a sale if the prospect was qualified at a trade show. Once a trade show contact is identified and judged to be a qualified lead, information regarding the lead should be carefully recorded. When a prospect enters a Xerox Corporation booth, a salesperson uses a few questions to qualify the lead and types the answers into an on-screen form. Xerox uses software developed by NewLeads on record and process data obtained from prospects who have been qualified by a salesperson working in the booth.[11]

A special event can be a baseball game, golf tournament, reception for a dignitary, or charity event. Bentley Motor Cars invited a number of potential clients to the famous Le Mans 24-hour endurance race. Prospects watched the Bentley racecar compete while sipping champagne. Back in America, charity events serve as a venue for cultivating wealthy clientele who can afford a Bentley automobile.[12]

Telemarketing and E-Mail

Telemarketing is the practice of marketing goods and services through telephone contact. It is an integral part of many modern sales and marketing campaigns. One use of telemarketing is to identify prospects. A financial services company used telemarketing to identify prospects for its customized equipment leasing packages. Leads were given to salespeople for consideration. Telemarketing also can be used to quickly and inexpensively qualify prospects for follow-up. Some marketers use the telephone to verify sales leads generated by direct mail, advertisements, or some other method.

Although the response rate for sales e-mails is quite low, they have proven to be a source of leads for many salespeople. Ideally sales e-mails should be sent only to existing customers or others who have "opted in" to receive them. When you use *broadcast* e-mails, there is the risk that you will be blocked and end up on a spammer blacklist. Online sales specialist Mac MacIntosh says those who use broadcast e-mails should stay within anti-spam laws by giving recipients the right to opt out of future e-mails.[13]

Bentley Motor Cars invited a number of potential clients to the famous LeMans 24-hour endurance race. This special event helped the company develop its prospect base.

Source: Hunter65/Dreamstime LLC-Royalty Free

Putting your company name in the subject line can help get e-mails opened by prospects who are familiar with it. Some salespeople send newsletters to current and prospective customers. Lee Levitt, director of sales for software consultant IDC, sends a monthly newsletter to current IDC clients and professionals at large technology companies. He wants to expose them to services his company can provide. Levitt says, "The key is to offer something of value they can quickly digest and use in day-to-day work."[14]

Direct-Response Advertising and Sales Letters

Many advertisements invite the reader to send for a free booklet or brochure that provides detailed information about the product or service. In the category of business-to-business marketing, advertising has strong inquiry-generating power. Some firms distribute postage-free response cards (also known as *bingo cards*) to potential buyers. Recipients are encouraged to complete and mail the cards if they desire additional information. In some cases the name of the person making the inquiry is given to a local sales representative for further action.

Sales letters, sent via e-mail or the U.S. postal service, can be incorporated easily into a prospecting plan. The prospecting sales letter is sent to persons who are in a position to make a buying decision. Shortly after mailing the letter (three or four days), the prospect is called and asked for an appointment. The call begins with a reference to the sales letter. To make the letter stand out, some salespeople include product information. All sales letters must be written with care. To get results, sales letters must quickly get the reader's attention.

Web Site

Thousands of companies and businesspeople have established Web sites on the World Wide Web. A **Web site** is a collection of Web pages maintained by a single person or organization. It is accessible to anyone with a computer and a modem. Large firms, such as Century 21, maintain Web sites that feature 20 to 30 Web pages. Web sites frequently offer prospects the opportunity

---

SOCIAL MEDIA AND SELLING TODAY

Locating Prospects with Social Media

Whether seeking business or consumer prospects, a number of social media channels are available to salespeople. The choice of a channel, such as a Web site, blog, Twitter, or Facebook, depends upon the time the salesperson can commit to the social media prospecting effort.

WEB SITES AND BLOGS. With Web sites and blogs, it is important to create a clear identity. Similar to a positioning statement, the appearance and writing style of your Web presence must be designed to be appealing and interesting to your prospective customer visitors. It is well established that visitors expect to find information or entertainment on your site, not the hard sell. It is important to keep your content fresh and reply rapidly to all comments received, which can make this channel time-consuming.

SOCIAL MEDIA SITES. Participating in social media sites such as LinkedIn, Facebook, and Twitter can take less time because you can join in a conversation when you wish. LinkedIn is especially attractive to sales professionals. It offers information and tools that can help you conduct research, find new customers, and expand your business contacts and prospects. Much of it is free; however, for some of the advanced features you may have to pay a subscription fee. Search or use an online service to find communities of users with characteristics similar to your best prospect profile. When you join in conversations, you will be influencing people most likely to become customers. When time permits, salespeople also participate in groups that discuss their kinds of products.

START YOUR OWN GROUP. If you cannot find a social media community that meets your criteria, start your own. For example, jmagroup.com describes the sales representative who started tweetandgreet.com. The representative e-mailed well-known online marketing professionals and Twitter followers, asking them questions about their cars and their memories of them. The excellent responses and stories received provided the representative's site with interesting and attractive content that appealed to potential car buyers and increased the likelihood the Web site will be cited by others.

RULES OF PARTICIPATION. The rules of participation are to create value with short tips and techniques you've learned as a product/industry expert. Use word-of-mouth promotion by asking readers to share your message with others. When performed effectively, those looking for information about your topic are more likely to follow you and turn to you when it's time to buy.

Research shows that it is much easier to identify good prospects and actually close sales at a trade show.

Source: George Doyle/Thinkstock

to acquire product information that can help them make a buying decision. Financial services companies describe home financing and refinancing options. Salesforce.com's Web site provides detailed descriptions of Salesforce.com products and solutions. When someone clicks on a Web page and requests information, they will likely become a prospect. Some Web sites offer an incentive to leave contact information.

Computerized Database

With the aid of electronic data processing, it is often possible to match product features with the needs of potential customers quickly and accurately. In many situations, a firm can develop its own computerized database. In other cases it is more economical to purchase the database from a company that specializes in the collection of such information. One example, Salesgenie, is offered by infoUSA. With the aid of this software, you can easily obtain lead generation and prospect selection information for different market segments. Gary Hand, president of Alliance Security Systems, needs to keep his sales team supplied with plenty of leads. Salesgenie provides him with a list of prospects by geographical location and by the value of each house. Salesgenie handles these two classifications easily and has therefore become a major time saver.[15] Salesgenie can provide salespeople with leads in such diverse market segments as medical services, engineering, architecture, agriculture, and education.

Another product available from infoUSA, OneSource, provides in-depth prospect information needed by sales personnel involved in complex, long-cycle sales. Let's assume you are part

Winemaker Applies Her Sales Skills

Gina Gallo is a third-generation family winemaker who knows a thing or two about personal selling. She not only knows how to make the wines offered by E.&J. Gallo Winery, but she also knows how to sell them. The year she spent as a member of the sales force helped her learn about consumers' buying habits and the needs of retailers who sell Gallo wines. Gina Gallo sees some similarities between winemaking and sales. The better you understand your vineyards, the soil, and the grapes, the greater the chance you have of creating an excellent wine. The better you understand your customer's needs, the better you can relate to and fulfill those needs.[b]

Source: E.J Gallo Winery/E&J Gallo

With Salesgenie salespeople find it is easy to obtain lead generation and prospect selection information for different market segments. Through analyzing the current customer base, Salesgenie will create a list of similarly qualified prospects to call on.

Source: Used with permission of Salesgenie.com.

of a sales team that wants to do business with a group of companies that appear to be highly qualified. OneSource will provide data needed to make sales projections for a specific geographic area and industry type. The real strength of OneSource comes in high-value sales where a thorough understanding of prospects is needed for the first sales call.[16]

With the aid of a personal computer (PC), salespeople can develop their own detailed customer files. Newer PCs provide expanded storage capacity at a lower price. This means that salespeople can accumulate a great deal of information about individual customers and use this information to personalize the selling process. For example, a PC can help an independent insurance agent maintain a comprehensive record of each policyholder. As the status of each client changes (marriage, birth of children, etc.), the record can be easily updated. With the aid of an up-to-date database, the agent can quickly identify prospects for the various existing and new policy options.

Cold Calling

With products, such as Alex Homer's custom clothing line offered by Tom James Company's, cold call prospecting is an effective approach to prospect identification. In **cold calling**, salespeople select a group of people they anticipate may become actual prospects and then call (by phone or personal visit) on each one. The sales representative for a wholesale medical supply firm might call on every hospital in a given community, assuming that each one is a potential customer. Many new salespeople must rely on the cold call method because they are less likely to get appointments through referrals.

With computers, salespeople can accumulate a great deal of information about individual customers and use this information to add value during the selling process.

Source: Yuri_arcurs/Dreamstime.com

Edward Jones Corporation, a financial services company, is a strong supporter of cold calling. Sales representatives knock on doors and introduce themselves with a friendly, professional message:

"Hi, my name is Brad Ledwith. I represent the Edward Jones Corporation, and we sell financial services. We're a unique firm because we try to do all of our business face-to-face. I just wanted to stop by and let you know that I've opened up a Jones office in the area and to find out if it's OK to contact you when I have an investment idea."[17]

Sales representatives such as Brad Ledwith connect personally with members of their communities.

Successful cold calls do not happen spontaneously. Some strategic thinking and planning must precede personal visits and telephone calls. Whom do you contact? What do you say during the first few seconds?

In order to appear confident and competent, carefully develop your opening remarks. If you appear to be nervous or unprepared, the prospect will assume you lack experience. Many salespeople who make cold call phone calls prepare a well-polished script. The script helps keep you on message and guarantees you will not leave out important information.[18]

Samantha Ettus, CEO of Ettus Media Management, a New York City public relations agency, says cold calls helped her firm land some of its biggest clients. Ettus does plenty of research before she reaches for the phone. She collects all the pertinent information she can find—memberships and professional affiliations, career history, awards received, and of course information regarding the prospect's business. Then she makes the call, which is as brief and precise as possible. Immediately after the call, she sends the prospect a personalized e-mail that summarizes what her firm has to offer. Ettus views the cold call as nothing more than a way to introduce herself and her company to a prospect.[19]

Networking

One of the most complete books on networking is *Dig Your Well Before You're Thirsty* by Harvey Mackay. He says, "If I had to name the single characteristic shared by all the truly successful people I've met over a lifetime, I'd say it's the ability to create and nurture a network of contacts."[20] Networking skills are of special importance to new salespeople who cannot turn to a large group of satisfied customers for referrals and leads. Professionals (accountants, lawyers, consultants, etc.), entrepreneurs, managerial personnel, and customer service representatives also must develop networking skills. Networking skills are also of critical importance to job seekers because at any given time about 80 percent of all available jobs are not posted in the classifieds or on Internet job boards.[21]

In simple terms, **networking** is the art of making and using contacts, or people meeting people and profiting from the connections. Although networking is one of the premier prospecting methods, some salespeople are reluctant to seek referrals in this manner. In addition, many salespeople do not use effective networking practices. Skilled networkers suggest the following guidelines for identifying good referrals:

1. *Meet as many people as you can.* Networking can take place on an airplane, at a Rotary Club meeting, at a trade show, or at a professional association meeting. Don't make the mistake of limiting your networking activities to business contacts. The term **social network**

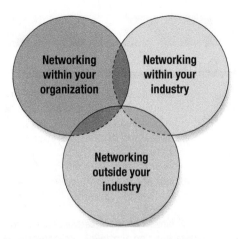

refers to your set of *direct and indirect contacts.* An indirect contact might be the brother
of a close friend. The brother works for a large company and can help you see more clearly
into the operation of this firm.[22]

2. *When you meet someone, tell the person what you do.* Give your name and describe your
position in a way that explains what you do and invites conversations. Instead of saying,
"I am in stocks and bonds," say, "I am a financial counselor who helps people make
investment decisions." Listen more than you talk.

3. *Do not do business while networking.* It usually is not practical to conduct business while
networking. Make a date to call or meet with the new contact later.

4. *Offer your business card.* The business card is especially useful when the contact attempts
to tell others about your products or services.

5. *Edit your contacts and follow-up.* You cannot be involved with all your contacts, so
separate the productive from the nonproductive. Send a short e-mail message to contacts
you deem productive and include business information, brochures—anything that
increases visibility.[23] Make sure your materials are professional. Use inexpensive contact
management software, such as Salesforce.com, to organize your contact information.

There are three types of networks salespeople should grow and nurture (Figure 2). Every
salesperson can be well served by networking within their own organization. You never know when
someone in finance, technical support, or shipping may be needed to help solve a problem or provide
you with important information. A second form of networking involves establishing contacts inside
your industry. Make contact with experts in your field, top performers, leaders, successful company
representatives, and even competitors. The third form of networking involves business contacts with
people outside of your industry such as bankers, government officials, developers, and other people
in your community. The local golf course is frequently a good place to make these contacts.[24]

Educational Seminars

Many salespeople are using educational seminars as a method of identifying prospects. Seminars
provide an opportunity to showcase your product without pressuring prospects to buy. Many
banks, accounting firms, wine merchants, and consulting companies use seminars to generate
new prospects. Previously we mentioned that Edward Jones's sales representatives often make
cold calls on prospects. They also schedule seminars that provide prospects with an opportunity
to acquire information regarding the potential benefits of investing in a mutual fund. Another
popular seminar topic is the benefits of tax-free investing. A complimentary lunch is usually
served before the informative presentation. When inviting prospects, be clear about the seminar's
content and always deliver what you promise.

Prospecting by Nonsales Employees

Should service technicians, receptionists, bank tellers, and other nonsales personnel be involved
in prospecting? In a growing number of organizations, the answer is yes. Prospecting does not
need to be the exclusive responsibility of the sales force. Janet Dixon, a UPS sales representative,
needed help making contact with an important prospect. This person wouldn't take her calls. She
talked to the UPS service provider (driver) who called on this account and requested his help. He

SELLING IN ACTION

Develop Your Prospect Base with Seminars

The use of educational seminars has become an important prospecting method. You can educate prospective customers with brochures, news releases, catalogs, or your Web site, but educational seminars offer the advantage of face-to-face contact. Barbara Siskind, in her book *Seminars to Build Your Business*, identifies 15 objectives for hosting seminars. A few of the most important ones follow:

Obtain sales leads. This is one of the most common objectives for seminars. You can obtain the names of attendees and arrange appointments for future sales calls. Seminars also may help identify actual product users, technical support people, or engineers who, although they may not be the decision maker, may influence the purchase decision.

Promote your place of business. Your place of business can become a destination for people who might otherwise not consider visiting it. You have an opportunity to create awareness of your company and develop a positive image for your entire operation and its capabilities.

Showcase and demonstrate your expertise. Seminars allow you to show a carefully targeted group of people that you really know your stuff. Salespeople can be supported by technical experts and others in the organization who can address clients' specific concerns.

Polaroid Canada advertised educational seminars across Canada where imaging specialists assisted prospective clients in exploring imaging solutions. Toronto-based Charon Systems, Incorporated, a systems integrator that deploys networks for organizations, regularly organizes seminars for 80 to 100 technology people from midsized firms. President David Fung estimates that 25 percent of prospects become clients.[c]

had serviced this company for years and was like part of the family. He knew the prospect personally and persuaded her to accept a call from the salesperson.[25]

Combination Approaches

In recent years, we have seen an increase in the number of prospecting approaches used by salespeople. In many cases, success in selling depends on your ability to use a combination of the methods described in this chapter. For example, the large number of prospects identified at a trade show might be used to develop an effective telemarketing program. Prospects are called and an effort is made to set up a personal call. Prospects identified at a trade show or educational seminar might be sent a sales-oriented newsletter, a sales letter, or an e-mail message inviting prospects to visit your Web page.

Qualifying the Prospect

One of the most important keys to success in personal selling is the ability to qualify prospects. **Qualifying** is the process of identifying prospects who appear to have a need for your product and should be contacted. Top salespeople use good research and analysis skills to qualify leads effectively.[26]

The qualifying process is also the first opportunity to consider what the needs of the buyer might be, and how those needs match with the product characteristics being sold.[27] Some sales organizations link the qualifying process with the need discovery step in the consultative sales process. In most cases, this linkage will depend on the nature and complexity of the prospect's buying process. The more complex the buying process, the more likely these two sales functions will be separate steps in the sales process.

Every salesperson needs to establish qualifying criteria. The process involves finding answers to several basic questions.

1. *Does the prospect have a need for my product?* If you sell copy machines, it might appear that every business firm is a prospect. However, a firm that is outsourcing its copy work to FedEx Kinko's may not be a legitimate prospect.

   Qualifying involves probing for real needs. Let's assume you sell real estate for a large agency. You receive a call from someone who believes that owning a home is a good tax benefit. At this point it's important to find out what else makes owning a home important for that person. Get permission to ask questions and then determine the person's real needs. In the final analysis you may decide it would be a waste of your time and the prospect's time to visit several homes that are on the market.[28]

2. *Does the prospect have the authority to buy my product?* Ideally you should talk to a person who has the authority to buy or can influence the buying decision. Talking to the right person within a large organization may involve collecting information from several sources. Some buying decisions are made by individuals and others are made by a committee. Expensive products often require the approval of a decision maker higher up in the organization.

3. *Does the prospect have the financial resources to buy my product?* It is usually not difficult to obtain credit information for consumer and business buyers. If you are selling products to a business, the *Dun & Bradstreet Reference Book* is an excellent source of credit information. A local credit bureau can provide credit information for a consumer buyer.

    Although the collection of credit information is not difficult, detecting financial instability can be much more complicated. In recent years we have seen a steady stream of corporate scandals involving accounting irregularities, inflated balance sheets, and outright fraud.[29] Salespeople must be aware of the possibility that a customer may provide incorrect or misleading information.

4. *Does the prospect have the willingness to buy my product?* Rick Page, author of *Hope Is Not a Strategy*, reminds us that many prospects evaluate products but do not buy. When an evaluation stalls, the prospect may have determined that the problem is not of great enough magnitude or urgency to make the purchase. Also, in some cases there is not enough support within the company to reach closure. Rather than walk away from this situation, some salespeople move higher in the organization to determine the level of support for the purchase.[30]

    A large number of senior executives say they get involved in the sale early in the decision process, yet salespeople have difficulty meeting with high-level decision makers. Most senior executives will not meet with salespeople who are making cold calls. When appointments are granted, the time allocated may be very short; 5 to 10 minutes is not uncommon. How do you establish credibility for yourself and your company in a short time period? Be sure you know a great deal about the company before the appointment and be prepared to demonstrate your knowledge of the company and the industry it serves. Do not propose solutions until you fully understand the buyer's problems. Be sure to communicate value.[31]

This list of questions can be revised to meet the needs of many different types of salespeople. A sales representative for an industrial equipment dealer may see the qualifying process differently from the person who sells commercial real estate. The main consideration is providing accurate answers to each question.

Collecting and Organizing Prospect Information

The Internet and information revolution continue to make acquiring and managing sales leads much easier.[32] When it comes to collecting and organizing prospect information, salespeople have a large assortment of computer-based systems available. Companies such as Salesforce.com, Oracle, NetSuite, Sage, and Microsoft all offer software applications designed to collect and organize prospect information. Most of these sales force automation (SFA) systems or customer relationship management (CRM) systems, as they are now known, have preset categories or fields that contain sales data on the prospect. This **sales data** is the information seen in most CRM systems, including the contact name, title, address, phone number, e-mail, and so forth. It also may include information about what products have been purchased, what sales opportunities exist in the future, who the various members or influencers are in the buying center, what their preferred communication styles are, past sales and forecasted sales, volume, and percentage change and date of closing the sale. All of the sales data information about a prospect in a CRM system is presented in the account screen report. Figure 3 shows an account screen report for Able Profit Machines. The information in this report, including any notes about previous sales calls, is accessed and studied before the salesperson makes a sales call.

When bringing new prospects into the database, it is expected that the salesperson will acquire this sales data and enter it into the records kept on the prospect. In most CRM systems

FIGURE 3

The CRM Account Screen Report

This account screen report shows sales data for Able Profit Machines. The sales data, including any notes from previous sales calls, was entered by sales representative Pat Silva, of SimNet Systems. Pat Silva has been calling on Able Profit Machines President Bradley Able. (For more information on SimNet Systems see CRM Case Study.)

Source: Courtesy of Salesforce.com.

Contacts [1] | Open Activities [0] | Activity History [5] | Notes & Attachments [0]

Account Detail   Edit Delete Sharing

Account Owner	Pat Silva [Change]	Phone	(800) 912-0934
Account Name	Able Profit Machines [View Hierarchy]	Fax	(800) 912-0933
Parent Account		Website	http://www.apm.com

▼ Sales Opportunity Information

Sales Process Stage	Needs Analysis	Probability	0.70%
Weeks to Close	8	Forecast	175,000
Total Potential Sale	250,000		

▼ Additional Information

Type		Employees	520
Industry	Architecture	Annual Revenue	
Description			

▼ Address Information

Billing Address	245 Alcala St. Houston, TX 77023	Shipping Address	

this information goes into a shared database that allows other members of the sales team to access the information and make additions as they work with prospects. In the event a new salesperson takes over an existing prospect database, all of this information can be accessed quickly and used to plan sales strategies to work effectively with prospects.

Sales Intelligence

In addition to collecting sales data, the collection of **sales intelligence** is necessary when the sale is complex and requires a long closing cycle. Sales intelligence goes beyond data, giving salespeople access to insights into the prospect's marketplace, their firm, their competitors, even about the prospects themselves. Sales intelligence is needed today over and above sales data because prospects are looking for insights and knowledge from salespeople above and beyond the product features and benefits. In many buying situations today, prospects using advanced search engines have already learned about features and benefits. In terms of sales intelligence, prospects expect salespeople to know answers to many of the following questions. Answers to these questions create much of the value that results in successfully turning prospects into long-term customers:

Do You Know Me? You need to know more than my name and title. Do you know my role, my goals, how I am evaluated, and how long I have been with the organization? Do you know the projects I am working on, my style of doing business, and what the requirements are for me to meet my objectives? Do you know about previous dealings I have had with your company? Do I have a favorable opinion of your company and do you know my role and the role of other influencers in the decision making process?

Do You Know My Company and My Marketplace? Do you know our company mission statement, culture, and vision for the future? Do you know clearly what we are doing, how we are performing in the marketplace, what issues keep us up all night, and who and what our competitors are doing? Do you know where we fit into the existing competitive landscape? Are we the leader or are we in the position of having to play catch-up to survive? Can you relate what you sell directly to what we need to accomplish our goals? Do you know who our partners are? What effect the current economy has on our business?

Do You Have Any Special Value-Add? You have a product or service you think we need, but what else can you bring to the table? Are there additional resources you can bring to bear to solve my problems or improve my internal business processes? Can you educate me on how you are truly different from the other players in your area of expertise so I can support my recommendation to work with you? Can you help me build a case for return on investment (ROI)?[33]

Answers to these questions come from many sources. CRM suppliers like Salesforce.com, infoUSA.com, Sales-i.com, and Vecta.net have programs that supply this kind of sales

Your OneSource for Global Business Information

OneSource delivers the most in-depth business information available, providing companies with the data needed to effectively approach targeted markets including; solutions for Sales, Marketing, M&A/Finance, Insurance, Procurement, Recruitment, Legal Compliance, Consulting, Research and more.

Global Business Information

♦Companies ♦Executives ♦Industries ♦Financials ♦Analysis Data ♦News

OneSource enables companies to:

- Access data via your web browser
- Integrate with CRM systems
- View rich company profiles
- Develop quality sales leads
- Improve pre-meeting planning
- Gain competitive intelligence
- Identify key executives
- Target new customers
- Analyze financial performance
- Research industry trends

OneSource.
Global Business Information

866-354-6936

www.onesource.com

OneSource goes beyond sales data, and supplies value-adding sales intelligence to salespeople involved in complex sales that have a long closing cycle. This prospect information is loaded into a customer's CRM system. Salespeople review this information to plan strategies for successfully moving the sale through the stages in the sales process.

Source: Used with permission of OneSource Global Business Information.

intelligence to companies and salespeople. infoUSA's OneSource is one example of a supplier of sales intelligence. OneSource supplies sales intelligence to Cardinal Logistics Management, a major provider of logistics, transportation, and supply-chain solutions to large retailers, manufacturers, and distribution companies. Cardinal's salespeople must know each prospect inside and out in order to sell logistics solutions effectively to their 5,000 customers. OneSource supplies 24/7, anywhere access to detailed customer profiles, executive contact data and biographies, financial statements, news trade articles, and analyst reports. A special feature keeps salespeople up-to-date on any and all developments within their customer's company and their industry, including both their customer's customer and their competitors.[34]

Most importantly, this information must be entered into the company's CRM system to get a 360-degree view of the prospect. This information will also be used to move the prospect through the steps in the sales process.

Managing the Prospect Base

High-performing salespeople today are focused on effectively managing sales activities for all prospects in their database. This means that the size and number of prospects are more carefully considered. Too few prospects in various stages of the sales cycle can quickly signal problems. Alternatively, too many customers can drain a salesperson's resources so that too little effort is focused on prospects with the best opportunities. This is a particular problem when salespeople spend too much effort on prospects that have limited potential. CRM software can help organize customer data into meaningful and easy-to-interpret information, as evident in Figure 4.

Account Name ↑	Industry	Sales Process Stage	Forecast	Account Owner	First Name	Last Name	Title	Phone	Email
Able Profit Machines	Architecture	Needs Analysis	175,000	Pat Silva	Brad	Able	President	(254) 555-1000 Ext: 4234	bable@pearson-sellingtoday.com
Aeroflot Airlines	Warehousing and Distribution	Qualified	60,000	Pat Silva	John	Poltava	VP Purchasing	(214) 555-6113 Ext: 567	jpoltava@pearson-sellingtoday.com
Big Tex Auto Sales	Retail	Needs Analysis	112,500	Pat Silva	Dwayne	Ortega	President	(972) 555-4094	dortega@pearson-sellingtoday.com
Bryan Enterprises	Architecture	Presentation	75,000	Pat Silva	Bill	Bryan	President	(214) 555-4567	bill.bryan@pearson-sellingtoday.com
Canton Group	Financial Services	Prospect	100,000	Pat Silva	Maya	Ying	Executive Vice-President	(717) 555-3700	maya.ying@pearson-sellingtoday.com
Cantor & Glick	Financial Services	Prospect	87,500	Pat Silva	Saul	Greenburg	Analyst	(972) 555-7900	saul@pearson-sellingtoday.com
Coleman Financial	Financial Services	Prospect	187,500	Pat Silva	Alonzo	Washington	Broker	(972) 555-1500	awashington@pearson-sellingtoday.com
Computerized Labs	Healthcare	Presentation	45,000	Pat Silva	Sam	Pearlman	Office Manager	(713) 555-5454	spearlman@pearson-sellingtoday.com
Computer Products	Engineering	Qualified	15,000	Pat Silva	Joanna	Barkley	Purchasing Agent	(713) 555-2345	jbarkley@pearson-sellingtoday.com
Designers Associates	Education	Qualified	-	Pat Silva	Simon	Sayers	Director	(972) 555-6866	ssayers@pearson-sellingtoday.com
Ellis Enterprises	Construction	Qualified	157,500	Pat Silva	Timothy	Ellis	Architect	(214) 555-1234	tellis@pearson-sellingtoday.com
Excellent Software, Inc.	Engineering	Negotiations	22,000	Pat Silva	Ian	Program	President	(214) 555-8979 Ext:34	iprogram@pearson-sellingtoday.com
General Contractors	Engineering	Needs Analysis	90,000	Pat Silva	Brian	Allan	Owner	(214) 555-2947	ballan@pearson-sellingtoday.com
International Studios	Electronics	Needs Analysis	20,000	Pat Silva	Robert	Kelly	President	(214) 555-3456 Ext 240	rkelly@pearson-sellingtoday.com
Johnson and Associates	Architecture	Qualified	123,750	Pat Silva	Ralph	Johnson	Engineer	(817) 555-3212 Ext 310	rjohnson@pearson-sellingtoday.com
Lakeside Clinic	Other	Needs Analysis	5,000	Pat Silva	Jeff	Gray	Manager	(214) 555-6600	jgray@pearson-sellingtoday.com
Landers Engineering	Engineering	Presentation	20,000	Pat Silva	Colleen	Landers	Engineer	(717) 555-6121	clanders@pearson-sellingtoday.com
Media Conglomerate	Media	Negotiations	60,000	Pat Silva	Joe	Romera	Planner	(214) 555-9090	jromera@pearson-sellingtoday.com
Mercy Hospital	Healthcare	Closed/Service	100,000	Pat Silva	Kerri	Mathers	MIS Coordinator	(214) 555-1880 Ext 35	kmathers@pearson-sellingtoday.com
Modern Designs	Architecture	Negotiations	100,000	Pat Silva	Cheryl	Castro	Chief Engineer	(214) 555-1098 Ext 556	ccastro@pearson-sellingtoday.com
Murray D'Zines	Retail	Closed/Service	10,000	Pat Silva	Karen	Murray	Owner	(713) 555-7644	karen@pearson-sellingtoday.com
New Castle Associates	Financial Services	Prospect	125,000	Pat Silva	Kaitlin	Vanderbilt	Vice-President	(214) 555-3797	kvander@pearson-sellingtoday.com
Piccadilly Studio	Engineering	Closed/Service	24,000	Pat Silva	Judith	Albright	Owner	(214) 555-3084	jalbright@pearson-sellingtoday.com
Quality Builders	Architecture	Qualified	17,500	Pat Silva	Sherry	Britton	President	(223) 555-0098	sbritton@pearson-sellingtoday.com
Grand Totals (24 records)									

FIGURE 4

The Prospect Base

This CRM record presents a partial list of SimNet salesperson Pat Silva's prospects. Note this list includes information on the forecasted amount of each sale and what stage of the sales process the prospect is in. In CRM systems like Salesforce.com, clicking on any of the prospects on this list will allow the user to drill down into detailed contact information and notes supporting the projections.

Source: Courtesy of Salesforce.com.

Competitive position

Strong ◄─────────────────────────────► Weak

High	**Strategic accounts** Attractive and necessary accounts. Need to be protected from competitive activity so must be serviced to meet their needs. Often the most resource-intensive accounts. **Intensive account coverage**	**Problem accounts** Attractive buy only if competitive weakness can be overcome. Require careful planning and execution and deserve some effort because of their potential. **Moderate account coverage**
Account opportunity	**Hold accounts** Moderately attractive if current sales can be maintained with a limited commitment of resources. Should be monitored closely to see when opportunities arise but care needs to be taken to ensure that they don't require too much resource commitment beyond their potential. **Moderate account coverage**	**Drag accounts** Limited if any resource commitments required. Could be better managed by methods other than personal selling. These accounts often require resource commitments beyond their potential and may improve your performance if they buy from a competitor. **Moderate account coverage**
Low		

FIGURE 5

The Portfolio Model

This portfolio model uses account opportunity (forecasted sales) and competitive position (the ability to capitalize on the opportunity) to classify how much sales effort should be made on individual accounts in the prospect database. Those prospects listed in the strategic accounts cell (high sales forecast and strong position for closing the sale) will receive the largest amount of sales effort, while those in the drag accounts cell will receive little, if any, attention.

To effectively and efficiently manage the prospect base, sales managers and salespeople often conduct an **account analysis** to estimate the sales potential for each prospect. It is a necessary step before deciding how to allocate sales calls across accounts. The portfolio model and the sales process model are two popular models salespeople use for performing account analysis and deciding how much time and effort, and what sale strategies, to use with the prospects in their database.

Portfolio Models

Portfolio models involve the use of multiple factors when classifying prospects. Figure 5 illustrates a typical four-cell model based on two factors: overall account opportunity for the seller and the seller's competitive position, that is, the ability to capitalize on these opportunities.[35]

The portfolio model provides an excellent framework to facilitate communication between salespeople and the various sales support personnel. Teamwork at this stage in the sales cycle can develop improved strategies for working successfully with difference accounts and contacts in the prospect base. Portfolio models are most effective where salespeople must understand individual customer needs and where relationship strength is important to sales success.

Sales Process Models

Sales process models, also referred to as *sales funnel models*, classify prospects based on where they are in the sales process. The **sales process model** is the total set of prospects being pursued at any given time. The sales process model is illustrated in Figure 6. This six-step sales process model includes Prospect, Qualified, Needs Analysis, Presentation, Negotiations, and Closed/Service. An account might be simply a prospect who has potential but has not been

FIGURE 6

The CRM Sales Funnel (or Sales Process) Dashboard

The sales funnel, or sales process dashboard as it is frequently called, classifies prospects according to where they are in the sales process. In this figure both the total sales potential funnel and the forecasted funnel are presented. The forecasted funnel amounts are arrived at by multiplying the total sale by the forecast amount or likelihood the salesperson projected for successfully closing the sale. The sales forecast needs to be accurate because it is the amount most firms use to project future operating results for the company. You can click any stage on these two charts and drill down to find the underlying data.

Source: Courtesy of Salesforce.com.

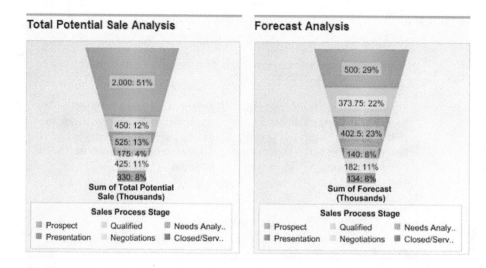

contacted, a qualified prospect ready for a needs analysis, or in serious negotiations with the salesperson. In sales process model reports like Figure 6, clicking on any part of any funnel graph will drill down into and report all the supporting data on prospects in each stage of the sales process. Where an account is in the sales process has implications for "if and when" the salesperson will be able to close the sale.

The sales cycle for complex technical sales such as networking installations might be several months in duration. The number of prospects in the sales process or funnel for selling networking installations may be small compared to the number for an insurance or real estate salesperson. Insurance salespeople know they need to contact a larger number of people to gain permission to make a smaller number of presentations, to make an even small number of sales. In any selling situation, it is important that salespeople balance their portfolio of prospects that are at various stages of the selling process.[36] A **balanced funnel** enables salespeople to know how many prospects and how much revenue is needed at each stage in the sales process to meet sales projections and quotas.[37] As indicated earlier with Joe Girard's "Ferris wheel" concept, this means that salespeople must ensure that sufficient prospects are regularly added to the funnel, so it does not become empty. In addition to the number of prospects, the quality of the prospects added to the funnel and the ability of the salesperson to manage the sales process will affect the number of sales opportunities that are successfully closed.

Salespeople need to ensure that they "work" the whole funnel so that it is always in balance. They should work on sales opportunities in the negotiation and close stages first; that is, close those that are near the end of the sales process. Then they should work on adding new prospects, and those that are in the earlier stages of the sales process. Prospecting is an activity that some salespeople dislike, but if it is not given sufficient attention there is a real danger that the funnel will empty. Finally, salespeople should work on those opportunities that are in the sales process, moving them along through the funnel and ensuring there are regular, predictable sales over time.[38]

CRM Technology for Pipeline Management

This process of managing all the prospects in the salesperson's sales funnel to ensure that sales objectives are being met is called **pipeline management**. CRM software provides an efficient and effective tool for forecasting and managing pipelines. Using sales data entered into the account detail, contact screens, notes applications, etc., sales forecasts can be continually updated as prospects move through the stages in the sales process. Prospects in the database who are no longer qualified, for whatever reason, can be quickly dropped from the sales funnel. Figure 7 shows part of a pipeline dashboard produced by a CRM software suite.

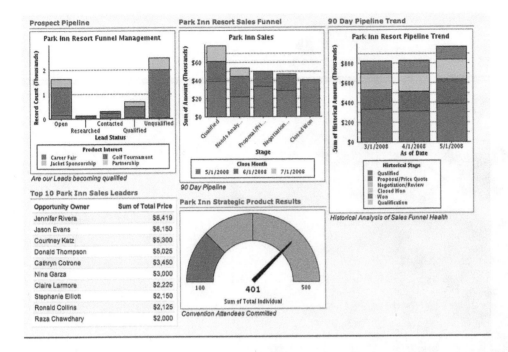

FIGURE 7

Pipeline Dashboards

These additional pipeline dashboards are at-a-glance visualizations that define, monitor, and analyze the relationships existing in the pipeline or funnel. Pipeline analytics exist in most modern CRM systems and are used to produce these important prospect movement reports. The salesperson can quickly and easily access detailed information on specific prospects, and then use this information to plan strategies for moving the prospect to the next stage of the sales process.

Source: Courtesy of Salesforce.com.

Pipeline analytics, defined as the ability to conduct sophisticated data analysis and modeling, are found in most CRM systems. Using pipeline analytics, new reports can be generated regarding the movement of the prospects through the sales funnel. These reports can be more clearly presented with the use of dashboards. **Pipeline dashboards** are at-a-glance visualizations that define, monitor, and analyze the relationships existing in the pipeline or sales funnel. Sales team members including the sales manager working together from a shared CRM database can collaborate to create value and enhance the sales strategies to help the salesperson move prospects through the pipeline to a successful sale. CRM pipeline dashboards allow the user to quickly and easily drill down into the reports and records supporting them. This provides for quick updates as prospects move through the sales funnel. Dashboards can also provide insight into the need to add new prospects, as existing ones are moved through the stages of the sales process.

GLOBAL BUSINESS INSIGHT

Doing Business in Germany

Germany represents the world's third largest economy and is America's largest European trading partner. If you are a salesperson planning a business trip to Germany, keep in mind that there is greater formality in the German business community.

- Germany has been described as a "low-context" culture in which words carry most of the information. Messages tend to be explicit and direct. In this culture, negotiations (verbal or written) tend to be explicit in defining terms of the agreement. By comparison, China is a high-context culture in which exact phrasing and the verbal part of the messages tend to be less significant than your relationship with the other person.

- There is a strong emphasis on punctuality, so avoid being late for appointments. Germans tend to make appointments far in advance.
- Lunch is the most common meal for business meetings. Dining etiquette in Germany involves eating continental style—holding the fork in the left hand continually and the knife in the right hand.
- The sales presentation should include data and empirical evidence that support your proposal. Brochures and other printed information should be serious and detailed, not flashy.[d]

Most salespeople use CRM software in the development of their prospecting and sales forecasting plan. This software allows the convenient preparation and management of prospect lists.

Source: Fancy Collection/Superstock Royalty Free

CHAPTER LEARNING ACTIVITIES

Reviewing Key Concepts

Discuss the importance of developing a prospect base

Prospect identification has been called the lifeblood of selling. A continuous supply of new customers must be found to replace those lost for various reasons. *Prospecting* is the systematic process of locating potential customers. Prospecting requires careful planning.

Identify and assess important sources of prospects

Analysis of both your product and your existing customers can help to identify, locate, and profile your prospects. Important sources of new customers include *referrals* (endless chain referrals and referral letters and cards), centers of influence, friends and family members, directories, trade publications, trade shows and special events, telemarketing and e-mail, direct-response advertising and sales letters, Web sites, computer databases, cold calling, education seminars, networking, and prospecting by nonsales employees. The use of social media to secure new prospects is also discussed.

Describe criteria for qualifying prospects

Prospecting techniques produce a list of names that must be evaluated using criteria developed by each salesperson. The process of prospect evaluation is called *qualifying*.

The qualifying process involves finding answers to several basic questions: Does the prospect have a need for my product? Can the prospect make the buying decision? Can the prospect pay for the purchase? Does the prospect have the willingness to buy my product? An estimate of the amount of sales that could be generated from this prospect and the prospect's credit rating also should be determined.

Explain common methods of collecting and organizing prospect information

Most companies rely on customer relationship management (CRM) systems to keep track of sales data. The collection of sales intelligence beyond sales data enables salespeople to impress their knowledgeable customers with insights that are above and beyond the product and/or service features and benefits.

Describe the steps in managing the prospect base

Salespeople need to allocate their resources wisely to make the most of the prospect base. They do so by conducting account analysis, using either the portfolio model or the sales funnel model.

Key Terms

Prospecting	Cold calling	Account analysis
Prospect	Networking	Sales process model
Prospect base	Social network	Balanced funnel
Referral	Qualifying	Pipeline management
Telemarketing	Sales data	Pipeline analytics
Web site	Sales intelligence	Pipeline dashboards

Review Questions

1. List and briefly explain the common causes of customer attrition.
2. During periods of economic uncertainty, the decision-making process often moves upward. What basic tips would you give a salesperson who is calling on senior executives?
3. Describe three steps progressive marketers are taking to improve the quality of the prospecting effort.
4. List the major sources of prospects.
5. Explain how the endless chain referral prospecting method works.
6. Discuss how direct-response advertising and sales letters can be used to identify prospects.
7. What is *networking*? How might a real estate salesperson use networking to identify prospects?
8. What does the term *qualifying* mean? What are the four basic questions that should be answered during the qualifying process?
9. What are the most common methods of organizing prospect information?
10. When is sales intelligence important? What are the three most important pieces of sales intelligence a salesperson needs to know?
11. Describe two popular models for performing the account analysis.

Application Exercises

1. Prior to getting involved in networking, it's a good idea to prepare an "elevator" presentation. This is a 30-second pitch that summarizes what you want people to know about you. You might think of yourself as a "product" to be sold to an employer who has a job opening. Make your presentation upbeat and brief. Who are you? What are you currently doing? What type of work are you looking for? Practice the presentation alone in front of a mirror and then present it to one or two class members.
2. You are a sales representative for Xerox Corporation. Assuming Xerox has just designed a new, less expensive, and better-quality copying machine, make a list of 15 prospects you would plan to contact. From the material in this chapter, identify the sources you would use in developing your prospect list.
3. You are in the process of interviewing for a sales position with CIGNA Insurance Company. In addition to filling out an application form and taking an aptitude test, one of the items the agency manager requests of you is to develop a list of prospects with whom

you are acquainted. He informs you that this list includes the prospects you will be working with during the first few weeks of employment. The agency manager recommends that you list at least 50 names. Prepare a list of 10 acquaintances you have that would qualify as prospects.

4. Sales automation software is most commonly used in the prospecting phase of selling. New-product releases are continually being developed that provide additional features and benefits to salespeople. The software used in this book is marketed by a leader in the field. Access www.salesforce.com and research the latest version of Salesforce. Click on and examine the latest demonstration copy of this popular sales automation software.

5. Locating companies to work for is a form of prospecting. Assuming you are interested in changing careers, develop a list of 10 companies for which you would like to work. Assign each company a priority according to your interest, from the most desirable (1) to the least (10). Organize your list in six columns showing the company name, telephone number, address, person in charge of hiring, prospect information, and priority. What sources did you use to get this information?

Role-Play Exercise

For this role-play, you will assume a sales position at a Lexus dealership. You have just completed a successful sale by signing the papers for the second new Lexus this customer has purchased in the past four years. Because you know your prospect has had a very successful experience with his first Lexus, you have decided to use the referral methods described in this chapter. Review the material on referrals and plan what you will say to your customer to build your prospect base. Pair off with another student who will assume the role of your customer. Explain that satisfied customers often know other people who would consider purchasing a Lexus. You might say, "Considering the positive experience you have had as a Lexus owner, you probably know others who appreciate fine automobiles. Is there anyone who comes to mind?" If, after probing, your customer doesn't recall someone immediately, ask permission to call him later to see if anyone has come to mind. Ask this person for actual names, addresses, and other qualifying information about prospective customers whom he knows. Also, ask the customer if he would write a referral note or letter that you could use.

Reality Selling Today Video Case Problem: Salesforce.com

Dave Levitt, featured at the beginning of this chapter, is a regional sales manager for Salesforce.com. The CRM solution provider is exclusively a cloud-computing vendor offering hosted applications. This model sets the company apart from competitors such as SAP, Oracle, or Microsoft, who are predominantly on-premise providers. Cloud-computing systems have a high degree of flexibility as they can be customized for each individual account and implemented within a very short time frame. Salesforce.com's unique selling proposition is therefore closely linked to the speed with which a client can gain the benefit: Cloud-computing implementation times are typically weeks or months, whereas competitive on-premise solutions can take years to be implemented. Therefore, the total cost of ownership is much lower, and the ROI is much higher and comes in faster.

Before getting in touch with a prospect, Levitt's sales representatives typically spend a substantial amount of time preparing for a sales call and keeping up with news releases. Such upfront investigative work is necessary to uncover such things as changes in top management or factors that are driving a company to change a business model. Working for a CRM company, Salesforce.com's salespeople have comprehensive access to additional news and information directly about each of their customers and prospects. Hence, by the time representatives have decided to pick up the phone to prospect, they already have a sense for why they are calling and what the value proposition is going to be specifically for that account.

For providers of enterprise software solutions, it is important to have contacts and relationships with three different types of individuals within the prospective customer company: (1) executive financial influencers who have ultimate responsibility for the budget and the project itself, (2) a coach who can give guidance on a day-to-day basis, and (3) IT specialists who can facilitate the process and who would be the custodians after the implementation of the solution. Therefore the sales representative has to be an orchestrator of resources within Salesforce.com for different buying influencers in the prospect's organization at different points in the sales cycle. For example, the salesperson would include a technical employee from Salesforce.com as part of the sales team that could apply the customer's needs to the product itself and perform demonstrations of software. One would also need to incorporate an internal sales executive that aligns with the customer's executive. Furthermore, the internal services organization or a third-party implementation partner is needed to explain and execute the implementation of the product. There could also be a wide variety of other specialists depending on which specific tasks have to be accomplished.

Typically, the sales representative would start to qualify the opportunity through conversations with the coach. Using various questioning techniques during the initial discovery process, the sales representative has to understand the following: What is the prospect's business model? Why might the prospect be interested in our offerings? What is their problem, and how big is it? What is the complexity of the problem the prospect is trying to address? Will there be a good fit? Is it worth investing the time and money it takes to win the account? What is their time frame? How are they going to measure success?

If the initial discovery shows that the problem can be addressed, the sales representative would then ask for access to the ultimate decision maker and all the other key stakeholders. Then he/she would perform a similar discovery as was done with the first person (i.e., the coach), constantly trying to qualify the value of the service solution offering and making sure that it is worth pursuing the opportunity (as for large opportunities, it could be a one-year investment to win it). So the sales representative has to make sure and qualify that (1) it is a legitimate opportunity, (2) it can be won, and (3) it is worth winning the opportunity. As Levitt emphasizes, it has to be a win-win perspective: "We do not sell a commodity, but a specialty. We do not compete on price alone, but on quality and value." (See the chapter opener and Reality *Selling Today* Role-Play 7 in the end-of-chapter appendix for more information).

Questions

1. Imagine you were in the position of Dave Levitt, selling CRM services to different business clients. What would be the most promising sources of prospects for you?
2. What criteria does Dave Levitt use for qualifying the prospect?
3. What questions does Dave Levitt ask to understand the needs of the customer?
4. What product features does Dave Levitt highlight that will help a user of Salesforce.com improve his business?
5. Does it appear that Dave Levitt is utilizing previously collected sales intelligence to impress the potential buyer with insights that are above and beyond the product features and benefits? Please specify.

CRM Case Study

Reviewing the Prospect Database

 Becky Kemley is the sales manager in the Dallas, Texas, office of SimNet Systems, which sells network products and services. The productivity and the critical mission of Becky's customers can be considerably enhanced by selecting and using the correct LAN (local area network), WAN (wide area network), or VPN (virtual private network) system. Becky's company is called a *value-added reseller (VAR)* because its people help customers maximize the value of the products bought through SimNet.

Becky's sales and technical support people may spend several months in the sales process (sales cycle). Salespeople telephone and call on prospects to determine whether they qualify for SimNet's attention. Time is taken to study the customer's needs (needs discovery). The expert opinion of SimNet's technical people is incorporated into a sales proposal that is presented to the prospective customer. The presentation may be made to a number of decision makers in the prospect's firm. The final decision to purchase may follow weeks of consideration within the firm and negotiations with SimNet.

Once a decision is made by a customer to buy from SimNet, Becky's people begin the process of acquiring, assembling, and installing the network system and then follow through with appropriate training, integration, and support services.

Becky's company must carefully prospect for customers. SimNet may invest a significant amount of time helping a potential customer configure the right combination of products and services. This means that only the most serious prospects should be cultivated. Further, Becky's people must ascertain that if the investment of time is made in a prospective customer, the prospect will follow through with purchases from SimNet.

Becky is responsible for assuring that prospect information is collected and used effectively. The network salespeople use Salesforce.com to manage their prospect information. The system allows salespeople to document and manage their sales efforts with each prospect.

Becky has just hired you to sell for SimNet. Becky has given you the files of Pat Silva, a salesperson who just has been promoted to SimNet's corporate headquarters. Becky has asked you to review the status of Pat's 24 accounts. Pat's customers have been notified that Pat is leaving and that a new salesperson, you, will be contacting them. Becky wants you to review each contact's record. You are to meet with Becky next Monday and be prepared to answer the following questions.

Refer to Appendix: Selling Today and Customer Relationship Management in the back of your book for instructions on how to access and review the 24 Salesforce.com prospect records of Pat Silva. If you haven't already done so, view the Sales Representative Fundamentals video classes at www.salesforce.com.

Questions

1. Which contact can you ignore immediately *as a contact* likely to make a purchase?
2. Referring only to the *weeks to close* field, which three contacts would you call immediately?
3. Referring only to the estimates in the *total potential sale* fields, which four accounts—not Prospects—would you call first? Does the *probability* field—the likelihood of closing percentage—have any influence on decisions concerning which prospects to call first? Why?
4. According to information on the records, what sources did Pat Silva use most to find new prospects? Give examples.

ROLE-PLAY EXERCISE

Developing a Customer Strategy

Scenario

You are a sales representative employed by the Park Inn International hotel and convention center. One of your primary responsibilities is to identify prospects and make sales calls that result in the development of new accounts. During each of these calls, you plan to build a relationship with the customer and describe selected value-added guest services and amenities offered by the Park Inn. You also try to learn as much as possible about the customer's buying process.

Customer Profile

Shannon Fordham is the founder and chief executive officer of USA Technologies, a growing high-tech firm with more than 300 employees. The company manufactures and sells security systems that can be used in residential homes, retail stores, and other commercial buildings. According to a recent article in the *Wall Street Journal*, USA Technologies is poised to grow very rapidly in the next year. The article described Shannon Fordham as a workaholic who usually puts in an 80-hour workweek. Delegation does not come easy to this personable, hard-charging entrepreneur.

Salesperson Profile

You have just completed the Park Inn sales training program and now want to develop some new accounts. In addition to taking care of established customers, you plan to call on at least four new prospects every week.

Product

Park Inn International is a full-service hotel and convention center located in Rockport, Illinois. The hotel recently completed a $2.8 million renovation of its meeting and banquet rooms.

Instructions

For this role-play activity, you will meet with Shannon Fordham, who appears to be a good prospect. During the first sales call, plan to learn more about the prospect as an individual and acquire more information about USA Technologies. This meeting will provide you with the opportunity to begin building a long-term partnership.

During the first meeting with a prospect, you like to present a limited amount of important product information. In this case the length of the appointment is 15 minutes, so you should not try to cover too much information. To prepare for the first sales call, read Employment Memorandum 1 in Appendix: Partnership Selling. This memo describes the value-added guest services and amenities offered by the Park Inn. For the purpose of this role-play, Shannon Fordham should be considered a consultative process buyer. You can assume that the prospect will need help identifying and evaluating possible solutions. As you prepare for the first call, think about what may take place during future calls. Review the steps in the typical buying process. Keep in mind that today's more demanding customers are seeking a cluster of satisfactions. Study the Product-Selling Model prior to meeting with the prospect.

Appendix: Reality Selling Today Role-Play Scenario
Reality Selling Today Role-Play 7, Salesforce.com

Dave Levitt
Salesforce.com

(This mock sales call role-play scenario is created exclusively for use with this chapter.)

Your Role at Salesforce.com

You are a sales representative for Salesforce.com (see Web site at Salesforce.com), just like Dave Levitt in the chapter Video Case Problem. Your company is the world leader in on-demand customer relationship management (CRM) services. Unlike most CRM applications, companies who use your services store customer and sales data on Salesforce.com. One of the benefits of on-demand CRM services is that customers neither incur upfront capital investment nor on-site administration. Your company also offers solutions that are customized to specific customer needs, such as creating different interfaces for different departments and work groups, and providing limited access to data for specific authorized work groups.

Your Customer: Rename Clothing Company

You will meet with Jesse Golden, the marketing director at Rename Clothing Company. A family-owned business in Garden Grove, California, the company is expanding at a fast pace not only in the United States, but also in Latin American markets that the company entered into two years ago. The company currently has a sales force of 20 people, and outsources its selling activities for overseas operations to local firms. Each salesperson is responsible for three to four customers. Although outsourcing has the advantage of capitalizing on market knowledge of local partners, the company realizes that it does not have full control over their selling efforts. Domestically, the company has strong relationships with its buyers, but there have been signs of work overload among the sales force. While Rename has three in-house brands that it distributes using its own channel, it does provide sourcing solutions to mid- and high-end department stores under their private labels. Rename works closely with its suppliers in more than five countries, mainly in Europe and Asia. It also has a small manufacturing facility in California for sample development and small-batch order production.

Quick Facts About Rename Clothing Company's Needs

The apparel industry is a sophisticated, fast-moving industry with several designs launched every season, and repeat orders must be met as fast as possible before end-users change their tastes. As a company that operates in middle- to high-end markets, Rename positions itself as a sourcing company with a fast turnaround for its customers. The nature of the industry requires salespeople to be highly diligent in market information gathering, processing, and dissemination across geographic areas and departments.

At present, the in-house salespeople use spreadsheets for almost all of their selling activities such as recording sales calls, reporting to sales managers, and tracking delivery of orders, to name just a few. Jesse joined the company two months ago and realized the current system showed clear signs of overload. Mistakes have started to occur more often, and the company has received quite a few complaints about shipment delays, wrong labeling on products, and wrong packaging. As marketing director, Jesse spent several days making sense of disparate information about Rename's domestic sales and has mixed reports about its overseas operation. Jesse's secretary lamented that the spreadsheets provided by the sales force are not in a uniform format, making it difficult to consolidate the database. Meanwhile, salespeople claim that their customers are not the same, and they need to customize their spreadsheets so that they can keep track of things more easily.

With high pressure for growth, Rename is looking for an efficient way to consolidate and manage its customer database. Jesse is also in the process of establishing a branch office in Mexico and will staff three local salespeople to manage Rename's business in this growing market. In overseas markets, the focus is more on customer acquisition and lead management, while in domestic markets, Jesse is more concerned with keeping Rename's existing customers happy.

Your Call Objectives

In your meeting with Jesse Golden, you hope to convince him that Salesforce.com is the right CRM solution for Rename. You can do this by providing him with interesting facts and benefits Salesforce.com can offer (see more information at www.Salesforce.com). Hopefully, you will close a deal by the end of the meeting.

Endnotes

1. Gerhard Gschwandtner, "Thoughts to Sell By," *Personal Selling Power*, 15th Anniversary Issue, 1995, p. 122.
2. Dorothy Leeds, "Where Are the Real Decision Makers?" *Personal Selling Power*, March 1993, p. 62; Gerhard Gschwandtner, "Getting Squeezed," *Selling Power*, May 2002, p. 10.
3. Terry Hill, "How Do You Sustain and Grow Your Customer Relationships," *American Salesman*, October 2007, p. 26.
4. For additional information on Joe Girard see "Joe Girard on Becoming the World's Greatest Salesperson," *Harvard Business Review*, July–August 2006, p. 25.
5. Gerhard Gschwandtner, "The Funnel Concept," *Personal Selling Power*, 15th Anniversary Issue, 1995, p. 23.
6. Joel R. Pecoraro, "Panning for Gold," *Sales & Marketing Management*, November 2004, p. 56.
7. "Skills Workshop," *Selling Power*, October 2000, p. 54.
8. Geoffrey James, "How to Earn Customer Referrals," *Selling Power*, July/August 2004, pp. 25–28.
9. *Business Network International*, www.bni.com (accessed February 14, 2005).
10. Thomas Petzinger Jr., "Selling a 'Killer App' Is a Far Tougher Job Than Dreaming It Up," *Wall Street Journal*, April 3, 1998, p. B1.
11. Daniel Tynan, "Tricks of the Trade Show," *Sales & Marketing Management*, January 2004, p. 27.
12. Ron Donoho, "Steering New Sales," *Sales & Marketing Management*, November 2001, pp. 31–35.
13. Henry Canaday, "Carefully Composed," *Selling Power*, May 2007, pp. 44–46.
14. Ibid., pp. 45–46.
15. Henry Canaday, "Zeroing In on Prospects," *Selling Power*, March 2006, p. 82.
16. Ibid., pp. 84–85.
17. Andy Cohen, "Man About Town," *Sales & Marketing Management*, June 2000, p. 29.
18. John Boe, "Selling Is a Contact Sport: Keys to Effective Phone Calling," *American Salesman*, January 2008, p. 26. For more information on cold calls, see Scott Stears, "Cold Calls Have Yet to Breathe Their Last Gasp," *Wall Street Journal*, December 14, 2006, p. D2.
19. Nicole Gull, "Warming Up to Cold Calls," *Inc.*, November 2004, pp. 41–43.
20. Maxwell Maltz, Dan S. Kennedy, William T. Brooks, Matt Oechsli, Jeff Paul, and Pamela Yellen, *Zero-Resistance Selling* (Paramus, NJ: Prentice Hall, 1998), p. 167.
21. Stacy L. Bradford, "Ten Job-Networking Tips," *News & Observer*, January 30, 2005, p. 7E.
22. Tuba Üstüner and David Godes, "Better Sales Networks," *Harvard Business Review*, July–August 2006, pp. 102–112.
23. Michele Marchetti, "Do You Have the Knack for Networking?" *Sales & Marketing Management*, January 1996, p. 30; Deb Haggerty, "Successful Networking Begins as a State of Mind," *Selling*, December 2004, p. 13.
24. Maxwell Maltz, Dan S. Kennedy, William T. Brooks, Matt Oechsli, Jeff Paul, and Pamela Yellen, *Zero-Resistance Selling* (Paramus, NJ: Prentice Hall, 1998), pp. 179–180.
25. Steve Atlas, "Trouble Connecting?" *Selling Power*, September 2001, p. 27.
26. "Are You Generating and Using Quality Leads?" *Value-Added Selling* 21, September 16, 2003, p. 4.
27. Thomas R. Watruba, "The Evolution of Selling," *Journal of Personal Selling and Sales Management*, Summer 1991, p. 7.
28. This example was adopted from "Skills Workshop" by William F. Kendy, *Selling Power*, January/February 2000, p. 26.
29. Mitchell Pacelle, "Former SEC Chairman Levitt Decries Business Ethics in U.S.," *Wall Street Journal*, June 17, 2002, p. C7; Shoshana Zuboff, "A Starter Kit for Business Ethics," *Fast Company*, January 2005, p. 91.
30. Rick Page, *Hope Is Not a Strategy* (Atlanta, GA: Nautilus Press, 2002), pp. 69–71.
31. "Senior Execs Share Insider Tips," *Selling*, March 2000, pp. 1, 14; Tom Reilly, "Selling to Mr. Big Is Tough, But . . . ," *Selling*, February 2001, pp. 1, 12.
32. Henry Canada, "Fishing for Big Ones," *Personal Selling Power* (Source Book 2008), p. 46.
33. Jim Dickie and Barry Trailer, "Proactive Sales Intelligence: The New Requirement for Getting into the Game," *Salesforce.com*, 2007.

34. Ibid., pp. 46–47.

35. H. F. Mackenzie et al., *Sales Management in Canada* (Toronto, ON: Pearson Education Canada, 2008), p. 140.

36. Tony Parinello, "Keeping Track of Prospects," www.entrepreneur.com/article/0,4621,306013,00.html, January 13, 2003 (accessed February 14, 2008).

37. Don Thomson, *Keeping the Funnel Full* (French Creek, BC: Mardon Publishing, 2004), p. 7.

38. H. F. Mackenzie et al., p. 141.

Endnotes for Boxed Features

a. Based on Sarah Lorge, "The Best Way to Prospect," *Sales & Marketing Management*, January 1998, p. 80.

b. Based on Chad Kaydo, "Becoming the Face of the Brand," *Sales & Marketing Management*, February 2000, p. 14.

c. Barbara Siskind, *Seminars to Build Your Business* (North Vancouver, BC: Self-Counsel Press, 1998), pp. 9–12; Sheldon Gordon, "Punch Up Your Profits," *Profit*, May 1999, pp. 17–22.

d. Barbara Pachter and Marjorie Brody, *Complete Business Etiquette Handbook* (Upper Saddle River, NJ: Prentice Hall, 1995), p. 278; "International Snapshot," *Sales & Marketing Management*, August 2001, p. 64; Jan Yager, *Business Protocol*, 2nd ed. (Stamford, CT: Hannacroix Books, Inc., 2001), pp. 116–117.

Chapter 5

Approaching the Customer
with Adaptive Selling

From Chapter 10 of *Selling Today: Partnering to Create Value*, 12/e. Gerald L. Manning. Michael Ahearne.
Barry L. Reece. Copyright © 2012 by Pearson Education. Published by Prentice Hall. All rights reserved.

Approaching the Customer with Adaptive Selling

Reality Selling Today Video Series

The worldwide Hilti Corporation (www.hilti.com) specializes in providing leading-edge technology to the global construction industry. With some 20,000 employees in more than 120 countries around the world, Hilti actively pursues a value-added orientation in all of its activities.

As part of this orientation, Hilti puts its new salespeople through a rigorous training curriculum that includes one-month pretraining on Hilti products and services, a three-week intensive training in product and services sales, and a two-week training on software applications. In addition, these salespeople also ride along with experienced sales managers to get hands-on experience. Furthermore, the company offers refresher courses to keep its salespeople updated on Hilti's products and services, the construction market, and corporate strategy. Equipped with this in-depth knowledge and the value orientation that is deeply rooted in the corporate culture, salespeople like Alim Hirani, on the right in the photo above, are always well prepared to approach customers to make sales presentations, demonstrate and explain Hilti's products and services, and show the customers both the tangible and intangible benefits that Hilti can offer.

With a direct sales model, Hilti relies heavily on its salespeople to make the connection and deliver its values to its global customers. Alim is a strong believer that he and his sales team are the face of the company. His credibility is embedded in Hilti's credibility and vice versa. He always makes sure that his sales presentations are well prepared in advance. More importantly, he builds and maintains rapport with his customers from the very beginning of the business relationship because such partnership mentality motivates the customers to disclose their actual concerns. In the end, customers only value solutions that address their actual needs, and Alim as a Hilti salesperson knows that by heart. ●

Selling Power, a magazine with a circulation of over 200,000, understands the importance of value-added selling. This audio sales training program shows how a strategically planned presentation adds value when it is based on carefully developed call objectives and a presentation plan to meet these objectives.

Source: Courtesy of Personal Selling Power.

Developing the Presentation Strategy

The presentation strategy combines elements of the relationship, product, and customer strategies. Each of the other three strategies must be developed before a salesperson can create an effective presentation strategy.

The **presentation strategy** is a well-conceived plan that includes three prescriptions: (1) establishing objectives for the sales presentation, (2) developing the presale presentation plan needed to meet these objectives, and (3) renewing one's commitment to providing outstanding customer service (Figure 1).

The first prescription reminds us that we need to establish one or more objectives for each sales call. High-performance salespeople like Alim Hirani understand that it is often possible to accomplish several goals during a single call. A common objective of sales calls is to collect information about the prospect's needs. Another common objective is to develop, build, or sustain a relationship with those who make the buying decision.

A carefully prepared presentation plan ensures that salespeople are well organized during the sales presentation and prepared to achieve their objectives. A six-step presentation plan is introduced later in this chapter.

Strategic/Consultative Selling Model*	
Strategic Step	**Prescription**
Develop a Personal Selling Philosophy	☑ Adopt Marketing Concept ☑ Value Personal Selling ☑ Become a Problem Solver/Partner
Develop a Relationship Strategy	☑ Adopt Win-Win Philosophy ☑ Project Professional Image ☑ Maintain High Ethical Standards
Develop a Product Strategy	☑ Become a Product Expert ☑ Sell Benefits ☑ Configure Value-Added Solutions
Develop a Customer Strategy	☑ Understand the Buying Process ☑ Understand Buyer Behavior ☑ Develop Prospect Base
Develop a Presentation Strategy	☑ Prepare Objectives ☑ Develop Presentation Plan ☑ Provide Outstanding Service

*Strategic/consultative selling evolved in response to increased competition, more complex products, increased emphasis on customer needs, and growing importance of long-term relationships.

FIGURE 1

The Strategic/Consultative Selling Model provides the foundation for a value-added consultative presentation strategy.

Establishment of objectives for the sales presentation and preparation of the presentation plan must be guided by a strong desire to offer outstanding customer service. Achieving excellence is the result of careful needs analysis, correct product selection, clear presentations, informative demonstrations, win-win negotiations, and flawless service after the sale. Salespeople who are committed to doing their best in each of these areas are richly rewarded.

Presentation Strategy Adds Value

How does precall planning add value? Value is added when you position yourself as a resource—not just a vendor. You must prove that you have important ideas and advice to offer.[1] A well-planned presentation adds value when it is based on carefully developed sales call objectives and a presentation plan needed to meet these objectives. Good planning ensures that the presentation is customized and adapted to meet the needs and time constraints of the prospect. Increasingly, customers' time is very limited and they want a concise and thoughtful presentation. Careful planning is the key to delivering more value and increasing your sales productivity.[2]

Salespeople need to be aware of the changing needs of their customers or risk losing out to the competition. Some salespeople do not pay enough attention to how they conduct business with their established customers. Without a precall plan, it's easy to miss opportunities to increase your knowledge of the customer's business, sell new products, or discover ways to improve service.[3]

Planning the Preapproach

Preparation for the actual sales presentation is a two-part process. Part one is referred to as the **preapproach**. The preapproach involves preparing presale objectives and developing a presale presentation plan. Part two is called the **approach** and involves making a favorable first impression, securing the prospect's attention, and transitioning to need identification (Figure 2). The preapproach and approach, when handled correctly, establish a foundation for an effective sales presentation.

The preapproach should be viewed as a key step in preparing for each sales presentation. Professional salespeople complete the preapproach for every presentation whether it involves a

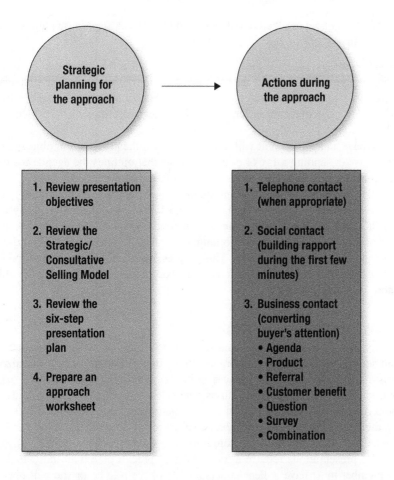

FIGURE 2

Preparing for the presentation involves planning for the activities that occur before meeting the prospect and for the first few minutes of actual contact with the prospect.

new account or an established customer. Top salespeople often spend two or three hours planning for a 25-minute sales call. The preapproach includes the first two prescriptions for developing a presentation strategy: establishing objectives and creating a presale presentation plan.

Establishing Presentation Objectives

Preparation for a sales call is part research, part planning, and part critical thinking. Sales representatives employed by Nalco Chemical Company prepare for each sales call by filling out a 13-point precall planner. One section of this form requires the salesperson to identify the objectives of the call. Nalco is a company that emphasizes professionalism, long-term partnerships, and staying focused on customer needs.[4]

When you are calling on a *consultative* or *strategic alliance* buyer, you will usually not cover all of the five stages of the typical buying process during a single sales call.

Multi-call sales presentations are especially common in complex sales. Therefore, it's best to develop presentation objectives suitable for each stage of the buying process. During the first stage—need awareness—customers may or may not be aware of their needs and problems. The need awareness stage is the "investigation" stage. Uncovering and clarifying needs will require the use of appropriate questions. The following presentation objectives would be appropriate during the first call on a new prospect:

- Establish rapport and begin building a relationship with the customer.
- Obtain permission to ask need identification questions.
- Obtain personal and business information to establish the customer's file.

During stage two of the buying process—evaluation of solutions—the customer is ready to consider possible problem solutions. In some cases, there may be several solutions that must be evaluated. Presentation objectives for stage two might include the following:

- Involve the customer in a product demonstration.
- Provide value justification in terms of cost reduction and increased revenues.

- Compare and contrast the features of, for example, a truck fleet lease plan with a fleet purchase plan.

Every sales call should have an **action objective**. An action objective is something that you want the customer to do during the sales presentation: provide specific financial information, schedule a visit to your manufacturing plant, agree to a trial use of your product, agree to a follow-up meeting, or place an order. An action objective brings a sharp focus to the sales presentation.[5]

Once you have an appointment with the prospect and the presentation objectives have been established, consider sending a fax or e-mail message that outlines the agenda for the meeting. This will confirm the appointment and clarify the topics to be discussed.[6]

Multi-call sales presentations are common in many areas, including the retail field. The sale of expensive recreational vehicles, leased automobiles, boats, and quality sound systems for the home or business often requires more than one sales call. Some clothing stores and independent tailors make office calls to sell tailored clothing. One example is Mitchells/Richards, with stores in Westport and Greenwich, Connecticut. This progressive retailer, with a reputation for superior customer service, makes office calls upon request. Working with a customer at his office usually requires more than one sales call.[7]

Team Selling Presentation Strategies

In today's ever-changing business environment, team selling has surfaced as a major development. Team selling is ideally suited to organizations that sell complex or customized products and services that require direct communication between customers and technical experts. Sales teams can often uncover problems, solutions, and sales opportunities that no individual salesperson could discover working alone.[8] In some situations the involvement of technical experts can shorten the selling cycle. The team approach often results in more precise need identification, improved selection of the product, and more informative sales presentations.

Team sales presentations require a more detailed precall plan than individual sales calls. Each team member must have a clear understanding of the role he or she will play during the sales call. Sales presentation objectives should be clearly stated. Team members should be given detailed information about the customer, understand the basics of a consultative sales presentation, and be prepared to add value.[9]

Companies that have moved to team sales have discovered that this approach is not easily executed. At Hickok Cole Architects in Washington, D.C., team selling is the primary approach used to obtain new accounts. However, the team selling process was not easily mastered by staff members. Determining who would communicate when, and determining how presentations would fall into place seamlessly, took months of practice among the company's teams, which often consisted of six or more people. Without sufficient practice, the staff at Hickok Cole discovered that team presentations were sometimes disorganized.[10]

A survey of 19,000 salespeople and sales managers found that about one-fourth of the people contacted use sales teams. A carefully conceived presentation strategy, with each participant having a clear understanding of the role and value he or she will add during the sales call, is essential.

Source: Yuri Arcurs/Shutterstock

SOCIAL MEDIA AND SELLING TODAY

Team Selling, Buying Committees, and "Chatter"

Sales of complex or customized products and services invariably involve two teams of people—the selling team and the buying committee or team. Important communications occur between and among members of the two teams. Information about technical and financial matters, information technology, facilities management, and other sales-related issues is exchanged throughout the sales process. Salesforce.com has introduced a system called "Chatter" to facilitate collaborative communication throughout the sales process.

Chatter is linked to the Salesforce.com CRM system and incorporates the benefits of social media. Chatter is a secure cloud-based online service similar to most social media systems. Members of both teams may create personal profiles similar to those on Facebook. This personalizes the people working together and makes it easy for anyone with access in both companies to get acquainted with everyone involved in the sales transaction. Users can follow selected personnel in either company, sort the profiles by expertise, and form networks of specialists. Messages are easily transmitted among all participants and recorded for reviewing later. Although it appears to be social media, wise users should retain a "casual business" writing style and avoid too much informality.

Chatter conversations can pertain to specific subjects so users receive real-time news feeds and participate in the development of each part of the solution. This creates value for the total transaction in that anyone in the buying company not involved in the solution development, such as a board of directors, can review the exchanges to understand the results achieved. Sections of the Chatter system are for people within the selling company to confidentially comment and exchange ideas on how to best solve problems and move the sale ahead. When it is time for the sales presentation, everyone following Chatter's continuous collaboration will be well prepared to confirm that the proposed solution is a good fit. The presentation contributions by sales team members can be better organized and coordinated. For more information, go to Salesforce.com/chatter.

A variation of the team approach to selling is used by some marketers. Salespeople are trained to seek the assistance of another salesperson or actually turn the customer over to another salesperson when problems surface. The other salesperson may bring to the selling situation greater ability to identify the customer's needs or select the appropriate product. Salespeople who have well-prepared presale objectives know when to seek assistance from another professional.

Strategies for Selling to a Buying Committee

In some cases salespeople must address and satisfy both the individual and collective concerns of each participant in a multi-buyer situation. The decision makers may be members of a well-trained buying committee, or a board of directors.

As in any type of selling situation, the salesperson should attempt to determine the various buying influences. When possible, the role of each decision maker, the amount of influence he or she exerts, and each decision maker's needs should be determined before the presentation. Careful observation during the presentation can reveal who may use the product (user influencer), who controls the finances (financial influencer), and who can provide the expertise necessary to make the correct buying decision (technical influencer).

When you make a presentation to a buying committee, make sure all parties feel involved. Any member of the group who feels ignored could prevent you from closing the sale. Be sure to direct questions and comments to all potential decision makers in the group. As early as possible, identify the most powerful influences.

Find out if there are any silent team or committee members. A *silent member* is one who can influence the buying decision but does not attend the presentation. Silent members are usually senior managers who have a major influence on the buying decision. If a silent member does exist, you must find a way to communicate, directly or indirectly, with this person.[11]

Adaptive Selling: Builds on Four Strategic Areas of Personal Selling

At the very heart of *adaptive selling* is the belief that every sales call must be tailored to the unique needs, wants, and concerns of the customer. Adaptive selling involves altering sales behaviors in order to improve communication with the customer. Identifying and responding to the customer's needs frequently requires complex behavioral adjustments before and during the sales call. These adjustments are based on the relationship needs and product needs of the customer. Salespeople today must develop a broader repertoire of selling strategies and apply more effective information acquisition skills.[12]

The strategic planning and preparation that takes place during the preapproach can greatly enhance the adaptive selling process. This planning includes a clear understanding of the relationship, product, and customer strategies. This planning and preparation enabled Lana and her sales team to create a presentation strategy that met the relationship and product needs of Ron, one of her largest customers.

The strategic planning that takes place during the preapproach can greatly enhance the adaptive selling process. This plan includes *strategies* that you use to position yourself with the customers and *tactics* you will use when you are face-to-face with a customer. Planning the approach involves consideration of how the *relationship, product,* and *customer strategies* can enhance the sales presentation.

REVIEW THE RELATIONSHIP STRATEGY Salespeople need to think of everything they say or do in the context of their relationship with the customer. Customers want a quality product and a quality relationship. Building and nourishing a long-term partnership with the customer often begins with attention to many small details. Confirming the appointment with a brief e-mail message and arriving for the appointment a few minutes early sends a positive message to the customer before the first face-to-face meeting.

The first contact between a salesperson and a prospect is very important. A positive or negative first impression can be formed in a matter of seconds. The customer is receiving a variety of verbal and nonverbal messages that can either facilitate or distract from the sales call. Your behaviors and appearance create an image that others observe and remember. Identification of the customer's preferred communication style should be given a high priority during the initial contact. Once you are in the presence of the customer, absorb the many clues that will help you with style identification. Then use *style flexing* to accommodate the needs of that person.

REVIEW THE PRODUCT STRATEGY During the preapproach you will learn some new things about the potential customer. You will no doubt acquire information that did not surface during the prospecting stage. If this is the case, it pays to take another look at your product. Now it will be easier to identify features with special appeal to the person you are calling on. In addition, you can more accurately identify questions that the prospect might raise.

Product knowledge, combined with knowledge of the customer, builds confidence. Salespeople who are confident in their ability to alter the sales approach as needed are much better prepared to engage in adaptive selling.[13] Customers today are eager to do business with salespeople who have developed "expert power."

REVIEW THE CUSTOMER STRATEGY Personal selling provides us with the opportunity to apply the marketing concept during every contact with the customer. All energies can be directed toward an individual who is likely to think and act differently from anyone else. Customers today have become increasingly sophisticated in their buying strategies. They have higher expectations for value-added products and long-term commitments. A customer strategy focuses on understanding the customer's needs, wants, and buying conditions. A careful review of information contained in the prospect database is an essential part of reviewing the customer strategy. With this understanding, adaptive selling strategies are formulated to meet both the relationship and product needs of the customer.

No Tech to High Tech

Account planning by the 70 sales representatives at Sebastiani Winery used to be a time-consuming process. Without the aid of modern technology, salespeople were forced to manually analyze two monthly reports that were inches thick. Preparing for a sales call was burdensome. Some salespeople said that they spent almost half their time analyzing reports. A major sales force automation (SFA) initiative was started. The project had these four objectives:

- Improve communication through the use of e-mail, file sharing, and intranet technology.

- Support needed development of multimedia presentations.
- Provide data analysis capabilities.
- Ease the administrative burden.

Each member of the Sebastiani sales force received a laptop loaded with Windows, PowerPoint, e-mail, and Business Objects—the software needed for analyzing data. The new technology was introduced during a three-day training program. Today, salespeople have the ability to do account planning that is much more effective than in the past.[a]

Developing the Six-Step Presentation Plan

Once you have established objectives for the sales presentation, the next step (prescription) involves developing the presentation plan. This plan helps you achieve your objectives.

Today, with increased time constraints, fierce competition, and rising travel costs, the opportunity for a face-to-face meeting with customers may occur less frequently. The few minutes you have with your customers may be your only opportunity to win their business, so careful planning is more critical than ever.

Planning the Presentation

Once you have collected background information, you are ready to develop a "customized" presale presentation plan. Preparing a customized sales presentation can take a great deal of time and energy. Nevertheless, this attention to detail gives you added confidence and helps you avoid delivering unconvincing hit-or-miss sales talks. The plan is developed after a careful study of the **six-step presentation plan** (Figure 3). In most cases, the sales process includes the following activities:

1. *Approach.* Preparation for the approach involves making decisions concerning effective ways to make a favorable first impression during the initial contact, securing the prospect's attention, and developing the prospect's interest in the product. The approach should set the stage for an effective sales presentation.
2. *Need discovery.* The need discovery process is one of the most critical parts of the selling process. If the salesperson is unable to discover the prospect's buying needs and select a product solution that meets those needs, the sale will likely be lost.
3. *Presentation.* Three types of need-satisfaction presentation strategies are available to adapt the sales presentation to the needs of the prospect. After deciding which strategy to use, the salesperson carefully prepares the presentations following the guidelines presented. Selling tools or proof devices are used to demonstrate and document the benefits presented.
4. *Negotiation.* Buyer resistance is a natural part of the selling/buying process. An objection, however, does present a barrier to closing the sale. For this reason, all salespeople should become skillful at negotiating resistance.
5. *Close.* As the sales presentation progresses, there may be several opportunities to confirm and close the sale. Salespeople must learn to spot closing clues.
6. *Servicing the sale.* The importance of developing a long-term value-adding relationship with the prospect has been noted in previous chapters. This rapport is often the outgrowth of postsale service. Learning to service the sale is an important aspect of selling.

The Six-Step Presentation Plan	
Step One: Approach	☐ Review Strategic/Consultative Selling Model ☐ Initiate customer contact
Step Two: Need Discovery	☐ Ask strategic questions ☐ Determine customer needs ☐ Select Product Solution
Step Three: Presentation	☐ Select presentation strategy ☐ Create presentation plan ☐ Initiate presentation
Step Four: Negotiation	☐ Anticipate buyer concerns ☐ Plan negotiating methods ☐ Initiate win-win negotiations
Step Five: Close	☐ Plan appropriate closing methods ☐ Recognize closing clues ☐ Initiate closing methods
Step Six: Servicing the Sale	☐ Follow through ☐ Follow-up calls ☐ Expansion selling

Service, retail, wholesale, and manufacturer selling

FIGURE 3

The Six-Step Presentation Plan

A presale plan is a logical and an orderly outline that features a salesperson's thoughts from one step to the next in the presentation.

Adapting the Presentation Plan to the Customer's Buying Process

A truly valuable idea or concept is timeless. The six parts of the presale presentation plan checklist have been discussed in the sales training literature for many years; therefore, they might be described as fundamentals of personal selling. These steps are basic elements of most sales and frequently occur in the same sequence. However, the activities included in the six-step presentation plan must be selected with care. Prior to developing the sales call plan, the salesperson must answer one very important question: Do these activities relate to the customer's *buying process*? Purchasing structures and buying procedures can vary greatly from company to company. In some cases, the steps in the buying process have been clearly defined by the organization and this information is available to vendors. Selling steps are of little value *unless* they are firmly rooted in your customer's buying process.[14]

GLOBAL BUSINESS INSIGHT

Doing Business in England

Linda Phillips, codirector of Executive Etiquette Company, says, "First and foremost is the British attention to detail." English businesspeople also tend to be more formal in terms of dress and person-to-person communication. It's helpful to study English business customs before visiting that country.

- Introductions in England tend to be very formal. The British look for whose name is spoken first. If you are calling on a client named Robert Timmons, the introduction of your sales manager would be, "Mr. Timmons, I would like you to meet Raymond Hill, my sales manager." In this case the client's name is first because he is the more important person. Never address someone by his or her first name unless you are invited to do so.

- Making decisions is often a time-consuming process, so don't expect a quick close.

- Do not use aggressive sales techniques, such as the hard sell, and avoid criticism of competing products. Focus on objective facts and evidence during the presentation.

- It would be poor manners to discuss business after the business day in England. This is true even when you have drinks or a meal with a businessperson.[b]

The Approach

After a great deal of preparation, it is time to communicate with the prospect, either by face-to-face contact, by telephone, or some other appropriate method of communication. We refer to the initial contact with the customer as the *approach*. A high-quality and professional approach is a powerful way to add value and differentiate yourself from your competitors.[15] All the effort you have put into developing relationship, product, and customer strategies can now be applied to the presentation strategy. If the approach is effective, you may be given the opportunity to make the sales presentation. If, however, the approach is not effective, the chance to present your sales story may be lost. You can be the best prepared salesperson in the business, but without a good approach there may be little chance for a sale.

The approach has three important objectives. First, you want to build rapport with the prospect. This will be accomplished with your *telephone and/or social contact*. Second, you want to capture the person's full attention with your *business contact*. These first two steps are extremely important in establishing how much *influence* you will have throughout the rest of the sales process. Never begin your sales story if the prospect seems preoccupied and is not paying attention. Third, you want to *transition to the next stage of the sales process*. In the early part of the sales process this will likely be the need discovery; in mult-call presentations it may be one of the other stages in the sales process such as the presentation, negotiaitions, or closing the sale. In some selling situations the first contact with the customer is a telephone call. The call is made to schedule a meeting or in some cases conduct the sales presentation. The face-to-face sales call starts with the social contact and is followed by the business contact. The telephone contact, social contact, and business contact are discussed in this section.

ESTABLISH YOUR CREDIBILITY EARLY During your approach, everything you do affects the amount of credibility and influence you will have throughout the sales process. Your actions will either increase your perceived value or detract from it.[16] Thomas A. Freese (www.qbsresearch.com/), author of *Secrets of Question-Based Selling*, says credibility is critical to your success in sales. Credibility is an impression that people often form about you very early in the sales process.[17] Sometimes little things can erode your credibility and influence before you have a chance to prove yourself. Strategic communications consultant and executive coach Mark Jeffries (www.markjeffries.com) in a new training video on *"The Art of Networking"* provides examples regarding how misspelled words or grammatical errors in an e-mail, arriving late for an appointment, answering a cell phone or reading an e-mail while with a customer, failing to maintain good eye contact, acknowledging only certain members of a buying group, or failing to send the prospect information that was promised can quickly weaken the amount of influence you have in a relationship. Failure to be well prepared for the sales call will also undermine your credibility. Credibility and influence grows when the customer realizes you are a competent sales representative who can add value throughout the sales process.

The Telephone Contact

A telephone call provides a quick and inexpensive method of scheduling an appointment. Appointments are important because many busy prospects may not meet with a salesperson who drops in unannounced. When you schedule an appointment, the prospect knows about the sales call in advance and can, therefore, make the necessary advance preparation.

Some salespeople use the telephone exclusively to establish and maintain contact with the customer. Inside salespeople rely almost totally on the telephone for sales. **Telesales**, not to be confused with telemarketing, include many of the same elements as traditional sales: gathering customer information, determining needs, prescribing solutions, negotiating objections, and closing sales. Telesales usually are not scripted, a practice widely used in telemarketing. In some situations, telesales are as dynamic and unpredictable as a face-to-face sales call.

Recall that some factors influence the meaning we attach to an oral message from another person. With the aid of this information, we can see that communication via telephone is challenging. The person who receives the call cannot see our facial expressions, gestures, or posture, and, therefore, must rely totally on the sound of our voice and the words used. The telephone caller has a definite handicap.

The Definitive Authority on Solution Selling

KEEPING THE FUNNEL FULL

Don Thomson

"Excellent coverage of the selling process. A must read for your sales library." **Mike Leavell, Vice President (retired) Hewlett Packard Company**

In *Keeping the Funnel Full*, author and award-winning Hewlett-Packard salesperson Don Thomson notes that "every prospect has a preferred method of communication." He states it is important to discover whether that contact method is by telephone, in person, or by e-mail. As one of HP's top-ranked sales pros, Don trailblazed new markets in the Pacific Northwest (awarded MVP for U.S. Western Sales Region), Western Canada (twice awarded HP Canada's Salesperson of the Year), and the Far East (doubled sales in nine countries in one year).

Source: Book cover from *Keeping the Funnel Full* by Don Thomson, Mardon Publishing Inc, French Creek, British Columbia.

The telephone has some additional limitations. A salesperson accustomed to meeting prospects in person may find telephone contact impersonal. Some salespeople try to avoid using the telephone because they believe it is too easy for the prospect to say no. It should be noted that these drawbacks are more imagined than real. With proper training, a salesperson can use the telephone effectively to schedule appointments. When you make an appointment by telephone, use the following practices:

Plan in advance what you will say. It helps to use a written presentation plan as a guide during the first few seconds of the conversation. What you say is determined by the objectives of the sales call. Have a calendar available to suggest and confirm a date, time, and place for the appointment. Be sure to write it down.

Capturing the customer's full attention is a major objective of the approach. Attention has become a very scarce resource in today's fast-paced world.

Source: EdBockStock/Shutterstock

Politely identify yourself and the company you represent. Set yourself apart from other callers by using a friendly tone and impeccable phone manners. This approach helps you avoid being shut out by a wary gatekeeper (secretary or receptionist).

State the purpose of your call and explain how the prospect can benefit from a meeting. In some cases it is helpful to use a powerful benefits statement that gets the prospect's attention and whets the person's appetite for more information. Present only enough information to stimulate interest.

Show respect for the prospect's time by telling the person how much time the appointment may take. Once the prospect agrees to meet with you, say, "Do you have your appointment calendar handy?" Be prepared to suggest a specific time: "Is Monday at 9:00 A.M. okay?"

Confirm the appointment with a brief note, e-mail message, or letter with the date, time, and place of your appointment. Enclose your business card and any printed information that can be of interest to the prospect.[18]

You should anticipate resistance from some prospects. After all, most decision makers are very busy. Be persistent and persuasive if you genuinely believe a meeting with the prospect can be mutually beneficial.

EFFECTIVE USE OF VOICE MAIL The growing popularity of voice mail presents a challenge to salespeople. What type of message sets the stage for a second call or stimulates a return call? It's important to anticipate voice mail and know exactly what to say if you reach a recording. The prospect's perception of you is based on what you say and voice quality. The following message almost guarantees that you will be ignored:

Ms. Simpson, I am Paul Watson and I am with Elliott Property Management Services. I would like to visit with you about our services. Please call me at 555-1500.[19]

Note that this message provides no compelling reason for the prospect to call back. It offers no valid item that would stimulate interest. The voice mail message should be similar to the opening statement you would make if you had a face-to-face contact with the prospect:

Miss Simpson, my name is Paul Watson and I represent Elliott Property Management Services. We specialize in working with property managers. We can help you reduce the paperwork associated with maintenance jobs and provide an easy way to track the progress of each job. I would like the opportunity to visit with you and will call back in the morning.[20]

Note that this message is brief and describes benefits that customers can receive. If Paul Watson wants a call back, then he needs to give the best time to reach him. He should give his phone number slowly and completely. It's usually best to repeat the number. If you are acting on a referral, be sure to say who referred you and why.

EFFECTIVE USE OF E-MAIL Many prospects and established customers like the convenience of e-mail correspondence and prefer it as an alternative to telephone contact. Your challenge is to make it easy for your correspondents to read and handle your e-mail. Always use a meaningful, specific subject line. People who receive large amounts of e-mail may selectively choose which ones to read by scanning the subject lines and deleting those of no interest. An e-mail with a subject line titled "Action Steps from Our 9/28 Meeting" is more likely to be read than a subject line like "Meeting Notes."[21]

The e-mail message should tell the reader what you want and then encourage a response. Identify the main point of your e-mail within the first or second paragraphs. Format the e-mail so it's easy to read. This may require the use of headings (with capitals or boldface print) to identify the main elements of the memo. Proofread all e-mails for proper grammar, punctuation, and spelling.[22] Always use the grammar and spell-check tools. Messages that contain errors may misrepresent your competence. Finally, use a signature file—a small block of text that automatically follows each e-mail you send. A typical signature file includes full name, title, affiliation, phone number, and in some cases a slogan.

During the telephone contact, CRM contact screens and note windows can be important sources of information for making effective value-added calls. The calendar function is being used by this salesperson to schedule and confirm the date, time, and place for the sales call.

Source: Supri Suharjoto/Shutterstock

The Social Contact—Building Rapport

According to many image consultants, "First impressions are lasting impressions." This statement is essentially true, and some profitable business relationships never crystallize because some trait or characteristic of the salesperson repels the prospective customer. Sales personnel have only a few minutes to create a positive first impression. Susan Bixler, author of *The New Professional Image*, describes the importance of the first impression this way:

> *Books are judged by their covers, houses are appraised by their curb appeal, and people are initially evaluated on how they choose to dress and behave. In a perfect world this is not fair, moral, or just. What's inside should count a great deal more. And eventually it usually does, but not right away. In the meantime, a lot of opportunities can be lost.*[23]

Building rapport should lead to credibility, which leads to trust. Once trust is established, the customer is likely to open up and share information. This information will provide clues regarding ways to create value.

The brief, general conversation that often occurs during the social contact should hold the prospect's attention and establish a relaxed and friendly atmosphere for the business contact that is to follow. There are three areas of conversation that should be considered in developing a social contact:

CUSTOMER RELATIONSHIP MANAGEMENT WITH TECHNOLOGY

Planning Personal Visits

Personally visiting prospects and customers helps build strong relationships, yet traveling is expensive and time-consuming. A salesperson is challenged to plan visits that optimize the investment represented by each trip. Access to customer relationship management (CRM) contact records helps salespeople quickly identify all the accounts in a given geographic area that can be visited during one trip.

CRM empowers salespeople to rapidly review and compare an area's contacts on the basis of their stage in the sales process, the potential size of the account or purchase, the likelihood of a sale, and the contribution the visit could make to information gathering and relationship building. A well-managed CRM database provides salespeople with appropriate business and social topics to discuss when calling selected prospects for an appointment. The CRM Application Exercise "Planning Personal Visits" describes how to find accounts within a city.

The goal of good social contact is to build rapport. Building rapport leads to credibility, which leads to trust. Once trust is established, the customer is likely to open up and share information.

Source: StockLite/Shutterstock

Comments on here-and-now observations. These comments may include general observations about an article in the *Wall Street Journal*, the victory of a local athletic team, or specific comments about awards on display in the prospect's office. Janis Taylor, sales representative with Trugreen Chemlawn, likes to start each new appointment by seeking "common ground" with her prospects. She looks for such items as a picture of the prospect's children or a trophy.[24]

Compliments. Most customers react positively to sincere compliments. Personal items in the prospect's office, achievements, or efficient operation of the prospect's business provide examples of what can be praised. A salesperson might say, "I learned recently that your company is ranked number one in customer satisfaction by J.D. Power and Associates."

Search for mutual acquaintances or interests. The discovering of mutual friends or interests can serve as the foundation for a strong social contact. Most people enjoy talking about themselves, their hobbies, and their achievements. Debra Fine, author of *The Fine Art of Small Talk*, says, "Small talk isn't stupid. It's the appetizer for all relationships."[25]

GUIDELINES FOR GOOD SOCIAL CONTACT The social contact should be viewed as rapport-building communication on a personal basis. This brief conversation establishes the foundation for the business contact, so it should never be viewed as an insignificant part of the presentation strategy. The following guidelines can help you develop the skills needed to make a good social contact.

1. *Prepare for the social contact.* Conduct a background check on topics of interest to the person you are contacting. This includes reviewing information in the prospect database, reading industry reports, and searching the Internet. Once you arrive at the customer's office, you will discover additional information about the person's interests. Most people communicate what is important to them in the way they personalize their work environment.

2. *Initiate social contact.* The most effective opening comments should be expressed in the form of an open-ended question, such as, "I understand you have just been elected president of the United Way?" You can improve the possibility of a good response to your verbal question by applying nonverbal communication skills. Appropriate eye contact, voice inflections that communicate enthusiasm, and a warm smile will increase the customer's receptivity to your opening comments.

3. *Respond to the customer's conversations.* When the customer responds, it is imperative that you acknowledge the message both verbally and nonverbally. The verbal response might be "That is really interesting" or any other appropriate comment. Nonverbally you let the customer know you are listening by taking notes, maintaining good eye contact, and occasionally nodding of your head. These gestures communicate you want her to continue talking.

4. *Keep the social contact focused on the customer.* Because you cannot control where a conversation might go, you may be tempted to focus the conversation on topics with which you are familiar. A response such as, "Several years ago I was in charge of our company's United Way campaign and we had a difficult time meeting our goal," shifts the focus of the conversation back to you. While an occasional short personal reference may be appropriate, it is best to keep the conversation focused on topics that are of interest to the customer. Dale Carnegie said that one of the best ways to build a relationship is to encourage others to talk about themselves.

Communication on a personal basis is often the first step in discovering a common language that can improve communication between the salesperson and the prospect. How much time should be devoted to the social contact? There is no easy answer to this question. The length of the conversation depends on the type of product or service sold, how busy the prospect appears to be, and your awareness of topics of mutual interest.

In many cases the rapport-building conversation will take place over lunch or dinner. Some sales professionals contend that social conversation should occur before the meal is served, reserving business conversation until later. In some cases it may be during a sporting event, such as a golf outing. It may also occur during a social event, such as a Broadway play that is offered in appreciation of prior or future business. Many successful sales have been closed during or after a social event. This explains why some companies enroll their sales staff and other customer contact personnel in dining etiquette classes.

The Business Contact

Converting the prospect's attention from the social contact to the business proposal is an important part of the approach. When you convert and hold your prospect's attention, you have fulfilled an important step in the selling process. Furthermore, without this step the door has been closed on completing the remaining steps of the sale.

Some salespeople use a carefully planned opening statement or a question to convert the customer's attention to the sales presentation. A statement or question that focuses on the prospect's dominant buying motive is, of course, more likely to achieve the desired results. Buyers must like what they see and hear and must be made to feel that it is worthwhile to hear more.

Converting the Prospect's Attention and Arousing Interest

Throughout the years, salespeople have identified and used a number of effective methods to capture the prospect's attention, arouse interest, and transition into the next step of the presentation. Seven of the most common are explained in the following material:

Agenda approach

Product demonstration approach

Referral approach

Customer benefit approach

Question approach

Survey approach

Premium approach

We also discuss combining two or more of these approaches.

Agenda Approach

One of the most effective methods to transition from the social contact to the business contact is to thank the customer for taking time to meet with you and then review the call objectives you have prepared for the meeting. You might say, "Thank you for meeting with me this morning. I would like to accomplish three things during the time you have given me." This statement shows you value the person's time and you have preplanned a specific agenda. Always be open to changing the agenda based on input from the customer.[26] This approach is welcomed by buyers in multi-call situations.

Product Demonstration Approach

This straightforward method of getting the prospect's attention can be achieved by showing the actual product, a sample, a mock-up, a video, or a well-prepared brochure either in print form or on a computer screen. It is a popular approach used by sales representatives who sell convention services, technical products, pharmaceuticals, photographic equipment, automobiles, construction equipment, office furniture, and many other products. In many multi-call situations, salespeople leave samples for the customer to examine and try out at a later date. Trish Ormsby, a sales representative for Wells Fargo Alarm Services, uses her portable computer to create a visual image of security systems that meet the customer's security needs.[27]

Referral Approach

Research indicates that another person is far more impressed with your good points if these points are presented by a third party rather than by you. The referral approach is quite effective because a third party (a satisfied customer) believes the prospect can benefit from your product. This type of opening statement has universal appeal among salespeople from nearly every field.

When you use the referral approach, your opening statement should include a direct reference to the third party. Here is an example: "Mrs. Follett, my name is Kurt Wheeler, and I represent the Cross Printing Company. We specialize in printing all types of business forms. Mr. Ameno—buyer for Raybale Products, Incorporated—is a regular customer of ours, and he suggested I mention his name to you."

Customer Benefit Approach

One of the most effective ways to gain a prospect's attention is to immediately point out benefits of purchasing your solution or value proposition. The benefit could focus on either the product, company, or salesperson. Begin with the most important issue (or problem) facing the client. When using this approach, the most important buyer's benefit is included in the initial statement. For example, the salesperson selling a portable Sony projector might open with this product benefit statement:

The Sony VPL-CS4 lightweight projector strikes a balance between cost, size, brightness, and convenience. It's a good choice for a quick business trip or for a work-at-home presentation.

Turn up the volume.

Cook's hard-working national consumer campaign will definitely drive up the volume moving through your meat case. Our significant TV presence is a big part of that effort.

Add to that, Cook's print advertising, which will reach your customers through a nonstop media schedule and couponing effort that includes leading national women's magazines, such as *Good Housekeeping, Woman's Day, Family Circle, Rosie* and many more. Plus, our public relations efforts targeting national and

local media, and an aggressive Web presence, will maximize the power of our campaign.

And Cook's offers a proven point-of-sale merchandising program tailored to the needs of your store. Of course, as always, our personalized service assures that your orders arrive when you want, the way you want.

We're turning up the volume to your customers. Stay tuned for more year-round exciting action.

© 2001 ConAgra Foods, Inc.

Cook's ham. Always good to the bone.®

A ConAgra Foods product

A straightforward product demonstration method for getting the grocery store meat manager's attention would be the use of this ad from Cook's, a division of ConAgra. The salesperson can explain the value of featuring meat products that are supported by a strong media promotion and point-of-sale merchandising program.

Source: Courtesy of ConAgra Foods, Inc.

A company benefit example taken from the financial services field is:

> *When you meet with a Charles Schwab investment specialist, you can obtain advice on over 1,200 no-load, no-transaction-fee mutual funds.*

The customer benefit approach is also used with what is sometimes referred to as the *elevator speech*. The **elevator speech** focuses on the benefit of working with the salesperson and is used to open the door and establish credibility to meet a need. It is about offering to take excellent care of the prospect. The elevator speech should be short, prepared well in advance, and extensively rehearsed before it is used. It is used most appropriately in the initial call on a prospect where the prequalifying research indicates the buyer is more interested in the benefits of working with a highly qualified salesperson than finding a new product solution or supplier. Here is an employment services example of a salesperson benefit statement using the elevator speech approach:

> *Hello, I'm Chad Leffler. I partner with companies like yours that need to find talented people to help their business grow and become more profitable.*

As noted, the key to achieving success with the customer benefit approach is advance preparation. Customers are annoyed when a salesperson cannot quickly communicate the benefits of meeting with them. Bruce Klassen, sales manager for Do All Industrial Supply, says, "Our salespeople begin the sales process by researching the prospect and the company. We need to be sure that our sales calls are going to benefit that prospect before we make even an initial sales approach."[28]

Question Approach

The question approach has two positive features. First, an appropriate question almost always triggers prospect involvement. Very few people avoid answering a direct question. Second, a question gets the prospect thinking about a problem that the salesperson may be prepared to solve.

Molly Hoover, a sales training consultant, conducts training classes for sales managers and car dealers who want to better understand the subtleties of selling to the new woman car buyers. She suggests an approach that includes a few basic questions such as:

> "Is the vehicle for business or pleasure?"
>
> "Will you be buying within the next week or so?"[29]

These opening questions are not difficult to answer, yet they get the customer mentally involved. Some of the best opening questions are carefully phrased to arouse attention. The authors of *The Sales Question Book* offer some good examples:

> "Are you aware that we just added three new services to our payroll and accounting package? Could I tell you about them?"
>
> "We are now offering all our customers a special auditing service that used to be reserved for our largest accounts. Would you be interested in hearing about it?"[30]

Once you ask the question, listen carefully to the response. If the answer is yes, proceed with an enthusiastic presentation of your product. If the answer is no, then you may have to gracefully try another approach or thank the prospect for his time and depart. The use of questions will be discussed in detail in the next chapter and will provide information on the specific types of questions to use to approach your customer.

Survey Approach

Robert Hewitt, a Monterey, California, financial planner, has new clients fill out a detailed questionnaire before the first appointment. This procedure is part of his customer strategy. He studies the completed questionnaire and other documents before making any effort to find a solution to any of the customer's financial planning needs. The survey or needs discovery, as it is also called, is an important part of the problem-solving philosophy of selling. It often is used in selling products where the need cannot be established without careful study.

The survey approach offers many advantages. It is generally a nonthreatening way to open a sales call. You simply are asking permission to acquire information that can be used to determine the buyer's need for your product. Because the survey is tailor-made for a specific business, the buyer is given individual treatment. Finally, the survey approach helps avoid an early discussion of price. Price cannot be discussed until the survey is completed.

The survey approach offers many advantages. It is generally a nonthreatening way to open a sales call. You simply ask permission to acquire information that can be used to determine the buyer's need for the product.

Source: carlosseller/Shutterstock

Premium Approach

The premium approach involves giving the customer a free sample or an inexpensive item. A financial services representative might give the customer a booklet that can be used to record expenses. Sales representatives for a large U.S. textbook publisher give faculty members a monthly planner. Product samples are frequently used by persons who sell cosmetics. Creative use of premiums is an effective way to get the customer's attention.

The agenda, product, referral, customer benefit, question, survey, and premium approaches offer the salesperson a variety of ways to set the stage for the presentation strategy. With experience, salespeople learn to select the most effective approach for each selling situation. Table 1 provides examples of how these approaches can be applied in real-world situations.

Combination Approaches

A hallmark of adaptive selling is flexibility. Therefore, a combination of approaches sometimes provides the best avenue to need identification. Sales personnel who have adopted the consultative style, of course, use the question and survey approaches most frequently. Some selling situations, however, require that one of the other approaches be used, either alone or in combination with the question and survey approaches (Figure 4). An example of how a salesperson might use a referral and question approach combination follows:

> *Salesperson:* Carl Hamilton at Simmons Modern Furniture suggested that I visit with you about our new line of compact furniture designed for smaller homes. He believes this line might complement the furniture you currently feature.
>
> *Customer:* Yes, Carl called me yesterday and mentioned your name and company.
>
> *Salesperson:* Before showing you our product lines, I would like to ask you some questions about your current product mix. First, what do you currently carry in the area of bedroom furniture?

Coping with Sales Call Reluctance

The transition from the preapproach to the approach is sometimes blocked by sales call reluctance. Fear of making the initial contact with the prospect is one of the biggest obstacles to sales

TABLE 1 Business Contact Worksheet

This illustrates how to prepare effective real-world approaches that capture the customer's attention.

METHOD OF APPROACH	WHAT WILL YOU SAY?
1. Agenda	1. (Office supply) "Thank you for meeting with me. During the next 45 minutes, I plan to accomplish three things."
2. Product	2a. (Retail clothing) "We have just received a shipment of new fall sweaters from Braemar International."
	2b. (Business forms manufacturer) "Our plant has just purchased a $300,000 Harris Graphics composer, Mr. Reichart; I would like to show you a copy of your sales invoice with your logo printed on it."
3. Customer benefit	3. (Real estate) "Mr. and Mrs. Stuart, my company lists and sells more homes than any other company in the area where your home is located. Our past performance would lead me to believe we can sell your home within two weeks."
4. Referral	4. (Food wholesaler) "Paula Doeman, procurement manager for Mercy Medical Center, suggested that I provide you with information about our computerized 'Order It' system."
5. Question	5. (Hotel convention services) "Mrs. McClaughin, will your Annual Franchisee Meeting be held in April?"
6. Survey	6a. (Custom-designed computer software) "Mr. Vasquez, I would like the opportunity to learn about your accounts receivable and accounts payable procedures. We may be able to develop a customized program that will significantly improve your cash flow."
	6b. (Retail menswear) "May I ask you a few questions about your wardrobe? The information will help me better understand your clothing needs."
7. Premium	7. (Financial services) "I would like to give you a publication titled *Guaranteed Growth Annuity*."

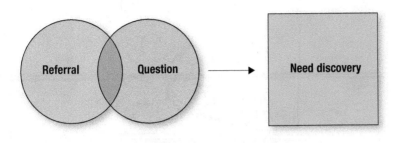

FIGURE 4

Combination approaches provide a smooth transition to the need discovery part of the consultative presentation.

success. For new salespeople, the problem can be career threatening. **Sales call reluctance** includes the thoughts, feelings, and behavioral patterns that conspire to limit what a salesperson is able to accomplish. It is an internal, often emotional, barrier to sales success. Sales call reluctance can be caused by several different thought patterns:[31]

- Fear of taking risks
- Fear of group presentations
- Lack of self-confidence
- Fear of rejection

Regardless of the reasons for sales call reluctance, you can learn to deal with it. These are some suggestions:

- *Be optimistic about the outcome of the initial contact.* It is better to visualize and anticipate success than to anticipate failure. Martin Seligman, professor of psychology at the University of Pennsylvania and author of the best-selling book *Learned Optimism*, says that success in selling requires a healthy dose of optimism.[32] It is important to frequently recommit yourself to the double-win value-adding approach to working with customers discussed earlier. The anticipation of failure is a major barrier to making the initial contact.
- *Practice your approach before making the initial contact.* A well-rehearsed effort to make the initial contact increases your self-confidence and reduces the possibility that you may handle the situation badly.
- *Recognize that it is normal to feel anxious about the initial contact.* Even veteran salespeople experience some degree of sales call reluctance, and this reluctance can surface anywhere in the sales process.
- *Develop a deeper commitment to your goals.* Abraham Zaleznik, professor emeritus at Harvard Business School, says, "If your commitment is only in your mind, then you'll lose it when you encounter a big obstacle. If your commitment is in your heart *and* your mind, you'll create the power to break through the toughest obstacles."[33]

Selling to the Gatekeeper

Many decision makers have an assistant or secretary who manages their daily schedule. This person is often referred to as the "gatekeeper." If you want to reach the decision maker, work hard to align yourself with the person who schedules this person's appointments. Rule number one is to treat the gatekeeper with respect. Learn their name and what they do. Keep in mind this person can be an important source of information. For example, the gatekeeper can tell you how the buying process works and provide information regarding new developments in the company. This person may be able to help you make a preliminary qualification before you reach the decision maker. When you treat the person as an expert by soliciting their views, you establish a relationship that can pay big dividends today and in the future.[34]

When possible, use personal referrals from someone the prospect knows. If you have met the prospect previously, describe the meeting and tell the gatekeeper why you feel a second meeting would be beneficial.

In some cases, a secretary, assistant, or receptionist may screen incoming telephone calls. Be prepared to convince this person that your call is important. Always treat the gatekeeper with respect and courtesy.

Source: Wall Street Journal, March 10, 1999, p. A23. Reprinted by permission of Mark Litzler.

"I don't think of myself as the Jenkins Doolittle & Bloom gatekeeper. I rather prefer lead blocker."

CHAPTER LEARNING ACTIVITIES

Reviewing Key Concepts

Describe the three prescriptions that are included in the presentation strategy

Developing a presentation strategy involves preparing presale objectives, developing a presale presentation plan, and providing outstanding customer service. The presentation strategy combines elements of the relationship, product, and customer strategies.

Discuss the two-part preapproach process

Preparation for the sales presentation is a two-part process. Part one is referred to as the *preapproach* and involves preparing presale objectives and developing a presale presentation plan. It's best to develop presentation objectives for each stage of the buying process. Part two is called the *approach* and involves making a good first impression, securing the prospect's attention, and transitioning to need identification.

Describe team presentation strategies

In recent years, team selling has surfaced as a major development. Sales teams can often uncover problems, solutions, and sales opportunities that no individual salesperson could discover working alone. Team sales presentations require a more detailed precall plan than individual sales calls. Without careful planning and extensive practice (rehearsal), team presentations are likely to be delivered in a disorganized manner.

Explain how adaptive selling builds on four broad strategic areas of personal selling

Adaptive selling involves altering sales behaviors in order to improve communication with the customer. Salespeople today are challenged to develop a broader repertoire of selling strategies. Salespeople skilled in adaptive selling consider how the relationship, product, and customer strategies can enhance the sales presentation.

Describe the six main parts of the presentation plan

After collecting background information, salespeople need to create a customized presale presentation plan. The plan is developed after careful study of the six-step presentation plan, which includes approach, need discovery, presentation, negotiation, close, and servicing the sale.

Explain how to effectively approach the customer

The approach may involve face-to-face contact, telephone contact, or some other appropriate method of communication. If the approach is effective, the salesperson will be given an opportunity to make the sales presentation. A major goal of the *social contact* is to make a good first impression, build rapport, and establish credibility. The *business contact* involves converting the prospect's attention from the social contact to the sales presentation.

Describe seven ways to convert the prospect's attention and arouse interest

Over the years, salespeople have identified several ways to convert the prospect's attention and arouse interest in the presentation. Some of the most common ways include the agenda approach, product demonstration approach, referral approach, customer benefit approach, question approach, survey approach, and premium approach.

Key Terms

Presentation strategy	Action objective	Elevator speech
Preapproach	Six-step presentation plan	Sales call reluctance
Approach	Telesales	

Review Questions

1. What is the purpose of the preapproach? What are the two prescriptions included in the preapproach?
2. Explain the role of objectives in developing the presale presentation plan.
3. Why should salespeople establish multiple-objective sales presentations? List four possible objectives that would be appropriate for stage one and stage two of the buying process.
4. Compare and contrast team sales presentations and individual sales calls.
5. Describe the major steps in the presentation plan. Briefly discuss the role of adaptive selling in implementing the presentation plan.
6. What are the major objectives of the approach?
7. Briefly describe the four guidelines that can help you make a good social contact.
8. What are some rules to follow when leaving a message on voice mail? On e-mail?
9. What methods can the salesperson use to convert the prospect's attention to the sales presentation?
10. Discuss why combination approaches are considered an important consultative selling practice. Provide one example of a combination approach.

Application Exercises

1. Assume that you are a salesperson who calls on retailers. For some time you have been attempting to get an appointment with one of the best retailers in the city to carry your line. You have an appointment to see the head buyer in one and one-half hours. You are sitting in your office. It will take you about 30 minutes to drive to your appointment. Outline what you should be doing between now and the time you leave to meet your prospect.
2. Tom Nelson has just graduated from Aspen College with a major in marketing. He has three years of experience in the retail grocery business and has decided he would like to go to work as a salesperson for the district office of Procter & Gamble. Tom has decided to telephone and set up an appointment for an interview. Write out exactly what Tom should *plan* to say during his telephone call.
3. Concepts from Dale Carnegie's *How to Win Friends and Influence People* can help you prepare for the social contact. Access the Dale Carnegie Training home page (www.dalecarnegie.com) and examine the courses offered. Search for the sales advantage course. Read the course description and review the two main things you will learn in this program. View the online sales action plan demo video to learn how Dale Carnegie's Web-based coaching program enhances what is learned in the course.

Role-Play Exercise

Research the type of computer that you would like to purchase in the future or one that you have just purchased. Strategically prepare to meet a potential customer who has been referred to you by a friend and who would like to purchase a similar computer. Using Table 1, prepare four different business contact statements or questions you could use to approach your prospect. Review the material in this chapter and then pair off with another student who will assume the role of your customer. First, role-play the telephone contact and set up an appointment to get your customer into your store to meet with you and look at the computer. Second, role-play the approach you will use when the customer actually comes into the store. Review how well you made the approach.

CRM Application Exercise

Planning Personal Visits

CRM software allows trip planners to examine the status of prospects in the geographic area to be visited. Access Salesforce.com and assume you wish to visit contacts in the city of Bedford, Texas. Using Salesforce.com, you can find all of the prospects in Bedford by selecting the Reports tab. Choose the Contact by Location report. Click on the "Edit" link in the Filtered By: field.

Filtered By: Edit

In the Edit Filters section, change the Field to "City" using the drop-down list and similarly change Operator to "equals." Enter the city name, Bedford, in the Value field.

Edit Filters

	Field	Operator	Value
	City ▼	equals ▼	Bedford
AND	--Select Field-- ▼	equals ▼	

Add filter logic
☐ Limit Rows ⓘ

The resulting preview report will list the 3 contacts in Bedford. Click on Run Report.

Save | Save As | Close | ⚙ Report Properties | ▶ Run Report

After arranging to visit a group of people like this, the salesperson may print the information contained in these records in case a paper report is convenient. To print the Bedford list, click on the "Printable View" button, which will download it to your computer in Excel format. Open Excel and the saved file, and then print. You should now have printed information about all customers in Bedford. Today, the Internet provides all details of a planned trip, including transportation, lodging, weather forecast and the street view of your destination.

Run Report ▼ | Hide Details | Customize | Save | Save As | Delete | Printable View | Export Details

Reality Selling Today Video Case Problem

The global construction industry is a lucrative market, with customer needs ranging from measuring products to sophisticated construction solutions. Hilti Corporation, the company featured at the beginning of this chapter, provides its customers around the world with leading-edge construction products and services with outstanding added value. Hilti prides itself for its direct sales model, which allows its salespeople and service teams to work directly *with* and *for* the customers.

Alim Hirani, an account manager for Hilti, adopts the relationship marketing approach in his selling strategy. He often starts his sales calls, which have been carefully preplanned, with icebreakers such as asking about the customer's family rather than making the sales immediately. His sales presentations may take place in the client's office or even at the construction site. Consequently, he must always plan well in advance the best way to make his sales presentations for specific sales calls. At all times he must attempt to establish his own and his company's credibility by demonstrating the premium value that Hilti's products and services can offer his clients. Whenever possible, he tries to get the customer involved in product demonstration because seeing is believing. Once the customers see for themselves the benefits of Hilti's product features, moving the customers from the investigation and evaluation stages to the action stage is just a procedure.

Alim sells not only individually but also as part of a team. For major clients who require a complete package of building/construction, mechanical/electrical, telecom, and interior finishing products and services, Alim works closely with his team members to make sure the information he acquires from the customer during initial contacts is made available to other salespeople and technical personnel of the team. In the construction industry, closing the sale is—most of the time—just the beginning. Well-trained product application specialists join Alim to offer the customers after-sales services, technical support, and training. (See the chapter opener and Reality Selling Today Role-Play 8 in the end-of-chapter appendix for more information.)

Questions

1. Why should Alim Hirani adopt the three prescriptions for the presentation strategy?
2. Salespeople are encouraged to establish multiple-objective sales presentations. What are some objectives Alim Hirani should consider when he calls on construction managers at the construction site?
3. What are some special challenges Alim Hirani faces when he makes his sales presentations in a non-office setting?
4. Put yourself in the position of a construction salesperson. Can you envision a situation when you might combine different ways to convert the prospect's attention and interests into action? Explain.

CRM Case Study

Establishing Your Approach

Becky Kemley, your sales manager at SimNet Systems, has notified Pat Silva's former prospects by letter that you will be calling on them soon. She wants to meet with you tomorrow to discuss your preapproach to your new prospects. Please review the records in the Salesforce.com database.

Questions

1. Becky wants you to call on Robert Kelly. Describe what your call objectives would be with Mr. Kelly.
2. Describe a possible topic of your social contact with Mr. Kelly and how you would convert that to a buying contact.
3. Becky has given you a reprint of a new article about using networks for warehouse applications. Which of your prospects might have a strong interest in this kind of article? How would you use this article to make an approach to that prospect?

Partnership Selling: A Role-Play/Simulation (see Appendix: Partnership Selling)

Developing a Relationship Strategy

Read Employment Memorandum 2, which announces your promotion to account executive. In your new position, you will be assigned by your instructor to one of the two major account categories in the convention center market. You will be assigned to either the *association accounts market* or the *corporate accounts market*. The association accounts market includes customers who have the responsibility for planning meetings for their association or group. The corporate accounts market includes customers who have the responsibility for planning meetings for the company they represent. (You will remain in the account category for the rest of the role-plays.)

Note the challenges you may have in your new position. Each of these challenges is represented in the future sales memoranda you receive from your sales manager.

Read Sales Memorandum 1 for the account category you are assigned. (Note that the "A" means association and your customer is Erin Adkins, and "B" means corporate and your customer is Leigh Combs.) Follow the instructions in the sales memorandum and strategically prepare to approach your new customer. Your call objectives are to establish a relationship (social contact), share an appealing benefit, and find out if your customer is planning any future conventions (business contact).

You may be asked to assume the role of a customer in the account category to which you are not assigned as a salesperson. Your instructor will provide you with detailed instructions for correctly assuming this role.

Appendix: Reality Selling Today Role-Play Scenario
Reality Selling Today Role-Play 8, Hilti Corporation

Alim Hirani
Hilti Corporation

(This mock sales call role-play scenario is created exclusively for use with this chapter.)

Your Role at Hilti Corporation

You will be a sales representative for Hilti (see Web site at www.hilti.com), working out of the same office as Alim Hirani, featured in the chapter Reality *Selling Today* Video. The company provides the global construction industry with innovative products and services. In addition to a wide variety of high-end products such as measuring systems, drilling and demolition, installation systems, foam systems, and screw fastening systems, the company also offers its customers customized training programs and consulting services. Hilti sales representatives work directly with customers rather than through intermediary parties. (Refer to the chapter opening vignette and case problem, and review the Reality *Selling Today* Video for more information.)

Your Customer: Ellis Exhibition Inc.

You will meet with Casey Smith, procurement manager for Ellis Exhibition Inc. The company owns a 100,000-square-foot exhibition center that hosts several local and regional events in Atlanta, Georgia. Some of these events have become a must-see for the local business community. Depending on the theme and the products being showcased, Ellis Exhibition offers exhibitors outstanding display services that include floor plans, display solutions, display installation, and booth dismantlement. After an event, the installation systems are reused, while installation accessories are generally discarded. Casey Smith believes that by buying the right type of installation accessories, Ellis can save a lot of money, and therefore offer their exhibitor customers more competitive prices.

Quick Facts About the Ellis Exhibition Inc.'s Needs

- Ellis Exhibition Inc. spends about $500,000 a year on installation accessories. These accessories are galvanized, but they can also be painted to match the color theme stipulated by exhibitors.
- Ellis uses a wide variety of installation accessories, from hexagon nuts and head screws to distance holders.
- Ellis does not want to stock these accessories. Exhibitors who want to use Ellis display services are required to place their order 3 months in advance. Then, an Ellis accountant will calculate the necessary accessories needed for each event.
- Ellis is extremely concerned with the quality of all of its installation systems and accessories.

Your Call Objectives

In your meeting with Casey Smith, you hope to identify the specific types and the expected quantity of installation accessories. You also want to know about delivery requirements. In addition, you might be able to cross-sell other Hilti products and services, such as sprinkler systems.

Endnotes

1. Malcolm Fleschner, "Too Busy to Buy," *Selling Power*, March 1999, p. 36.
2. Gina Rollins, "Prepped to Sell," *Selling Power*, September 2006, pp. 74–77.
3. Bradford Agry, "Every Client Meeting Provides a Dynamic New Opportunity," *Selling*, April 2002, pp. 1, 4.
4. Malcolm Fleschner, "Anatomy of a Sale," *Selling Power*, April 1998, p. 76; Gina Rollins, "Prepare for the Unknown," *Selling Power*, July/August 2003, pp. 26–30.
5. Tom Reilly, "Prepare Like a Pro," www.TomReillyTraining.com (accessed April 8, 2007).
6. "Set the Agenda," *Personal Selling Power*, May/June 1995, p. 79.
7. Donna Fenn, "Because His Family Business Makes an Art of Customer Service," *Inc.*, April 2005, p. 94; telephone interview with Pamela Miles, staff member at Mitchells/Richards, March 22, 2005.
8. Philip Kotler and Gary Armstrong, *Principles of Marketing*, 10th ed. (Upper Saddle River, NJ: Prentice Hall, 2004), p. 531.
9. Rick Page, *Hope Is Not a Strategy* (Atlanta, GA: Nautilus Press, 2002), p. 25.
10. Betsy Cummings, "Group Dynamics," *Sales & Marketing Management*, January/February 2007, p. 8.
11. James F. O'Hara, "Successful Selling to Buying Committees," *Selling*, February 1998, p. 8.
12. George R. Franke and Jeong-Eun Park, "Salesperson Adaptive Selling Behavior and Customer Orientation: A Meta-Analysis," *Journal of Marketing Research*, November 2006, pp. 693–702; Leroy Robinson, Jr., Greg W. Marshall, William C. Moncrief, and Felicia G. Lassak, "Toward a Shortened Measure of Adaptive Selling," *Journal of Personal Selling and Sales Management*, Spring 2002, pp. 111–119.
13. The role of confidence in adaptive selling is discussed in Leroy Robinson, Jr., Greg W. Marshall, William C. Moncrief, and Felicia G. Lassak, "Toward a Shortened Measure of Adaptive Selling," *Journal of Personal Selling and Sales Management*, Spring 2002, pp. 111–119.
14. Neil Rackham and John R. Vincentis, *Rethinking the Sales Force* (New York: McGraw-Hill, 1999), p. 217.
15. Graham Roberts-Phelps, "How to Add Value to Every Sales Call," *Selling Power*, March–April 2010, p. 19.
16. Ibid.
17. Thomas A. Freese, *Secrets of Question-Based Selling* (Naperville, IL: Sourcebooks, Inc., 2003), p. 114.
18. Based on John Fellows, "Your Foot in the Door," *Selling Power*, March 1996, pp. 64–65.
19. Adapted from Art Sobczak, "Please, Call Me Back!" *Selling*, March 1999, p. 12.
20. Ibid.
21. Deborah Dumaine, "Managing Customers with E-Mail," *Selling Power*, March 2004, p. 94.
22. Rachel Zupek, "Reply All and Other E-Mail Gaffes," *Business.com*, September 2007, p. 26.
23. Susan Bixler and Nancy Nix-Rice, *The New Professional Image* (Holbrook, MA: Adams Media Corporation, 1997), p. 3.
24. Steve Atlas, "How to Cultivate New Turf," *Selling Power*, January/February 2003, p. 26.
25. Maxine Clayton, "60 Seconds on Small Talk," *Fast Company*, November 2004, p. 43.
26. Dean A. Goettsch, "Make Your First Meeting Count," *Selling*, July 2004, pp. 1, 4.
27. Melissa Campanelli, "Sound the Alarm," *Sales & Marketing Management*, December 1994, pp. 20–25.
28. Carolee Boyles, "Prewarm Cold Calls," *Selling Power*, July/August 2001, p. 30.
29. Abner Littel, "Selling to Women Revs Up Car Sales," *Personal Selling Power*, July–August 1990, p. 50.
30. "Six Great Upselling Questions," *Personal Selling Power*, April 1993, p. 44.

31. Theodore Kinni, "How to Identify and Remove the Problems Underlying Call Reluctance," *Selling Power*, November/December 2004, pp. 69–71; "Types of Call Reluctance," *Value-Added Selling* 21, February 14, 2005, p. 4.

32. Alan Farnham, "Are You Smart Enough to Keep Your Job?" *Fortune*, January 15, 1996, pp. 34–42.

33. "The Disappointment Trap," *Selling Power*, January/February 1999, p. 14.

34. Roy Chitwood, "Still Trying to Slip Past Gatekeepers? Forget It." *Value-Added Selling* 21, December 16, 2003, pp. 1–2.

Endnotes for Boxed Features

a. Based on Jay Winchester, "Ripe for Change," *Sales & Marketing Management*, August 1998, p. 81.

b. "International Snapshot," *Sales & Marketing Management*, February 2001, p. 92; Jan Yager, *Business Protocol*, 2nd ed. (Stamford, CT: Hannacroix Books, Inc., 2001), pp. 114–115.

c. Byran Ziegler, "Your Business Card Can Be a Powerful Tool," *The Des Moines Register*, August 2, 1999, p. 17-B; Kemba J. Dunham, "Here's My Card," *Wall Street Journal*, May 14, 2002, p. B12.

Chapter 6

Chapter 6

Determining Customer Needs with a Consultative Questioning Strategy

Chapter Preview

When you finish reading this chapter, you should be able to

1 Outline the benefits of the consultative sales process

2 Describe the four parts of the need-satisfaction model

3 Discuss the use of questions to discover customer needs

4 Describe the importance of active listening and the use of confirmation questions

5 Select solutions that match customer needs

▶ Adaptive Selling Today Training Video Series

The effective use of questions is the starting point of the consultative sales process. Questions are used to build adaptive-style selling relationships, discover customer needs, and adapt and present product solutions that meet those needs. Questions span the entire sales process and are also used to successfully negotiate, close, and service a sale.

"Questions, Questions, Questions," the second video in our Adaptive Selling Today Training Video Series, introduces and shows how to use the four adaptive selling questions described in this chapter. An Internet telephone systems sales representative featured in the video learns one of his largest accounts may be going with another supplier. The salesperson's company brought in a new sales training program on how to use questions effectively, and the salesperson is the first to learn the system. With his newly acquired knowledge and skills, the salesperson schedules another call to see if he can, with the use of questions, reestablish his relationship and salvage the sale.

In this follow-up call, we find out how well he has learned to adapt and use questions to discover and better understand the customer's needs, create value, solve the customer's buying problem, and retain the account. Throughout the three-part video, our salesperson learns about the following four-part multiple questioning strategy and what these questions will reveal during the consultative sales presentation.

Survey Questions	*Reveal*	Problems and situation
Probing Questions	*Reveal*	Pain and implications
Need-Satisfaction Questions	*Reveal*	Pleasure and need satisfaction
Confirmation Questions	*Reveal*	Mutual understanding

The use of an effective questioning strategy, so important to the consultative sales process, is one of the greatest challenges facing salespeople. Need discovery and questioning will be explored in this chapter (Figure 1). ●

From Chapter 11 of *Selling Today: Partnering to Create Value*, 12/e. Gerald L. Manning. Michael Ahearne. Barry L. Reece. Copyright © 2012 by Pearson Education. Published by Prentice Hall. All rights reserved.

Extensive research regarding the use of questions in the sales process reveals the importance of developing and perfecting a multiple questioning strategy to understand and solve customer needs. The Adaptive Questions video dramatically presents how these questions are used in the sales process.

The Six-Step Presentation Plan

Step One:
Approach

- ☑ Review Strategic/Consultative Selling Model
- ☑ Initiate customer contact

Step Two:
Need Discovery

- ☐ Ask strategic questions
- ☐ Determine customer needs
- ☐ Select Product Solution

Step Three:
Presentation

- ☐ Select presentation strategy
- ☐ Create presentation plan
- ☐ Initiate presentation

Step Four:
Negotiation

- ☐ Anticipate buyer concerns
- ☐ Plan negotiating methods
- ☐ Initiate win-win negotiations

Step Five:
Close

- ☐ Plan appropriate closing methods
- ☐ Recognize closing clues
- ☐ Initiate closing methods

Step Six:
Servicing the Sale

- ☐ Follow through
- ☐ Follow-up calls
- ☐ Expansion selling

Service, retail, wholesale, and manufacturer selling

FIGURE 1

Creating the Sales Presentation

The consultative sales process involves adding value by accurately determining the prospect's needs and selecting an appropriate product or service.

The Consultative Sales Process Adds Value

A growing number of salespeople, like the Internet telephone system salesperson pictured above, have adopted the consultative sales process. New competitive structures and customer demands have forced companies to continuously adapt and redefine their value-adding processes.[1] Consultative selling, is a value-adding process. Consultative selling involves meeting customer needs by asking strategic questions, listening to customers, understanding—and caring about—their problems, selecting the appropriate solution, creating the sales presentation, and following through after the sale. Consultative selling is a very customer-centric form of selling that creates value for the customer and, in the process, creates value for the firm.[2] This approach is very different from product-oriented selling. As one author noted, "Product-oriented selling can easily lapse into product evangelism." Product-oriented selling is usually inefficient and ineffective.[3, 4]

New entrants in the field of personal selling sometimes wonder why some people excel in selling products or services, while others, who seem to work just as hard, fall short of meeting company or personal selling goals. The answer can be found by reviewing the behaviors displayed by top sales performers from *Fortune* 500 and smaller entrepreneurial-based companies. High-performance sales personnel have learned how to skillfully diagnose and solve problems better than their competitors.[5] This consultative problem-solving capability translates into the following:

INCREASED CUSTOMER SATISFACTION Customers prefer to purchase solutions that truly meet their needs. The solution that is "just right" for the customer adds value, maximizes satisfaction, and sets the stage for a partnership relationship and repeat business. In some cases the right solution will cost more than the customer planned to pay, but the added value will usually compensate for the higher price.

Jeff Thull, author of *Mastering the Complex Sale* and *The Prime Solution,* states, "In too many buyer–seller relationships, there is a value gap where the customer is not getting the satisfaction they believe was promised."[6] Consultative salespeople with the ability to diagnose and solve customer problems are able to close this value gap.

MORE SALES CLOSED The extra time taken to carefully solve the customer's buying problem will set the stage for closing more sales. A certain amount of buyer resistance surfaces in nearly every selling situation. Understanding your customer's needs and configuring the most suitable solution from available options adds value to both your customer and your company. It will help you avoid unnecessary objections from the customer.

FEWER ORDER CANCELLATIONS AND FEWER RETURNS It is always disappointing to have a customer cancel an order a few days after the sale was closed. The frequency of order cancellations can be reduced with consultative-style selling. Returned merchandise is another serious problem. Whether the product is returned or needs to be reconfigured, the expense will often wipe out the profit earned on several sales.

INCREASED REPEAT BUSINESS AND REFERRALS Many business firms do not make a profit on the first sale. In fact, some firms do not earn a profit until the customer has placed the third or fourth order. The same is true for the salesperson. Without repeat business and a steady list of referrals, the salesperson will generally not experience certain financial and psychic rewards. If at any point the customer does not feel the treatment was fair, the time and cost invested in partnership building and obtaining the initial order, as well as future sales, may be lost. Repeat business also builds a sense of pride within everyone associated with the business.

Satisfied customers represent a potent form of sales promotion. A group of satisfied customer forms what might be called an "auxiliary" sales force. Through word-of-mouth advertising, especially with the availability of social media and blogging, these people are referring potential customers and building new business for both the salesperson and the firm. Most of us can't resist sharing positive experiences with friends and business acquaintances.

The sales environment is changing. In competitive markets, success increasingly hinges on developing and maintaining mutually rewarding customer relationships.[7] Salespeople using the consultative sales presentation model are able to create more value and gain competitive advantage in their markets.

The Four-Part Need-Satisfaction Model

To be most effective, the salesperson should think of the sales process as a four-part model. The Consultative Sales Process Guide features these four parts (Figure 2).

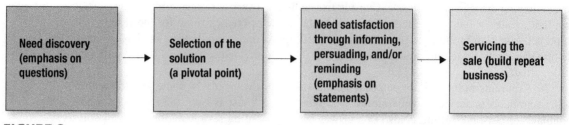

FIGURE 2

The Consultative Sales Process Guide

To be most successful, the salesperson should think of the sales presentation as a four-part process.

Part One—Need Discovery

Since the emergence of a marketing concept where the activities of a firm revolve around the needs of the customer, need discovery forms the essence of salespeople being able to create value, meet the needs of their customers, and execute the firm's commitment to the marketing concept. A review of the behaviors displayed by high-performance salespeople helps us understand the importance of precise need discovery. They have learned how to skillfully diagnose and solve the customer's problems better than their competitors. This problem-solving capability translates into more repeat business and referrals and fewer order cancellations and returns.[8]

Unless the selling situation requires mere order taking (customers know exactly what they want), need discovery in the information economy is a critically important part of the sales presentation. It may begin during the qualifying stage of building the prospect database or during the approach if the salesperson uses questions or a survey during the initial contact with the customer. Need discovery generally begins after you transition from the approach. In multi-call situations, need discovery may be the primary call objective during the first or second call. In most multi-call settings, it is wise to reconfirm the needs discovered in earlier calls.

The pace, scope, depth, and time allocated to inquiry depend on a variety of factors. Some of these include the sophistication of the product, the selling price, the customer's knowledge of the product, the product applications, and, of course, the time available for dialogue between the salesperson and the prospect. Each selling situation is different, so a standard set of guidelines for need discovery is not practical. Additional information on need discovery is presented later in the chapter.

Pharmaceutical salespeople generally have only a short time to present their product. In some situations, the doctor may immediately indicate a willingness to prescribe. However, in other situations the salesperson may be asked to make an informative need satisfaction presentation to several members of the practice.

Source: Custom Medical Stock Photo/Alamy Images Royalty Free

Part Two—Selection of the Solution

The emphasis in sales and marketing today is on determining customer needs and then selecting or configuring custom-fitted solutions to satisfy these needs. Therefore, an important function of the salesperson is product selection and recommendation. The salesperson must choose the product or service that can provide maximum satisfaction. When making this decision, the salesperson must be aware of all product options, including those offered by the competition.

Salespeople who have the ability to conduct an effective value-added needs analysis achieve the status of trusted adviser. Mary Langston, personal shopper at Nordstrom's Michigan Avenue store in Chicago, helps customers update their wardrobes. When asked what her days are like, she says, "It starts and ends with being a good listener." She promises her customers that she will never let them walk out of the store with clothing that does not look right.[9]

Part Three—Need Satisfaction Through Informing, Persuading, or Reminding

The third part of the consultative sales process consists of creating a need-satisfaction sales presentation and communicating to the customer, both verbally and nonverbally, the satisfaction that the product or service can provide. The salesperson places less emphasis on the use of questions and begins making value-adding statements. These value-adding statements are organized into a presentation that informs, persuades, or reminds the customer of the most suitable product or service. In several of the remaining chapters we discuss specific strategies used in conjunction with the sales presentation/demonstration, negotiating buyer resistance, and closing and servicing the sale.

Part Four—Servicing the Sale

Servicing the sale is a major way to create value. These activities, which occur after closing the sale, ensure maximum customer satisfaction and set the stage for a long-term relationship. Service activities include expansion selling, making credit arrangements, following through on assurances and promises, and dealing effectively with complaints.

In those cases in which a sale is normally closed during a single sales call, the salesperson should be prepared to go through all four parts of the Consultative Sales Process Guide. However, when a salesperson uses a multi-call approach, preparation for all the parts is usually not practical. The person selling networking systems or investments, for example, almost always uses a multi-call sales process. Need discovery (part one) is the focus of the first call.

Creating Value with Need Discovery

A lawyer does not give the client advice until the legal problem has been carefully studied and confirmed. A doctor does not prescribe medication until the patient's symptoms have been identified. In like manner, the salesperson should not recommend the purchase of a product without thorough need identification. You start with the assumption that the client's problem is not known. The only way to determine and confirm the problem is to get the other person talking. Effective relationship builders are willing to listen to better understand customer challenges. They ask questions that lead to consultative conversations, which open doors to greater opportunities.[10] You must obtain information to properly clarify the need, propose a single solution, or offer a range of solutions.

Customers may not realize that they actually have a problem. Even when they are aware of their need, as noted earlier by Salesforce.com's Dave Levitt, given the wide range of solutions and new products available today they may not realize that an actual solution to their problem exists. Bringing new insights regarding both their buying problem and enhanced solutions creates value for your customer.

Need discovery (sometimes called *need analysis* or *needs assessment*) begins with precall preparation when the salesperson is acquiring background information on the prospect. This part of need discovery is also referred to as *qualifying the prospect*. Need discovery, and in some cases the qualification process, continues once the salesperson and the customer are engaged in a real dialogue. Through the process of need discovery, the salesperson

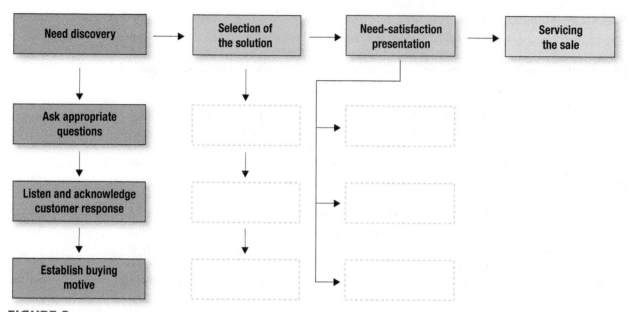

FIGURE 3

Three Dimensions of Need Discovery

establishes two-way communication by asking appropriate questions and listening carefully to the customer's responses. These responses usually provide clues concerning the customer's dominant buying motives (Figure 3).

Need Discovery—Asking Questions

The effective use of questions to achieve need identification and need satisfaction is one of the greatest challenges facing most professional salespeople. The types of questions you ask, the timing of those questions, and how you pose them greatly impact your ability to create customer value. In many situations, asking high–value-added questions that enlighten your prospect both about their needs and possible solutions results in an immediate sale.

The strategic approach to asking questions has been the focus of two major studies. These studies were conducted in response to the emergence of a marketing concept and evolution of consultative and strategic selling eras. The research was conducted by Neil Rackham for his book *SPIN Selling* and SPIN Selling Sales Training programs, and Xerox Learning Systems for their successful Personal Selling Skills (PSS) course.

THE SPIN SELLING MODEL According to research conducted during the strategic selling era on more than 35,000 salespeople by Neil Rackham, mastering the use of questions can increase one's success in sales by 17 percent.[11] Questions help clarify the exact dimensions of the problem, help the customer evaluate a range of solutions, and assist the customer in evaluating the potential outcome of the solution that is implemented.[12] Rackham's research focused on strategies for making large-ticket sales and is based on a close examination of successful salespeople. Rackham found the investigative or need discovery stage of the sales process has the most impact on the buyer's decision to purchase a product. He recommends a multiple-question approach that involves using four types of questions in a specific sequence (see Selling in Action). SPIN sales training programs are presented by Huthwaite, Inc. (www.huthwaite.com).

PERSONAL SELLING SKILLS MODEL The importance of questioning to establishing two-way communication was revealed in another study conducted during the consultative selling era. Research conducted by Xerox Learning Systems was used to develop the original Xerox Personal Selling Skills training program. Sales personnel were interviewed to identify the characteristics of a successful sales call. The results were quite surprising. A successful sales call lasts an average of 30 minutes. During this period the salesperson asks an average of 13.6 questions, discusses an average of 7.7 product features, and describes approximately six product benefits. During the successful sales call the customer asks approximately eight questions.[13] This 18-month study of behavioral differences among high-, average-, and low-performance salespeople illustrates that a successful sales call is a model of good two-way communication. Regarding the specific use of questions, the results revealed high performers:

- Use effective questions to gather information and build a clear, complete, mutual understanding of customer needs.
- Guide the direction of a sales call by striking an appropriate balance between open and closed questions.
- Use their questioning strategy to facilitate an open exchange of information.[14]

This study has been used to create and update the very successful Personal Selling Skills training program, now presented by AchieveGlobal (www.achieveglobal.com/solutions/sales).

The art and science of using questions was also discussed by Socrates more than 2,500 years ago. He noted, among other things, that questions tend to make people think. It's nearly impossible to remain passive when confronted with a direct question. Today there are sales training programs such as Michael Hargrove's "Using the Socratic Selling Methods" and books such as Kevin Daley's *Socratic Selling: How to Ask the Questions That Get the Sale* that include many of the observations of Socrates.[15]

In every selling situation, you want the prospect to be actively thinking, sharing thoughts, and asking questions. Appropriate questions reduce tension and build trust in a selling situation because they communicate interest in the other person's welfare. Until the person begins to talk freely, the salesperson will have difficulty diagnosing and solving the customer's problems.

The Four-Part Consultative Questioning Strategy

Table 1 illustrates the use of a multiple questioning strategy to discover customer needs. This strategy is based upon the research studies discussed earlier, as well as that conducted for the "Questions, Questions, Questions" sales training video described in the opening material for this chapter. The four types of questions are situation questions, probing questions, confirmation questions, and need-satisfaction questions. Developing skill in the use of these questions will work best if the consultative salesperson develops the mindset that it is more important to understand the customer than it is to persuade the customer. You will note similarity to the SPIN Selling and personal selling skills questioning strategies, as well as those found in other popular selling books.

TABLE 1 Types of Questions Used in Conjunction with Consultative Selling

A salesperson is selling fractional ownership of a jet aircraft to a well-known golf professional on the Professional Golf Association (PGA) Tour. The prospect is currently using commercial air travel.

TYPE OF QUESTION	DEFINITION	WHEN USED	EXAMPLES
Survey	*Discovers basic facts* about the buyer's *problem* and existing situation	Usually at the beginning of a sale	"Can you describe the problems you experience traveling to each of the pro golf tournaments?"
Probing	*Designed to uncover pain, and clarify the circumstances and implications* surrounding the customer's problem	When you feel the need to obtain more specific information to fully understand the problem	"Are the travel problems affecting your concentration when you are preparing for the event?"
Confirmation	*Used throughout the sales process to verify* the accuracy and assure a mutual understanding of information exchanged by the salesperson and the buyer	After important information has been exchanged	"So you think the uncertainty associated with commercial air travel is having some effect on your game?"
Need-Satisfaction	*Designed to move the sales process toward commitment and action*; focuses on the *pleasure* or payoff achieved from the proposed solution	When you change the focus from the problem to a discussion of the solution	"With fractional ownership of your own jet, what personal benefits would this bring to your performance in the 30 tournaments you play each year?"

SURVEY QUESTIONS REVEAL CUSTOMER'S *PROBLEMS* At the beginning of most sales presentations, there is a need to collect basic facts about the buyer's existing situation and problem. **Survey questions,** or *information gathering questions*, as they are sometimes called, are designed to obtain this knowledge. To accomplish this, there are two types of survey questions.

General survey questions help the salesperson discover facts about the buyer's problem and existing situation and are often the first step in the partnership-building process. Rackham refers to these as Situation Questions. Here is a sampling of general survey questions that can be used in selected selling fields:

> "I understand that your regional facilities don't necessarily use the same delivery carriers, is that correct?" (Shipping Service)
>
> "Tell me about the new challenges you are facing in the area of data storage." (File Server)
>
> "What is your current rate of employee turnover?" (Customer Service Training)
>
> "Can you provide me with information on the kinds of meetings and conventions you plan for your clients and employees?" (Hotel Convention Services)
>
> "Can you describe the style of home furnishings you prefer?" (Retail Home Furnishings)

In most selling situations, general survey questions are followed by specific survey questions.

Specific survey questions are designed to give prospects a chance to describe in more detail the problem, issue, or dissatisfaction they are experiencing from their point of view. These specific survey questions (see Selling in Action) or problem questions as they are referred to in the SPIN Selling sequence are designed to delve more deeply into the customer's buying situation. Five examples of specific survey questions are:

> "Has it occurred to you that by not consolidating your shipping with one carrier, you're likely spending more than is really necessary?" (Shipping Service)
>
> "How do you feel about installing another server to your system?" (File Server)
>
> "To what extent is employee turnover affecting your customer service?" (Customer Service Training)
>
> "What meal function features are most important to your guests?" (Hotel Convention Services)
>
> "Are you looking for an entertainment center that blends in with your existing furniture?" (Retail Home Furnishings)

Survey questions, general or specific, should not be used to collect factual information that can be acquired from other sources, such as your CRM prospect database prior to the sales call. The preapproach prospect qualification effort is especially important when the salesperson is involved in a large or complex sale. These buyers expect the salesperson to do their homework and not waste the buyer's time asking general survey questions and discussing basic factual information that is available from other sources. Rackham's research revealed that more experienced salespeople tended to ask more specific survey or problem questions, and ask them sooner.

Although survey questions are most often used at the beginning of the sales process, they can be used at other times. Gaining a better understanding of the customer's situation or buying problem may be necessary at any time during the sales presentation. We present the four types of questions in a sequence that has proven to be effective in most selling situations. However, it would be a mistake to view this sequence as a *rigid* plan for every sales presentation. High-performing salespeople spend time strategically preparing tentative questions before they make the sales call. Table 2 provides some examples. Note that both open and closed questions are listed. **Open questions** require the prospect to go beyond a simple yes/no response. **Closed questions** can be answered with a yes or no, or a brief response.

Open questions are very effective in certain selling situations because they provoke thoughtful and insightful answers. The specific survey question "What are the biggest challenges you face in the area of plant security?" focuses the prospect's attention on problems that need solutions. Closed questions, however, can be equally effective when the sales conversation needs to be narrowed or focused on a specific issue.

TABLE 2 Need Discovery Worksheet

Preplanned questions (sometimes used in conjunction with company-supplied forms) are often used in service, retail, wholesale, and manufacturer selling. Salespeople, such as Johnny in the P3 Questions video, who use the consultative approach frequently record answers to their questions and use this information to correctly select and recommend solutions in subsequent calls in their multi-call sales situations. Open and closed questions used in the area of financial services appear in the following list.

PREPLANNED QUESTIONS TO DISCOVER BUYING MOTIVES	CUSTOMER RESPONSE
1. "Now, as I understand it, you're currently pursuing an Internet phone system to offset your high cellular costs?" (Closed/General Survey/Situational)	
2. "Are you aware that with the system you are currently using, your brokers may have to keep their laptop 'on' in order to make and receive Internet calls?" (Closed/Specific Survey/Problem)	
3. "So what happens if, say, your broker is waiting for an important return call and then inadvertently logs off their laptop without a way to roll over the client's return call into a centralized system?" (Open/Probing/Pain/Implication)	
4. "Let's see if WE understand this—the brokers won't support the system you're considering because it doesn't include instant messaging? And, since the brokers would be the primary users of the new system, you're concerned that the system will fail without their support, is that correct?" (Closed/Summary Confirmation)	
5. "What if we could develop a communications system for you that included I.M. and met the SEC requirements? What positive impact could that have on your situation?" (Open/Need Satisfaction/Pleasure)	
6.	
7.	
8.	

PROBING QUESTIONS REVEAL CUSTOMER'S *PAIN* Early in the sales process, the salesperson should make every effort to fully understand the buying problem and the pain, implications, or consequences surrounding the problem. This is especially important when the problem is difficult to describe, the solution is complex, and the potential impact of a wrong decision is enormous.[16]

Probing questions help you uncover and clarify the pain, implications, and circumstances surrounding the customer's buying problem. They are used more frequently in large, complex sales. These questions often uncover the current level of customer concern, fear, or frustration related to the problem. The following probing questions, also referred to as *implication* questions in Rackham's *SPIN Selling,* are more focused than the survey questions presented earlier.

"But, doesn't every incorrect label cost you to ship to an incorrect address, then cost you again to have it shipped back to you?" (Shipping Service)

"What would be the consequences if your choose to do nothing about your current server situation?" (File Server)

"How does senior management feel about employee turnover and the related customer service problem?" (Customer Service Training)

"Is poor service at the meal function negatively affecting the number of people returning to your seminar?" (Hotel Convention Services)

"Is it important that you have easy access for connecting your DVD, TIVO, and your wireless LAN network?" (Retail Home Furnishings)

Probing or implication questions help the salesperson and customer gain a mutual understanding of *why* a problem is important. Asking effective probing questions requires extensive knowledge of your company's capabilities, much insight into your customer's buying problem, and a great deal of practice.

The best sales presentations are characterized by active dialogue. As the sales process progresses, the customer becomes more open and shares perceptions, ideas, and feelings freely. A series of appropriate probing questions stimulates the prospect to discover things not considered before.

Neil Rackham conducted studies of 35,000 sales calls and from this research developed the material for his books *SPIN Selling* and *The New SPIN Selling Fieldbook*. SPIN is an acronym for Situational, Problem, Implication, and Need-Payoff Questions. According to Rackham, "more than half the Fortune 100 companies are using the SPIN Selling Model to train their sales forces."

Book cover from *The Spin Selling Fieldbook* by Neil Rackham. Copyright © 1996. Reprinted by permission of The McGraw-Hill Companies, Inc.

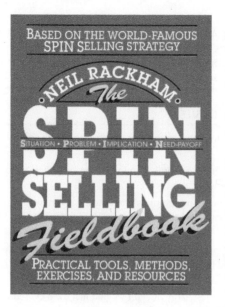

CONFIRMATION QUESTIONS REVEAL *MUTUAL UNDERSTANDING* Confirmation questions are used throughout the sales process to verify the accuracy and assure a mutual understanding of information exchanged by the salesperson and the buyer (see Table 1). They are also used to gain commitment, a critically important part of achieving success in larger complex sales. Without commitment throughout the sales process, the chances of a successful sale evaporate rapidly.

These questions, which are an important update to the research on the use of questioning strategies, help determine whether there is mutual understanding of the problems and circumstances the customer is experiencing, as well as the possibilities for a solution. Throughout the sales process there is always the potential for a breakdown in communication. Perhaps the language used by the salesperson is too technical. Information and initial needs discovered during the qualifying stage of the need discovery may have changed. Maybe the customer is preoccupied and has not listened closely to what has been said. Many confirmation questions are simple and to the point.

> "If I understand you correctly, the monitoring system we are looking at for data storage must be set up for both your corporate headquarters and the manufacturing operation. Is that correct?" (File Server)

> "I want to be sure I am clear that you feel there is a direct relationship between employee turnover and the problems that exist in customer service?" (Customer Service Training)

> "Did you say that your seminar attendance dropped 12 percent last year?" (Hotel Convention Services)

> "So you want a new entertainment center that blends with your current light-colored oak furniture?" (Retail Home Furnishings)

The length of the sales process can vary from a few minutes during a single-call presentation to weeks or even months in a complex multi-call sales presentation. As the sales process progresses, the amount of information available to the salesperson and the customer increases. As the need discovery progresses, the customer's buying criteria or buying conditions surface. **Buying conditions** are those qualifications that must be available or fulfilled before the sale can be closed. The customer may buy only if the product is available in a certain configuration or can be delivered by a certain date. In some selling situations, product installation or service after the sale is considered an important buying condition by the customer. In a large, complex sale, several buying conditions may surface. The salesperson has the responsibility of clarifying, confirming, and gaining commitment on each condition. The same is true for gaining commitment of each of the specific benefits presented to the customer.

One of the best ways to clarify, confirm, and gain commitment on several buying conditions is with a **summary-confirmation question**. To illustrate, let us consider a situation in which Alexis Rodriguez, sales manager at a major hotel, has interviewed a prospect who wants to schedule a large awards banquet. After a series of survey, probing, and confirmation questions, Alexis feels confident that the information collected is complete to prepare a proposal. However, to be sure all the facts have been collected, Alexis asks the following summary-confirmation question to gain commitment on the important buying conditions:

> "Let me summarize the major items you have mentioned. You want all banquet attendees served within an eight-minute time frame after the opening speaker has finished his speech? And, you need a room that will comfortably seat 60 people banquet style and 10 of these people will be seated at the head table. Is this correct?"

Once all the buying conditions are confirmed, Tammy can prepare a proposal that reflects the specific needs of her customer. The result is a win-win situation for the customer and the salesperson. The chances of closing the sale greatly improve. In multi-call sales processes, it is wise to begin subsequent calls with summary-confirmation questions that reestablish what was discussed in the previous call(s):

> (Re-qualifying the new prospect) "I would like to revisit the information we have in our database about your company's purchasing procedures. You prefer limiting your suppliers and developing long-term partnerships where they are committed to your profitability and your customers' total customer satisfaction. You also require e-commerce linkages that allow your people to review the status of their order, delivery dates, and the projected costs including transportation and financing. Is that correct?"

> (The second call in a multi-call sale situation) "Let me begin by going over what we discussed in our last visit. Your current shipper gives you a 50 percent discount and provides their own custom label printer?" If the customer responds in the affirmative, the salesperson continues with another summary-confirmation question. "You also have to buy fairly expensive custom labels and, at around $90 a pack, you're spending over $20,000 just on labels, is that still correct?"

This enables the salesperson to verify that the previously discovered buying conditions have remained the same and not changed since the last meeting. Summary-confirmation questions are also used to effectively clarify, confirm, and gain commitment to several product benefits after they have been presented, generally one at a time. Commitment to the value of the benefits usually results in transitioning the presentation to the closing and servicing of the sale.

NEED-SATISFACTION QUESTIONS REVEAL *PLEASURE* The fourth type of question used in the sales process is fundamentally different from the other three. **Need-satisfaction questions** are designed to focus on the solution and the benefits of the solution. These are helpful questions that move the sales process toward commitment and action. The chances of closing the sale greatly improve because need-satisfaction questions, or as they are sometimes called *solution* or *pleasure questions*, focus on specific benefits and build desire for a solution.

Survey, probing, and confirmation questions focus on understanding and clarifying the customer's problem. Need-satisfaction questions help the prospect see how your product or service provides a solution to the problem you have uncovered. The opportunity to close the sale greatly improves because you have cast the solution in a pleasurable light.

In most cases, these questions are used after the salesperson has created awareness of the seriousness of the buyer's problem. The need-satisfaction questions you ask will replace their current levels of concern, pain, or frustration with pleasurable thoughts about a solution. The following examples provide insight into the use of need-satisfaction, or as SPIN Selling refers to them need-payoff, questions:

> "And if I told you that I can offer you cost savings of at least 5 percent over your current shipping expenses, would that be meaningful?" (Shipping Service)

> "Tests on similar applications show a new file server can increase data storage by 30 to 40 percent. How much of an increase do you feel you would achieve?" (File Server)

SELLING IS EVERYONE'S BUSINESS

Selling a Product That Doesn't Exist

Some creative entrepreneurs start selling their product before it even exists. Greg Gianforte wanted to start an Internet software company in the late 1990s. He noted that no one seemed to be making a good product that would help companies respond to e-mail from customers. Armed with a product feature sheet, Gianforte started trying to sell a nonexistent product. He called customer-support managers at hundreds of companies. After reviewing the product features, he explained that the product would be ready in 90 days. Some of these potential customers mentioned features he had not thought of. This input helped him develop a better product. After two weeks of cold calls, he knew exactly what customers wanted and he began the development of RightNow software. It was ready for customer use in 90 days. He then hired his first three employees—all of them salespeople. Gianforte says, "Sales is really the most noble part of the business because it's the part that brings the solution together with the customer's need." Today, more than 1,200 organizations worldwide use RightNow solutions.[a]

Selling in Action

The use of questions to discover needs and present solutions is discussed in several popular personal selling books. For comparison purposes, the approximate equivalents to the four types of questions described in this chapter are listed.

Selling Today by Manning, Ahearne, and Reece	The SPIN Selling Fieldbook by Rackham	The New Solution Selling by Eades	The New Conceptual Selling by Heiman, Sanchez, with Tuleja	Secrets of Question Based Selling by Freese
SURVEY	SITUATION	OPEN\	CONFIRMATION	STATUS
PROBING	PROBLEM	CONTROL	NEW INFORMATION	ISSUE
CONFIRMATION	IMPLICATION	CONFIRMING	ATTITUDE	IMPLICATION
NEED-SATISFACTION	NEED-PAYOFF		COMMITMENT	SOLUTION
			BASIC ISSUE	

The questions above are listed in the sequence presented by the authors. To determine the exact definition of each type of question, check the source.

In many selling situations, a product demonstration is an essential stage in the sales process. In this case, the salesperson might use the following need-satisfaction question:

> "What benefits do you see if we provided a demonstration of one of the training modules to senior management so they can understand what you and I have discovered about reducing employee turnover?" (Customer Service Training)

Once the prospect needs are clearly identified, need-satisfaction questions can be valuable closing tools. Consider this example:

> "Considering the benefits we have summarized and agreed on, and noting the fact that our staff will deliver an outstanding meal function, would you like to sign this confirmation so we can reserve the rooms and schedule the meals that you need?" (Hotel Convention Services)

Need-satisfaction questions such as these are very powerful because they build desire for the solution and give ownership of the solution to the customer. When the prospect understands which parts of the problem(s) your solution can solve, you are less likely to invite objections. In some cases you may identify problems that still need to be clarified. When this happens, you can use survey, probing, or confirmation questions to obtain more information.

At this point you have received an introduction to the four most common types of questions used during the selling process. (For more insight into the application of questions to the sales process, view the three videos in the "Questions, Questions, Questions" series referred to in this chapter's opening vignette. Also refer to the Role-Play Application Exercises.) We will revisit these important sales tools later in this chapter.

Qualifying to Eliminate Unnecessary Questions

It is important to avoid the use of unnecessary questions during a sales call. Pre-qualifying the prospect is especially important when the prospect is a business buyer. Successful salespeople acquire as much information as possible about the prospect before the first meeting. They use sources such as the prospect's Web site, LinkedIn, previous phone calls or e–mails, and information recorded in the salesperson's CRM system. This prior understanding of the prospect allows the salesperson to direct the qualifying conversation using effective confirmation questions like: "Your Web site mentions your company has recently expanded into a new product market. Can you tell me more about that?" Buyers expect the salesperson to be well informed about their operation and not waste time asking a large number of basic survey questions. Confirmation questions communicate this prior knowledge and allow the salesperson and customer to move ahead in the consultative sales process with more important probing and need-satisfaction questions.

Action Selling at CARQUEST

CARQUEST Auto Parts promises to deliver what customers need. To achieve this lofty goal, the company enrolled its 1,200 outside sales force members in *Action Selling*. A major objective of this sales training program is to help salespeople become trusted business consultants. They learned that asking—not telling—is the key to sales success. Emphasis throughout the course is placed on asking more and better questions. Duane Sparks, who developed *Action Selling*, says "The success rate of sales calls rises significantly when more than two specific customer needs are uncovered by questioning."[b]

Duane Sparks, *Action Selling*

Source: Duane Sparks, Courtesy of The Sales Board, Inc.

Robert Jolles, author of *Customer-Centered Selling*,[17] suggests that salespeople be careful when determining whether the person they are meeting with has the authority to make the purchase decision. According to Jolles, asking a survey question like "Are you the one who will be making the decision on this purchase?" encourages prospects without decision-making authority to lie in order to maintain their pride in the situation. Instead, Jolles recommends the question, "Who, besides yourself, will be responsible for this purchase decision?" This subtle, yet strategic rephrasing to a confirmation/survey question allows the prospect to tell the truth and maintain his or her dignity.

Need Discovery—Listening and Acknowledging the Customer's Response

To fully understand the customer, we must listen closely and acknowledge every response. The authors of *First Impressions* offer these words of advice to salespeople who use questions as part of the need-identification process:

> "What you do after you ask a question can reveal even more about you than the questions you ask. You reveal your true level of interest in the way you listen."[18]

Most of us are born with the ability to hear, but we have to learn how to listen. The starting point is developing a listening attitude. Always regard the customer as worthy of your respect and full attention.[19] Salespeople with high levels of customer orientation truly care about customers, and thus engage in actions that customers value such as listening to customer feedback and solving customer problems. Once you have made a commitment to becoming a better listener, develop active listening skills.

DEVELOPING ACTIVE LISTENING SKILLS **Active listening** is the process of sending back to the prospect what you as a listener think the person meant, both in terms of content and in terms of feelings. Active listening requires intense involvement as you concentrate on what you are hearing, exhibit your listening attitude through your nonverbal messages, and feed back to the prospect what you think he or she meant.[20]

CUSTOMER RELATIONSHIP MANAGEMENT WITH TECHNOLOGY

Reviewing Account Status

Salespeople regularly review the status of their prospects' records in their customer relationship management (CRM) databases. In some cases, this is done on the computer screen. In other situations, a printed copy of the records can enhance the process.

Salespeople review their files to ascertain at what phase in the Consultative Sales Presentation Guide each prospect is in the sales cycle. Then they decide which action to take to help move the prospect to the next phase. Sales managers can be helpful with this process, especially for new salespeople. Managers can help

salespeople evaluate the available information and suggest strategies designed to move to the next phase.

Even experienced salespeople count on their sales managers to help plan presentations. Managers can help salespeople evaluate their contacts' needs, select the best solution, and plan a presentation most likely to succeed. The CRM Application Exercise "Printing the Customer Database" describes how to plan for a review of your Salesforce.com records.

Developing active listening skills involves three practices that can be learned by any salesperson willing to make the commitment.

FOCUS YOUR FULL ATTENTION This is not easy because the delivery of the messages we hear is often much slower than our capacity to listen. Thus, we have plenty of time to let our minds roam, to think ahead, and to plan what we are going to say next. Our senses are constantly feeding us new information while someone is trying to tell us something. Staying focused is often difficult and involves use of both verbal and nonverbal messages.[21] To show that you are paying attention, lean toward the prospect while saying "uh-huh," "okay," or "I understand" and nodding in agreement when appropriate. Avoid nodding rapidly or saying "uh-huh" rapidly because this will communicate impatience or a desire to turn the conversation back to yourself.[22]

Lisa Ciampi, account executive for Design Display Inc. in Birmingham, Alabama, believes consultative selling is about being a marketing advisor and problem solver. This approach creates value within the sales process.

Source: The Sales Board Inc.

It is important to listen to the emotion involved in your customer's comments. A poor listener listens to facts; a good listener listens to emotions. Theoretically, 20 percent of communications is strictly facts and 80 percent is emotion—the emotion we all have and put into every thought. Listening for the emotions in your client's conversation enables you to receive the entire message.[23]

Within every sales presentation there will be times when silence should be welcomed. Use silence to control the flow of information and draw out the customer. Customers are often inclined to fill silence by talking. Throughout an effective sales presentation the customer should be talking more than the salesperson.[24]

PARAPHRASE THE CUSTOMER'S MEANING After the customer stops talking, pause for two or three seconds and then state in your own words, with a confirmation question, what you think the person meant. This technique not only helps ensure understanding but also is an effective customer relations strategy. The customer feels good knowing that not only are you listening to what has been said but you are also making an effort to ensure accuracy.

In addition to paraphrasing the content, use questions to dig for full understanding of the customer's perceptions.[25] The use of survey or probing questions is appropriate any time you need to clarify what is being said by the prospect.

TAKE NOTES Although note taking is not necessary in every sales presentation, it is important in complex sales in which the information obtained from the customer is critical to the development of a buying solution. Taking accurate notes is a good way to demonstrate to the customer that you are actively listening. When you take notes, you increase your memory of what you heard. Your notes should be brief and to the point.[26] If the information you receive from the customer is too technical or unfamiliar, do not hesitate to ask for clarification of information you don't understand.

Need Discovery—Establishing Buying Motives

The primary goal of questioning, listening, and acknowledging is to uncover prospect needs and establish buying motives. Our efforts to discover prospect needs can be more effective if we focus our questioning on determining the prospect's primary reasons for buying. When a customer has a definite need, it is usually supported by specific buying motives.

The greatest time investment in personal selling is on the front end of the sales process. First, you must plan the sales call and then, once you are face-to-face with the customer, you can begin the need discovery stage. It is during the early stage of the sales process that you can create the greatest value for the customer.[27]

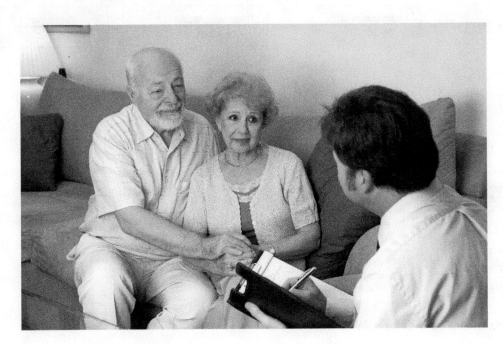

In many selling situations, note taking will demonstrate a high level of professionalism.

Source: Lisa F. Young/Shutterstock

Selecting Solutions That Create Value

Salespeople are no longer selling just a "product"; instead they are providing a valuable "solution" to customer problems.[28] Consultative salespeople act as product experts and generally provide a customized solution. The second part of the consultative sales process consists of selecting or configuring a solution that satisfies the prospect's buying motives.

As we have noted, most salespeople bring to the selling situation a variety of products and/or services. In today's information economy, salespeople are increasingly selling related services as a part of their product solution. This is especially true in the Western industrialized countries where profit margins on B2B goods-related solutions are declining. In Germany, for example, six of the 30 largest firms have established specific organization units to offer services.[29] The challenge to select the correct solution is growing. Digesting relevant information, perceiving patterns, and determining the unique solution that will work in each unique selling situation requires a considerable amount of time and effort.[30] This process done correctly can create significant value for the customer and build a long-term partnership of repeats and/or referrals.

After identifying the buying motives, the salesperson carefully reviews the available product options. At this point the salesperson is searching for a customized solution to satisfy the prospect's buying motives. Once the solution has been selected, the salesperson makes a recommendation to the prospect (Figure 4). The following customer response to this process illustrates the value created when this process is done correctly: "She listened to and worked with the ideas that I had concerning my desires and preferences, as well as made recommendations that complemented and enhanced the vision that I had for my home."[31]

Selecting Solutions—Match Specific Benefits with Buying Motives

Products and services represent problem-solving tools. People buy products when they perceive that they fulfill a need. We also note that today's more demanding customers seek a cluster of satisfactions that arise from the product itself, from the company that makes or distributes the product, and from the salesperson who sells and services the product. Tom Reilly, author of *Value-Added Selling*, says, "Value-added salespeople sell three things: the product, the company, and themselves. This is the three-dimensional bundle of value."[32] When possible, the salesperson should focus on benefits related to each dimension of value. Of course, it is a mistake to make benefit statements that do not relate to the specific needs

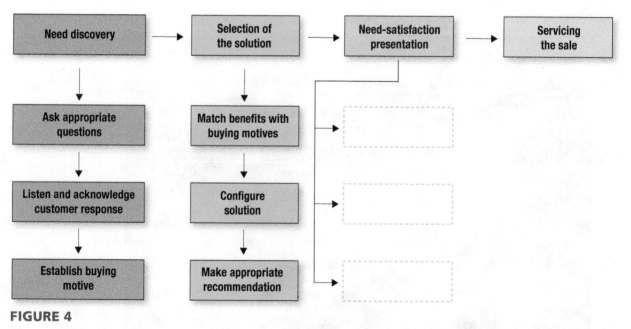

FIGURE 4

Three Dimensions of Product Selection

of the customer. High-performance salespeople present benefits that are precisely tailored to the customer's needs. Benefits that are not relevant to the customer's needs waste time and may invite objections.[33]

Selecting Solutions—Product Configuration

Most salespeople bring to the sale a variety of products or services. Salespeople who represent food distributors can offer customers a mix of several hundred items. Most pharmaceutical sales representatives can offer the medical community a wide range of products. Best Buy, a large retailer of electronics, offers customers a wide range of audio and visual entertainment options. The customer who wants to purchase an entertainment system, for example, can choose from many combinations of receivers, speakers, and so on. Selecting the right solution is referred to by many sales organizations as *product configuration.*

If the sale involves several needs and the satisfaction of multiple buying motives, selection of the solution may take several days or even weeks and may involve the preparation of a detailed sales proposal. In addition, research conducted by Neil Rackham revealed that top-performing salespeople tend to introduce their solutions later in the sale—after several problems were uncovered.

A company considering the purchase of automated production equipment would likely present this type of challenge to the salesperson. The problem needs careful analysis before a solution can be identified.

Configuration Solutions (www.configsc.com) is one of many providers of product configuration solutions. Their software applications help configure-to-order organizations quote, market, and sell highly customized and complex products and service offerings. Their advanced technology and industry-focused solutions help salespeople automate a wide range of customer product solutions—regardless of the complexity or variability of their products, processes, or services.[34]

Electronic catalogs also play an increasingly important role in the product selection or product configuration process. Software programs such as Configure One's (www.configureone.com) Web-based *Concept E-Catalog* enable salespeople to rapidly implement and easily maintain electronic catalog solutions for business-to-business and business-to-consumer applications. *Concept E-Catalog* software enables salespeople to find product solutions faster. Their electronic catalog fully integrates with their other products (e-commerce and configurator software) or can stand alone. With their e-commerce software, salespeople and customers can have access to product solutions 24/7.

Salesforce.com with their AppExchange integration program also provides product selection and electronic catalog capability. BigMachines, voted Best Quote App in 2009, provides on-demand product configuration, pricing, and proposal capabilities that can be easily added to Salesforce.com's on-demand CRM solution. BigMachines enables salespeople to streamline the entire opportunity-to-quote-to-order process, all within the familiar Salesforce.com CRM interface. Capabilities include guided selling, product configuration, complex pricing and discounting, approval workflow, and proposal generation.[35] Electronic product configurators and product catalogs and e-commerce enable salespeople to create value for the customer by providing time-sensitive, professionally prepared, information-rich alternatives in selecting solutions that meet the unique needs established during the need discovery. For many salespeople the use of sales force technology has changed their methods of selling.[36]

In some selling situations, the salesperson will solely create the solution based on the needs analysis. In more complex selling situations, however,[37] both the salesperson and the customer often play an active role and together co-create the solution. This co-creation process takes place through conversations between the customer and the salesperson. Research reveals this process often helps customers better understand their own needs and conceive of possible solutions that fit those needs. This process creates value and, as a consequence, customers make smarter buying choices that conform to the salesperson's solutions and sales propositions.

Selecting Solutions—Make Appropriate Recommendations

The recommendation strategies available to salespeople are similar to those used by a doctor who must recommend a solution to a patient's medical problem. In the medical field, three possibilities for providing patient satisfaction exist. In situations in which the patient easily understands the medical problem and the appropriate treatment, the doctor can make a recommendation, and the patient can proceed immediately toward a cure. If the patient does not easily understand the medical problem or solution, the doctor may need to discuss thoroughly with the patient the benefits of the recommended treatment. If the medical problem is not within his medical specialty, the doctor may recommend a specialist to provide the treatment. In consultative selling the salesperson has these same three counseling alternatives.

RECOMMEND SOLUTION—CUSTOMER BUYS IMMEDIATELY The selection and recommendation of products to meet customer needs may occur at the beginning of the sales call, such as in the product approach; during the presentation just after the need discovery; or near the end, when minor resistance has been negotiated. At any of these three times, the presentation of products that are well matched to the prospect's needs may result in an immediate purchase.

RECOMMEND SOLUTION—SALESPERSON MAKES NEED-SATISFACTION PRESENTATION This alternative requires a presentation of product benefits including demonstrations and negotiating objections before the sale is closed. In this situation the customer may not be totally aware of a buying problem, and the solution may not be easily understood or apparent. Because of this, the salesperson needs to carefully define the problem and communicate a solution to the customer. The need-satisfaction presentation will be discussed later in the book.

RECOMMEND ANOTHER SOURCE Earlier, we indicated that professional salespeople may recommend that a prospect buy a product or service from another source, maybe even a competitor. If, after a careful needs assessment, the salesperson concludes that the products represented do not satisfy the customer's needs, the consultative salesperson should recommend another source.

Paul Roos, a sales representative for Hewlett-Packard (HP), once met with a customer who wanted to buy a newly introduced HP product for an application that would not work. He explained why the application would not work and then took time to configure a competing product to meet the customer's needs. He lost that sale to a competitor, but the assistance provided confirmed his integrity and made a lasting impression on the customer. That customer later became a high-value account.[38] In situations like Paul Roos's, where the unique needs of a customer cannot be solved and an alternative recommendation is made to buy from another supplier, long-term partnerships are often created that result in future sales and/or referred business. This creates value for the customer who is looking for a unique solution.

Need Discovery and the Transactional Buyer

Throughout this chapter, you have been given a comprehensive introduction to the consultative sales process. It is important to keep in mind that the fundamentals of consultative selling must be customized to meet the individual needs of the customer. For example, some of the guidelines for developing an effective consultative presentation must be abandoned or greatly altered when you are working with a transactional buyer. In most cases, transactional buyers understand what product they need and when they need it. The Internet has armed many transactional buyers with a great deal of information, so the salesperson that spends time asking survey questions or making a detailed informative presentation may be wasting the customer's time. Most of these buyers want the salesperson to configure a product solution that focuses on pricing and delivery issues.[39]

When working with the transactional buyer, it is important to understand the difference between a transaction and a consultative relationship. Transactions create one-time value; consultative relationships create long-term value and a stable business foundation.[40]

Involving the Prospect in the Need Discovery

In most selling situations there is a certain amount of time pressure. Rarely does a salesperson have an unlimited amount of time to spend with the customer. As noted earlier the salesperson is often allotted only 30 minutes for the sales call. Some buyers limit all their appointments to 30 minutes or less.

Figure 5 illustrates an ideal breakdown of time allocation between the salesperson and the prospect during three parts of the sales process. In terms of involvement, the prospect

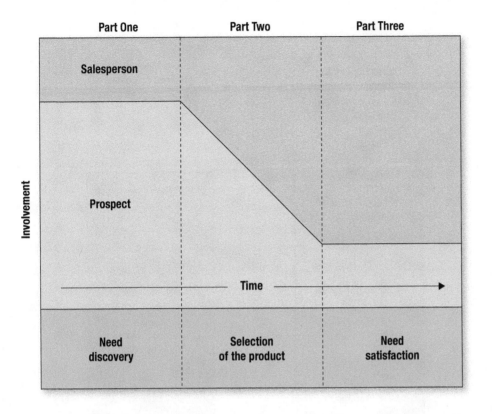

FIGURE 5

Time Used by Salesperson and Customer During Each Part of the Consultative Sales Presentation

assumes a greater role during the need discovery stage. As the salesperson begins the product selection process, the prospect's involvement decreases. During the need-satisfaction stage, the salesperson is doing more of the talking, but note that the prospect is never excluded totally.

Transitioning to the Presentation

There is a need to make an effective transition from the approach to the need discovery stage. There is the same need to transition from the need discovery/product selection stage to the need-satisfaction presentation stage. As noted earlier, if your customer buys immediately, you will transition to the close and conduct those activities associated with servicing the sale. If you and your customer decide another supplier might better meet their needs, you might transition directly to servicing the sale to achieve a future sale or a referral.

If it is decided a need-satisfaction presentation is needed to communicate specific features and benefits, a statement such as "I would like to point out some of the specific benefits of the solution we have agreed upon." If the need-satisfaction presentation is made during a separate call of a multi-call presentation, the transition should include a summary-confirmation question covering the buying conditions discussed. The summary-confirmation question would be used in closing the existing call and opening the next call.

Planning and Execution—Final Thoughts

The importance of strategic planning and execution of the need discovery and product selection parts of the consultative sales presentation model is explained in this chapter. Figure 6 summarizes the key concepts that must be addressed during the planning and execution process. These planning and execution activities will impact your ability to create customer value and build a partnering relationship. This approach can be used in the three major employment settings: service, B2B, and B2C.

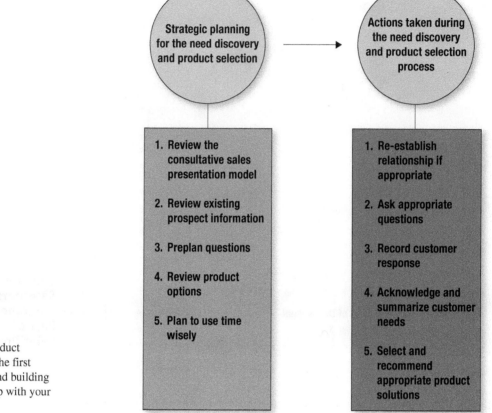

FIGURE 6

Need discovery and product selection activities are the first step in creating value and building a partnering relationship with your customer.

CHAPTER LEARNING ACTIVITIES

Reviewing Key Concepts

Outline the benefits of the consultative sales process

Salespeople use the consultative sales presentation because this customer-focused selling model results in increased customer satisfaction, more closed sales, and more repeat and referred business. Research indicates high-performance salespeople have learned how to skillfully use the consultative model to diagnose and solve their customers' buying problems better than their competitors.

Describe the four parts of the need-satisfaction model

A well-planned and well-executed consultative sales process is an important key to success in personal selling. To be most effective, the presentation should be viewed as a four-part process: need discovery; selection of the solution; need satisfaction through informing, persuading, or reminding; and servicing the sale.

Discuss the use of questions to discover customer needs

The most effective sales process is characterized by two-way communication. It should be encouraged with survey, probing, confirmation, summary-confirmation, and need-satisfaction questions.

Describe the importance of active listening and the use of confirmation questions

Beware of assuming information about the prospect, and be sure the language of your presentation is clearly understood. Listen attentively as the prospect responds to your questions or volunteers information. The effective use of confirmation questions to enhance active listening assures a mutual understanding of buying motives.

Select solutions that match customer needs

After making a good first impression during the approach and getting the customer's full attention, the salesperson begins. During the process of, or shortly after determining and/or confirming customer needs, the process of configuring a solution begins. The salesperson's ability is tested during this part of the sale because this is where the prospect's buying motives are matched with benefits, a solution is configured, and appropriate solutions are recommended.

Key Terms

Need discovery
Survey questions
General survey questions
Specific survey questions
Open questions

Closed questions
Probing questions
Confirmation questions
Buying conditions

Summary-confirmation
   question
Need-satisfaction questions
Active listening

Review Questions

1. List and describe the four parts of the Consultative Sales Process Guide.
2. Describe the findings of the two major research projects on the strategic use of questions in selling.
3. List and describe the four types of questions commonly used in the selling field.
4. Define the term *buying conditions*. What are some common buying conditions?
5. Describe the process of active listening, and explain how it can improve the listening efficiency rate.
6. Discuss the three dimensions of need discovery.
7. Describe the three dimensions of selecting a product solution.
8. Describe the ideal time allocation for each part of the consultative sales presentation between the salesperson and the prospect.
9. Describe the nature of the need discovery process when working with a transactional buyer.
10. Describe how to transition to the presentation part of the consultative sales presentation model.

Role-Play Application Exercises for "Questioning" Video Series

Most sales skill development exercises used in the classroom are product-oriented. As noted earlier in the chapter, "Product-oriented selling can easily lapse into product evangelism." This three-part video series on questioning focuses on the customer's buying process, consultative selling, and building high-quality partnerships.

The goal of this series is the identification and clarification of the customer's problem and finding a solution. The first video focuses on the appropriate use of survey and confirmation questions to identify the customer's problem. The second video introduces the use of probing and need-satisfaction questions. Probing questions examine and clarify the potential issues surrounding the customer's problem, while need-satisfaction questions focus the sales process on the appropriate solution. The third video demonstrates the use of these questions in a challenging yet typical contemporary sales setting.

The role-play exercises presented here challenge the participant to understand, apply, and integrate questioning skills presented in this chapter and in the video series. Product information needed for these exercises is found in Appendix: Partnership Selling. Customer information will be found in the B. H. Rivera Contact Report (disregard any other information). You will assume the role of a newly hired salesperson as described in the Position Description. Refer to the questioning material and examples presented on earlier. Use a Need Discovery Worksheet like the one presented earlier in the chapter for developing your questions.

After viewing the video "Questions—Discovering and Confirming Customer Problems," study the information presented in Appendix: Partnership Selling, Part One. Refer to the Contact Report (as noted, disregard any other information on this page). Assume you were assigned to this account and you are meeting B. H. Rivera to inquire about additional information regarding dates when the meeting will be held, and what audiovisual equipment might be needed. Prepare a list of general survey and specific survey questions that reveal when, during the next month, the meeting will be held and what, if any, audiovisual equipment might be needed. Plan to use a summary-confirmation question to verify the existing four items on the contact sheet. Using the questions you have created, role-play this part of the need discovery process.

After viewing the video "Questions—Discovering Pain and Pleasure," and reviewing the information you prepared in the previous role-play, prepare three probing questions. These questions should clarify and reveal a mutual understanding of issues and consequences regarding food service, facility design, and audiovisual equipment. Also, using the information in Part One, prepare five need-satisfaction questions that reveal how the features of your convention center provide a solution to the buying situation. Select appropriate proof devices to demonstrate these specific benefits. Using these questions, meet again with B. H. Rivera, and role-play this part of the questioning process. Prepare and use confirmation questions as the need arises.

After viewing the video "Questions—Getting It Right," and using the information in the first two role-plays, prepare a need-satisfaction presentation to Cameron Rivera, a new meeting planner just hired at Graphic Forms. Cameron, a cousin of B. H., had been previously employed as a training coordinator at West College. Due to extensive growth in the company, B. H. has turned all meeting planning over to Cameron. Cameron will make the final selection of a facility for the meeting described in Employment Memorandum 1, plus 11 more identical meetings to be scheduled in the next 12 months. You have also been informed that the Marriott and Sheraton Hotels will be making presentations (note the comparative room, parking, and transportation rates). You will travel to Graphic Forms to make your presentation. Prepare appropriate survey, probing, confirmation, and need-satisfaction questions and presentation strategies that will help secure this important account—then role-play this presentation.

CRM Application Exercise

Printing the Customer Database

Sales managers regularly help salespeople review the status of their accounts. These strategic account review meetings often involve examining all the information available on the salespeople's most prómising prospects. Both the sales manager and the salesperson have a copy of all information currently available for the accounts either on their computer screens or on paper. To produce a paper record of the important planning information contained in the Salesforce.com database, click the Reports tab and select the Sales Pipeline report. Click "Printable View," download the Excel file, open it, and print the report.

Next, click on the Salesforce.com Documents tab and choose the "Pat Silva Notes" link. On the following record click on the link, "Click here to view this file." This will open a PDF file with all of the notes taken by the salesperson that preceded you. The Excel report and the notes document will provide sufficient information to analyze the accounts. You might wish to keep a copy of this information for later assignments.

Folder	SimNet Product Information
Author	Pat Silva [Change]
File Extension	pdf
MIME Type	application/pdf
Size	224KB
Description	Notes taken by previous salesperson during sales calls and meetings
Keywords	notes
	View file

Case Problem

When Deborah Karish wakes up in the morning, she does not have to worry about a long commute to work. Her office is in her home. As an Amgen (www.amgen.com) pharmaceutical sales representative, Deborah spends most of her day visiting hospitals, medical clinics, and doctors' offices. She spends a large part of each day serving as a consultant to doctors, head nurses, pharmacists, and others who need information and advice about the complex medical products available from her company. As might be expected, she also spends a considerable amount of time conducting informative presentations designed to achieve a variety of objectives. In some situations she is introducing a new product and in other cases she is providing up-to-date information on an existing product. Some of her presentations are given to individual health care professionals, and others are given to a group. Each of these presentations must be carefully planned.

Deborah uses informative and reminder presentations almost daily in her work. Informative presentations are given to doctors who are in a position to prescribe her products. The verbal presentation often is supplemented with audiovisual aids and printed materials. Reprints of articles from leading medical journals are often used to explain the success of her products in treating patients. These articles give added credibility to her presentations. Some of her informative presentations are designed to give customers updates on the prescription drugs she sells. Reminder presentations are frequently given to pharmacists who must maintain an inventory of her products. She has found that it is necessary to periodically remind pharmacists of product delivery procedures and policies and special services available from Amgen. She knows that without an occasional reminder, a customer can forget information that is beneficial.

In some cases a careful needs analysis is needed to determine whether her products can solve a specific medical problem. Every patient is different, so generalizations concerning the use of her products can be dangerous. When doctors talk about their patients, Deborah must listen carefully and take good notes. In some cases she must get additional information from company support staff. If a customer needs immediate help with a problem, she gives the person a toll-free 800 number to call for expert advice. This line is an important part of the Amgen customer service program.

Deborah's career in pharmaceutical sales has required continuous learning. In the beginning she had to learn the meaning of dozens of medical terms and become familiar with a large number of medical problems. If a doctor asks, "What is the bioavailability of Neutogen?" she must know the meaning of the medical term and be knowledgeable about this Amgen product.

Deborah also spends time learning about the people with whom she works. She recently said, "If I get along with the people I work with it, makes my job a lot easier." When meeting someone for the first time, she takes time to assess his communication style and then adjusts her own style to meet his needs. She points out that in some cases the competition offers a similar product at a similar price. In these situations a good relationship with the customer can influence the purchase decision.

Questions

1. Would need discovery be an important part of Deborah Karish's sales process with a new medical practice? Explain.
2. Would Deborah use the same questioning strategy with medical personnel such as the office manager or receptionist that she would with medical professionals such as nurses or doctors?
3. Describe the nature of the multi-call sales process that Deborah might use.
4. Describe what Deborah might plan to do in the first call, in the second call, and in a third call on the same medical practice.

CRM Case Study

Planning Presentations

Becky Kemley, your sales manager at SimNet Systems, wants to meet with you this afternoon to discuss the status of your accounts. Becky wants to know what phase each account is in and, particularly, which accounts may be ready for a presentation.

Questions

1. Which five accounts already have had a needs analysis?
2. Which accounts should be scheduled for a needs analysis?
3. Which accounts have had a needs analysis and now need a product solution?
4. For those accounts listed next that are ready for your sales presentation, which strategy would you use for each: informative, persuasive, or reminder?
   a. Able Profit Machines
   b. Big Tex Auto Sales
   c. Lakeside Clinic
5. Which accounts appear to be planning to buy without a needs analysis discovery or product configuration/proposal? What risks does this pose?

Partnership Selling: A Role-Play/Simulation (see Appendix: Partnership Selling)

Understanding Your Customer's Buying Strategy

Read Sales Memorandum 2. Your customer has called you back because you made such a good approach in call 1 and wants to visit with you about a convention recently assigned. In this call, you are to use the information gathered in sales call 1 to reestablish a good relationship, discover your customer's convention needs, and set an appointment to return and make a presentation.

Follow the instructions carefully and prepare survey questions prior to your appointment. Keep your survey questions general and attempt to get your customer to openly share information. Use specific survey questions later during the appointment to gain more insight. Be careful about doing too much of the talking. In the need discovery, your customer should do most of the talking, with you taking notes and using them to ask confirmation and summary-confirmation questions to check the accuracy of your perceptions concerning what the customer wants. After this meeting, you will be asked to prepare a sales proposal from the information you have gathered.

Your instructor may again ask you to assume the role of a customer in the account category that you are not assigned to as a salesperson. If so, you will receive detailed customer instructions that you should follow closely. This will provide you with an opportunity to experience the strategic/consultative/ partnering style of selling from a customer's perspective.

Endnotes

1. Olaf Ploetner, "The Development of Consulting in Goods-Based Companies," *Industrial Marketing Management* 37, February 6, 2008, p. 329.

2. V. Kuman, Rajkuma, Rajkuman Venkatesan, and Werner Reinartz, "Performance Implications of Adopting a Customer-Focused Sales Campaign," *Journal of Marketing* 72, September 2008, p. 50.

3. *Going the Distance: The Consultative Sales Presentation* (Pasadena, CA: Intelecom); "The Amgen Difference," www.amgen.com (accessed June 11, 2010).

4. Louise E. Boone and David L. Kurtz, *Contemporary Marketing*, 11th ed. (Mason, OH: South-Western Publishing, 2004), p. 576; Geoffrey James, "Consultative Selling Strategies," *Selling Power*, April 2004, pp. 17–20.

5. Jack R. Snader, "Developing Consultative Sales Skills," *Pace*, October 1985, p. 49.

6. Jeff Thull, *The Prime Solution*, (Chicago, IL: Dearborn Publishing, 2005), p. 35.

7. Othman Boujena, Wesley J. Johnston, and Dwight R. Merunka, "The Benefits of Sales Force Automation: A Customer's Perspective," *Journal of Personal Selling and Sales Management*, 24, Spring 2009, p. 137.

8. Duane Sparks, *Questions—The Answer to Sales* (Minneapolis, MN: The Sales Board, 2005), p. vii.

9. Rose A. Spinelli, "Listening—A Priority in Shopping for Others," *Chicago Tribune*, November 30, 2003, p. 55.

10. Gerhard Gschwandtner, "What Makes Sales Relationships Work?" *Selling Power*, May–June 2010, p. 9.

11. Research for the SPIN model was conducted in the late 1970s and early 1980. Neil Rackham, *SPIN Selling* (New York: McGraw-Hill, 1988); www.huthwaite.com.au/research-ip.html (accessed June 8, 2010).

12. Geoffrey James, "Driving the High-Stakes Sales," *Selling Power*, May 2007, p. 51.

13. "What Do Good Salespeople Have in Common?" *Training*, December 1984, p. 21.

14. Research for the Professional Selling Skills model was conducted in the late 1960s and early 1970s. "Professional Selling Skills," www.achieveglobal.co.nz/_literature.../Professional_Selling_Skills (accessed June 7, 2010).

15. Michael D. Hargrove, "Using the Socratic Selling Method," www.bluinc.com/news/socraticselling.html (accessed June 6, 2010).

16. Geoffrey James, "Driving the High-Stakes Sales," p. 52.

17. Robert Jolles, *Customer-Centered Selling: Mastering the Art of Urgency*, 2nd ed. (New York: The Free Press, 2009), pp. 105–106.

18. Ann Demarais and Valerie White, *First Impressions—What You Don't Know About How Others See You* (New York: Bantam Books, 2004), pp. 68–69.

19. Fernando Jaramillo and Douglas B. Grisaffe (Spring 2009), "Does Customer Orientation Impact Objective Sales Performance?" *Journal of Personal Selling and Sales Management*, 24(1), p. 167.

20. Barry L. Reece and Rhonda Brandt, *Effective Human Relations: Personal and Organizational Applications*, 10th ed. (Boston: Houghton Mifflin Company, 2008), p. 40.

21. Ibid., p. 40.

22. Demarais and White, *First Impressions*, p. 70.

23. Abner Little, "Are You Listening," *Selling Power*, May–June 2010, p. 34.

24. William F. Kendy, "The Silence Play," *Selling Power*, July/August 2007, pp. 29–30.

25. Matthew McKay, Martha Davis, and Patrick Fanning, *Message: The Communication Skills Book* (Oakland, CA: New Harbringer, 1995), p. 15; Susan Scott, *Fierce Conversation* (New York: Viking, 2002), p. 157.

26. William F. Kendy, "How to Be a Good Listener," *Selling Power*, April 2004, p. 43.

27. Tom Reilly, *Value-Added Selling* (New York: McGraw-Hill, 2003), p. 130.

28. Adam Rapp, Raj Agnihotri, and Lukas P. Forbes (Fall 2008), "The Sales Force Technology–Performance Chain: The Role of Adaptive Selling and Effort," *Journal of Personal Selling and Sales Management*, 28(4), p. 335.

29. Olaf Ploetner, "The Development of Consulting in Goods-Based Companies," p. 329

30. Geoffrey James, "How to Use the Intuitive Model to Sell," *Selling Power*, May–June 2010, p. 40.

31. Decorating Den Interiors, www.decoratingden.com/meet-our-decorators.html (accessed June 12, 2010).

32. Tom Riley, *Value-Added Selling*, pp. 17, 167.

33. Kerry L. Johnson, "The Things Sales Masters Do," *Value-Added Selling* 21, April 16, 2007, p. 3.

34. Consona Corporation, www.configsc.com (accessed August 12, 2010).

35. Big Machines, www.bigmachines.com/salesforce.php (accessed September 14, 2010).

36. Rapp, Agnihotri, and Forbes, "The Sales Force Technology–Performance Chain: The Role of Adaptive Selling and Effort," p. 335.

37. Willem J. Verbeke, Frank D. Belschak, Arnold B. Bakker, and Bart Dietz (July 2008), "When Intelligence Is (Dys)Functional for Achieving Sales Performance," *Journal of Marketing*, 72, p. 44.

38. Paul F. Roos, "Just Say No," *Selling Power*, October 2003, p. 50.

39. Neil Rackham and John DeVincentis, *Rethinking the Sales Force* (New York: McGraw-Hill, 1999), p. 17.

40. Ibid., p. 9.

Endnotes for Boxed Features

a. Emily Barker, "Start with . . . Nothing," *Inc.*, February 2002, pp. 67–73; "About RightNow Technologies," www.rightnow.com (accessed April 4, 2005).

b. Duane Sparks, *Questions—The Answer to Sales* (Minneapolis, MN: The Sales Board, 2005), p. vi; "CARQUEST Cares," www.carquest.com (accessed September 7, 2010).

Index

Page references followed by "f" indicate illustrated figures or photographs; followed by "t" indicates a table.